THE JACOBITES & THE UNION

T0382394

JAMES FRANCIS EDWARD STEWART
Chevalier de St George

THE JACOBITES
AND THE UNION

BEING A NARRATIVE OF THE
MOVEMENTS OF 1708, 1715, 1719

BY SEVERAL CONTEMPORARY HANDS

EDITED BY

CHARLES SANFORD TERRY

LITT.D. Cantab., MUS.D. (Hon.) Edin.

BURNETT-FLETCHER PROFESSOR OF HISTORY
IN THE UNIVERSITY OF ABERDEEN

CAMBRIDGE
AT THE UNIVERSITY PRESS
1922

CAMBRIDGE
UNIVERSITY PRESS

University Printing House, Cambridge CB2 8BS, United Kingdom

Published in the United States of America by Cambridge University Press, New York

Cambridge University Press is part of the University of Cambridge.

It furthers the University's mission by disseminating knowledge in the pursuit of education, learning and research at the highest international levels of excellence.

www.cambridge.org
Information on this title: www.cambridge.org/9781107425927

© Cambridge University Press 1922

First published 1922
First paperback edition 2014

A catalogue record for this publication is available from the British Library

ISBN 978-1-107-42592-7 Paperback

PREFACE

I HAVE set myself to construct out of contemporary materials a full narrative of Jacobite effort at the four periods of its activity—in 1708, 1715, 1719, and 1745. These pages deal with the first three movements: the Forty-Five is treated in another volume published simultaneously with the present one.

The scope of these pages is somewhat more restricted than that of a volume which I contributed over twenty years ago to the "Scottish History from Contemporary Writers" series, entitled *The Chevalier de St George and the Jacobite movements in his favour*, 1701—1720 (David Nutt: 1901). That book is no longer procurable, and an edition of it printed more recently for the University of London is also inaccessible.

Only in the language and from the outlook of those who took part in it or watched its unfolding is it possible to recover the romantic atmosphere which irradiates the story. With no more than a connecting word here and there I have let the actors in it tell its incidents in their own way, piecing their prose so that it reads as a consecutive narrative. I venture to think it the fullest and most vivid account of the events it records.

To the University Tutorial Press I am indebted for the courteous permission to use the block illustrating the Battle of Glenshiel.

C. S. T.

KING'S COLLEGE,
OLD ABERDEEN.
August, 1922.

CONTENTS

ILLUSTRATIONS

ERRATUM

p. 210 note l. 3 *for* 9th Dragoons *read* 9th Lancers.

LIST OF AUTHORITIES

AND THE ABBREVIATIONS BY WHICH
THEY ARE INDICATED

B. A.   *Accounts of the Burning of the Villages of Auchterarder, Crieff, Blackford, Dalreoch, and Dunning, about the beginning of the year* 1716.
Printed in the Maitland Club's *Miscellany*, vol. III, 443–74. Edinburgh: 1843.

C. A.   Campbell, Robert, *The Life of the Most Illustrious Prince John, Duke of Argyle and Greenwich.* London: 1745.

      John Campbell, 2nd Duke of Argyll and Duke of Greenwich (1678–1743), eldest son of the 1st Duke (d. 1703), an active agent in bringing about the Union, served under Marlborough in Flanders 1706–9, commander-in-chief in Scotland 1712, repressed the '15, created Duke of Greenwich 1719.

C. H. N.   Hooke, Nathaniel, *The Secret History of Colonel Hooke's Negotiations in Scotland, in Favour of the Pretender; in* 1707. *Including the Original Letters and Papers which passed between the Scotch and Irish Lords and the Courts of Versailles and St Germains. Never before Published. Written by Himself. With a Translation of Letters, containing a Narrative of the Pretender's Expedition into Scotland in* 1708, *and his Return to Dunkirk, transmitted to the French Court by the commanding Officers of the Squadron.* London: 1760.

      An edition of the work was published at Edinburgh in the same year.

      Nathaniel Hooke (1664–1738), educated at Dublin, Glasgow, and Cambridge, employed by Monmouth to raise London against James II 1685, served under Dundee 1689, Jacobite agent in Ireland and Flanders, undertook secret missions to Scottish Jacobites on behalf of Louis XIV 1705 and 1707.

H. R.   *The Historical Register, containing An Impartial Relation of all Transactions, Foreign and Domestic. Volume IV. For the Year* 1719. London: 1720.

J. A.   *The Jacobite Attempt of* 1719. *Letters of James Butler, second Duke of Ormonde, relating to Cardinai Alberoni's project for the invasion of Great Britain on behalf of the Stuarts, and to the landing of a Spanish expedition in Scotland.* Edited by William Kirk Dickson. Edinburgh: Scottish History Society. 1895.

James Butler, 2nd Duke of Ormonde (1665–1745), succeeded to dukedom 1688, joined William of Orange 1688, Lord Lieutenant of Ireland 1703–5, 1710–11, 1713, Captain-General 1712, impeached and attainted as a Jacobite 1715, accepted command of Spanish expedition for James' restoration 1719, thereafter resided chiefly at Avignon.

K. M.   *A fragment of a Memoir of Field-Marshal James Keith, written by himself,* 1714–1734. Edinburgh: Spalding Club. 1843.

James Francis Edward Keith (1696–1758), brother of George K. 10th Earl Marischal (1693?–1778), took part in the '15, escaped to France, engaged in the '19, entered Russian service, made Field-Marshal by Frederick the Great 1747, mortally wounded at Hochkirch 1758.

L. L. E.   *The Loch Lomond Expedition, MDCCXV. Reprinted and illustrated from original documents.* Edited by James Dennistoun. Glasgow: 1834.

L. M.   Lockhart, George, *Memoirs concerning the Affairs of Scotland, from Queen Anne's Accession to the Throne, to the Commencement of the Union of the Two Kingdoms of Scotland and England, in May,* 1707. *With an Account of the Origine and Progress of the Design'd Invasion from France, in March,* 1708. *And some Reflections on the Ancient State of Scotland. To which is prefix'd an Introduction shewing the Reason for Publishing these Memoirs at this Juncture.* London: 1714.

George Lockhart, of Carnwath (1673–1731), arrested as a Jacobite 1715, confidential agent of the Chevalier in Scotland 1718–27. His 'Memoirs' and 'Papers' are among the most valuable Jacobite documents. Together they cover the period 1707–1728.

L. P.   *The Lockhart Papers: containing Memoirs and Commentaries upon the Affairs of Scotland from* 1702 *to* 1715, *by George Lockhart, Esq. of Carnwath, his Secret Correspondence with the Son of King James the Second from* 1718 *to* 1728, *and his other political Writings; Also, Journals and Memoirs of the Young Pretender's Expedition in* 1745, *by Highland Officers in his Army.* 2 vols. London: 1817.

M. C. F. *Memoires du Comte de Forbin.*

The Count's narrative of the Chevalier's voyage to Scotland in 1708 is printed in vol. 75 of A. Petitot and Monmerqué's "Collection des Mémoires relatifs a l'histoire de France, depuis l'avénement de Henri IV jusqu'a la Paix de Paris conclue en 1763." Paris: 1829.

Comte Claude Forbin, French Admiral, a Provençal, born 1656, retired from service 1710 after the voyage to Scotland in 1708, his 'Memoirs' published 1730, died 1733.

M. D. A. Mar's *Distinct Abridgement of some Materiall Poynts relateing to Scotts Affairs.*

This narrative of the Attempt of 1719 was sent by Mar to Lord Nairn in August 1719. It is printed at p. 450 of T. L. Kington Oliphant's *The Jacobite Lairds of Gask.* London: 1870.

John Erskine, 6th or 11th Earl of Mar (1675–1732), Secretary of State 1713, dismissed 1714, headed the Rising 1715, created Duke by James 1715, lost James' favour 1724.

M. J. *A Journal of the Earl of Marr's Proceedings, from his First Arrival in Scotland to his Embarkation for France. Printed in France by Order of the Earl of Marr.* Second Edition. London: 1716.

The *Journal* is also printed as an appendix to Patten's *History* (Second Edition) and substantially is identical with a pamphlet entitled "A Letter from an Officer in the King's Army, after it had march'd northward from Aberdeen, to his friend in London, February 17$\frac{15}{16}$."

P. C. *A Journall of Severall Occurences from 2d November* 1715, *in the Insurrection (began in Scotland) and concluded at Preston in Lancashire, on November* 14, *MDCCXV., kept by Peter Clarke.*

Printed in the "Miscellany of The Scottish History Society (First Volume)." Edinburgh: 1893.

The author describes himself in 1715 as clerk to Mr Craikenthorpe, attorney-at-law in Penrith. His 'Journal' is an illuminating document upon the events of the fortnight with which it deals.

P. H. Patten, Robert, *The History of the Late Rebellion. With original Papers, and Characters of the Principal Noblemen and Gentlemen concern'd in it. The Second Edition, with Large Additions.* London: 1717.

The author was curate of Allendale in 1715, joined Forster and became his chaplain, was made prisoner at Preston, and afterwards turned King's evidence. Two editions of his 'History' were published in 1717, of which the second and enlarged edition contains a narrative of the rising in Scotland with a separate pagination.

P. P. *A true account of the Proceedings at Perth; the Debates in the Secret Council there; with the Reasons and Causes of the suddain finishing and breaking up of the Rebellion. Written by a rebel.* The Second Edition. London: 1716.

Gives a full account of the Councils held at Perth on January 28, 1716, and following days, at which the retreat was resolved upon. Chambers, in his 'History' and Maidment, in vol. II of the 'Miscellany' of the Spottiswoode Society (where it is reprinted), ascribe it wrongly to the Master of Sinclair.

R. Rae, Peter, *The History of the Rebellion rais'd against His Majesty King George I by the Friends of the Popish Pretender.* London: 1746.

The author, originally a clockmaker, was minister of Kirkconnel 1732–48. The first edition of his 'History' appeared in 1718. He died 1748.

S. M. *Memoirs of the Insurrection in Scotland in* 1715. *By John, Master of Sinclair. With notes by Sir Walter Scott, Bart.* Edinburgh: Abbotsford Club. 1858.

John Sinclair, Master of Sinclair (1683–1750), served under Marlborough in Flanders, court-martialled for shooting Captain Alexander Shaw, whose brother the Master had mortally wounded in a duel 1708, pardoned 1712, came 'out' in 1715 but without enthusiasm, attainted and remained abroad till 1726, when he was pardoned, died 1750 aged sixty-seven. His 'Memoirs' show him to have been on bad terms with Mar, and his judgments need to be examined with caution.

CHAPTER I

1708

The[1] Union commenced upon the First of May, 1707, a Day never to be forgot by Scotland, a Day in which the Scots were stripped of what their Predecessors had gallantly maintained for many Hundred Years, I mean their Independency and Soveraignty.

I shall leave this Melancholy subject with adding a few Observes that some were pleased to remark.

First, That the first Article of the Union was approven the fourth Day of November, which was the Birth-day of our Dutch ironical Saviour, King William, being the Day preparatory to Gunpowder-Treason.

Second, That the Peerage was renounced the eighth of January, which was the Date of the Warrant for the Religious Murder of Glenco, upon which Day likewise the Earl of Sta[ir], Signer of the said Warrant, after he had with more than ordinary Zeal appeared that Day in Parliament, was found dead in his Bed, or, as was reported, hanged himself.

Third, The Ratification of the Articles of the Union was upon the sixteenth of the Date of the Sentence of the Royal Martyr, King Charles the First.

Fourth, The Dissolution of the Scots Parliament or Kingdom was upon the Twenty-fifth of March, being the first of the Year in England, and a handsome new Years Gift to that Kingdom.

Fifth, The Equivalent (*alias* Price of Scotland) came to Edinburgh on the Fifth of August, the Day the Earl of Gourie designed to perpetrate his horrid Conspiracy against King James VI....

I proceed next to give an account of what happened after the Commencement of the Union, particularly of the Projects that

[1] *L. M.* 339.

were set on foot to subvert the same and restore the King[1]. It is not to be expected I can discover all the secret Transactions at the time I write this, for many of them were carried on in France, and others, though at home, were kept very Secret; yet you'll perceive I have come at the Knowledge of so much as will sufficiently enable you to Understand the true Origine and Progress of the designed Invasion from France in March 1708.

To begin then. No sooner was the First of May past, than the Ministry (now of great Britain) took care to establish the Union of the two Kingdoms, and as by the Articles it was agreed their should be the same Regulations, Impositions, &c., of Trade throughout the united Kingdom (that is to say, that the Laws relative to Trade in England should take place in Scotland), Immediately two Commissioners were appointed, one for managing the Customs, the other the Excise of Scotland, which consisted partly of English, partly of Scotsmen (though these latter had no pretentions to intitle them to that Name, save their being born in that Country; they and all that were employed afterwards as Commissioners for managing the Equivalent, or advanced to any of the new Posts, being down right Renegadoes, and rewarded on no other account than the Assistance they gave in selling their Country); at the same Time vast Numbers of Surveyers, Collectors, Waiters, and in short, all or most of the Officers of the Customs and Excise were sent down from England, and these, generally speaking, the very Scum and Canalia of that Country, which remembers me of a very good Story: Sometime thereafter, a Scots Merchant Travelling in England, and shewing some apprehensions of being Robbed, his Landlady told him he was in no hazard, for all the Highwaymen were gone, and upon his enquiring how that came about; why truly, replied she, they are all gone to your Country to get Places.

These Fellons treated the Natives with all the Contempt, and executed the new Laws with all the Rigour imaginable; so that before the first Three Months were expired, there were too apparent Proofs of the Truth of what had been often asserted in

[1] James Francis Edward Stewart, Chevalier de St George, titular James III and VIII, a pensioner of Louis XIV at St Germain-en-Laye.

relation to the bad Bargain Scotland had made: 'tis true indeed, some particular Merchants made vast gain at this Juncture; for, the Duties upon Wine and most other Foreign Commodities, being much less in Scotland than in England, great Quantities were imported into the former before the Commencement of the Union, afterwards carried into England, [and] returned an extraordinary Profit; but as discerning People saw that was only the accidental Consequence of what could not be well avoided at this Juncture, and that these Sun shine Days would be soon over Clouded (as the Merchants have since effectually experimented), it did no Ways lessen the dreadful Apprehensions of the Consequences of the Union, and the People of all Ranks and Perswasions were more and more chagrin'd and displeased, and resented the loss of the Soveraignty, and were daily more and more perswaded that nothing but the Restoration of the [Stewart] Royal Family, and that by the means of Scotsmen, could restore them to their Rights. So that now there was scarce one of a Thousand that did not declare for the King; nay the Presbyterians and Cameronians were willing to pass over the Objection of his being Papist; for said they (according to their predestinating Principles), God may convert him, or he may have Protestant Children, but the Union can never be good; and...on all Occasions, in all Places, and by all People of all Perswasions, nothing was to be heard throughout all the Country save an universal Declaration in favour of the King, and Exclamations against the Union and those that had promoted it.

Nay, so great a length did their Indignation lead them, that the Presbyterian Ministers became universally Hated and Dispised, and lost all their Interest with the Commons, these not sticking to tell them publickly, that they were Time-servers, and had Preached up against the Union whilst they thought their Kirk not well enough secured, but that once being done, they valued not the Country nor the Peoples Liberties. And thus were the Commons come to this lucky pass, that they would have entered into and prosecuted any Measure without the previous Advice and constant Concurrance of the Ministers, who formerly, on all other Occasions, acted only with a view to themselves, could never be guided by the Nobility and Gentry,

4

and rendered the Commons immanageable by the influence they had over them.

As these were the Peoples Inclinations, so likewise was there an universal Expectation of the King's coming over to them; whence this came I cannot tell, but People were over all parts prepossessed and pleased themselves with an Opinion it would happen very soon; so that for several Months they were in a constant Expectation of him, and this was before any Measure for the Purpose was finally concluded, and in such Countries where few or none were privy to the Concert; besides, they acted consequentially to this their be[lie]f and expectation, preparing themselves to receive and assist him; for the Western Shires had their private Deligates from each Parish to meet and concert Measures together, and amongst others, they appointed several of their number to apply themselves towards getting of Intelligence; they named their Officers who should head them till once the Nobility and Gentry took the Command upon them; they had Arms making in all Places, and appointed People to buy Horses; so that a worthy Friend of mine in the Shire of Air assured me, That very Summer Twelve or Fifteen Hundred good Horses had been brought over from Ireland, which were picked and brought up by Country People, and carried where no body knew; and some of these Ringleaders and Delegates in Clydsdale did come to Mr Lockhart of Carnwath, telling him they were ordered by a considerable Party to enquire of him against what time he thought the King would Land; and upon his answering that he wondered how they could ask such a Question of him! and that he knew nothing of these Matters, they answered, he might indeed be shy in divulging his Mind to them, but they doubted not but he knew, and they would be glad to know likewise, that each of them might spare one or two of their best Horses from Work, and have them in good Condition against he landed. And on another occasion, one of the chief Cameronians told him they were content to join in an Army with the Episcopalians, for it was not now a time for Scotland to be divided amongst themselves....

It is not to be doubted but these Accounts would soon reach the Ears of those at St Germains and Versails. For in the first

Place, during the time that the Articles of the Union were
under the Consideration of the Scots Parliament, the English
Ministry allowed, or rather encouraged, their News-Mongers to
ascribe the opposition they met with to a Spirit of Jacobitism;
and next, care was taken to inform how averse the People were
to the Union, and pressing the King's coming over as the
luckiest opportunity for restoring of him, and advancing the
Affairs of France by giving a diversion to the English Arms;
and the French King[1], by the bad success of his Arms during the
last Campaign [1706] (wherein he lost the Battles of Audenard[2]
and Turin and several strong Towns), being brought to a weak
pass, began to relish the Proposal and seemed in earnest to do
something for our King; for which end he sent over Colonel
Hookes to get Intelligence and Treat with the People of
Scotland.

I have...good Grounds to believe he was palmed upon the
Court of St Germains, being pitched upon by the French King
as one that would follow his Directions and be true to his Interest;
and indeed he was not disappointed, for the Colonel show'd
more concern to raise a Civil War at any rate (which was what
the French King chiefly wanted), then so to manage and adjust
Measures as tended most for King James's Service and to
encourage his Subjects to do for him.

Now it will be proper to remember that the two Dukes of
Hamilton and A[thol]e had for sometime been in bad Terms
with one another; the first claim'd Merit upon the account of
his past Actions, his Interest and Qualifications (which are
seldom undervalued by great Men); the other thought he was
to be valued, and would yield to none because of the Interest he
had of late got with the North Country Gentry, and the great
number of Men he could raise; but he never considered these
would have join'd the King, not out of Affection or Obedience
to him (tho' he might have a considerable stroke with them, and
was therefore to be valued), but from a Principle of Loyalty,
which they had manifested on all occasions.

These Dukes had their several Friends; some Honest Men,

[1] Louis XIV.
[2] A slip on Lockhart's part. Oudenarde was fought in 1708.

being disgusted at the Duke of Hamilton on the Account of his Behaviour during the last Parliament[1], inclined to think the Duke of Athole would venture further for the King; which, as it picqued the one, so it elevated the other, nay, to so great a degree, that the Duke of A[thol]e and his Partizans railed openly against the Duke of Hamilton, and pretended to do all themselves.

There were others again, who, remembring the Duke of A[thol]e's Conduct at and on several occasions since the Revolutions, were afraid he was not thoroughly well founded, but acted more from a desire of revenging himself of the Courtiers, who had slighted him, than a true Principle of Loyalty; and considering that he was by no means qualified to be the Head of a Party, tho' in general an useful Man in promoting so good a Design, thought he was to be humoured, but not so as to disgust the Duke of Hamilton altogether. For tho' the last's Behaviour in all Points was not approved of by them, yet being thoroughly convinced that he was altogether Loyal, and tho' perhaps a little too Cautious, or rather Timorous in concerting of Measures, would infallibly join the King and venture as far to serve him as any Man alive; and it being evident to a Demonstration, that he was absolutely necessary to be with the King because of his Interest, Courage and Conduct, and particularly his dexterity in managing the different Parties in the K[i]ngdom; Upon these Considerations, I say, they thought he was to be valued, respected, and advised with, and having notified the same to the Earl of Midleton (who agreed with them in it), and he again to the K—g, the Duke of Perth, who was of a quite different Interest from the Earl of Midleton, soon made up with the Duke of A[thol]e, and having more interest with the Priests and Roman Catholicks than the Earl of Midleton, prevailed so far with the Court of France, or at least with Hookes himself, that when Hookes arrived in Scotland, he should make his chief Application to his Correspondent, the Duke of A[thol]e....

These being premised, I go to acquaint you, That Hookes set Sail from France and Landed in the Northern Parts of Scotland

[1] Cf. Terry, *A History of Scotland to* 1843 [Cambridge, 1920], chap. 24.

some time about the later end of February or beginning of March 1707.

Immediately[1] upon receiving the King's[2] orders in the month of January last [1707], to hold myself in readiness to go over to Scotland for his service, I wrote to the duke of Hamilton, begging of him to give notice to the well-affected of my journey, and that I was to bring them arms and ammunition. This resolution being soon after changed, and new orders being given to me to go over to that country only to treat with the principal men of the nation, I likewise acquainted the duke of Hamilton with this, and entreated him to concert every thing before-hand with the other chiefs, who were then assembled to attend the parliament, and to send some one well instructed and fully authorised from them to wait upon me at the Earl of Errol's, the Lord High Constable, where I was to land, and to whom also I gave notice of my journey....

Upon my arrival in Scotland, I found that the Union had been ratified by the parliament[3], to the great discontent and hearty dislike of the nation, and that all the peers and other Lords, together with the members of parliament, had returned to the country, their ordinary residence, (for in Scotland only the merchants and some lawyers make their constant abode in the cities), and that there remained only at Edinburgh the High Constable, the Duke of Hamilton, the Lord Marshal, the two last being dangerously ill.

The Countess of Errol, mother to the High Constable, who had come on purpose to the castle on the sea coast to wait upon me, put into my hands several letters of her son, in which he testified a great impatience to see me, adding, that all the well-affected would exert themselves to the utmost on this occasion as their last resource, being persuaded that at the worst they would obtain better conditions sword in hand than those of the Union. She told me also, that the Duke of Hamilton had sent

[1] *C. H. N.* 14. This Report was drawn up and submitted by Colonel Nathaniel Hooke to Michel de Chamillart, the French Secretary of State, on July 29, 1707.

[2] Louis XIV.

[3] On March 19, 1707.

Mr Hall, a priest, and his confident, to her, and that he had
waited for me a month. She gave me a letter from him, in which
Mr Hall informs me that the Duke of Hamilton entreats me to
come to him at Edinburgh, where he would take care that I
should be well lodged; that he would trust himself to none but
me only; that he and all his friends are ready to risk every thing
for the K— of England, provided that Prince comes in person;
that without his presence there will be nothing done; that if the
fatigue of the voyage hinder me from beginning my journey
directly, the Duke begs of me to send him the letters which I
may have for him.

The Countess of Errol at the same time told me, that she
advised me not to be in great haste; that the Duke of Hamilton's
affairs were greatly altered within a few months past; that all
the world had abandoned him, and all the well-affected had
come to an open rupture with him; that the only man that
stuck by him was lord Kilsyth; the high constable and great
marshal also observing some measures with him, on account of
their antient intimacy; that he had been suspected of holding a
correspondence with the court of London; therefore, that I
would do well to be upon my guard before I trusted much to
him, and that the high constable her son would tell me more....

The high constable came to his castle at the time he had fixed.
I found him very much dissatisfied with the duke of Hamilton.
He told me that the duke for two months past had testified the
utmost impatience to see me, but that he no sooner heard of my
arrival than he changed his tone. He said that I had come too
late, and that the animosity of the nation against the English
was greatly abated. Mr Hall had made a mistake in decyphering
my letter, for instead of explaining that I had letters from the
king [of France] and the K— of England for the duke, he wrote
that the letters were from the king and the queen, upon which
the duke of Hamilton cried out that his letters of two years date
were plainly not agreeable to the K—, and that as his majesty
had not written to him, it was a proof that he wished him not to
be concerned in the affair; that for the time to come, therefore,
he would think only of the means of securing his own safety.

The earl of Errol added, that all this was only a pretext which the duke used to cover his secret designs; that for some time past he had endeavoured to persuade his friends that there was nothing to be expected from the king; that his majesty was prevented by the state of his affairs from thinking upon them, and that if he appeared disposed to do any thing, it was only with a view to rid himself of the K— of England before the peace, or to excuse himself from doing any other thing for that prince, in case his subjects should refuse to receive him with a few troops; that the nation therefore should take some other measures for securing its liberties and independancy.

This discourse, he said, had given great offence to many, and his secret intrigues with the duke of Queensberry and the earl of Stairs (which lord Saltoun had already given me a hint of) had encreased their distrust; that the duke of Athol was the first who discovered that intrigue, with which he reproached the duke of Hamilton, who at first denied it, but the duke of Athol proving it plainly, the other was at length forced to confess it, entreating the duke of Athol to believe that he had no other design but to intimidate or gain the two chiefs of the English faction; that this excuse having given satisfaction to nobody, the well-affected had dropped all intercourse with him; that the duke of Athol continued still to treat with him, till he had proposed in parliament to agree to the succession of Hanover, provided the English would desist from pressing the Union; that then the duke of Athol openly broke with him, being persuaded the duke of Hamilton had only made that motion in hopes, that if the well-affected had agreed to it, that proceeding would have made them lose all their credit with the people, who wish only for the K— of England.

That when all the counties and all the cities of Scotland declared against the Union by their addresses to the parliament, the presbyterians of the west of Scotland, who are all armed, sent to inform the duke of Hamilton that they were preparing to march to Edinburgh to disperse the parliament [1706]; that if he thought the enterprise too bold, he need not concern himself with it, but only leave them to act; and that the duke had charged them not to make any disturbance, saying, it was not yet time[1]....

[1] Cf. W. L. Mathieson, *Scotland and the Union* [Glasgow, 1905], 134.

I asked him, how the duke, who was neither rich, nor powerful in the number of his vassals, had acquired so great a credit with the people. The earl of Errol answered, that by means of the dutchess dowager of Hamilton, his mother, he had acquired great credit among the presbyterians; but that his late refusal to permit them to arm had entirely lost him their favour, and that they had since addressed themselves to the dukes of Gordon and Athol. That the greatest credit of the duke of Hamilton was owing to the court of St Germain, several orders having come from thence to the friends of the K— of England to do nothing without him, and that those orders had been repeated on occasion of my voyage. As a proof of this he gave me a letter of Mr [Lewis] Innes, almoner to the queen of England, dated the 17th of last January, in which, after relating that I was soon to go over to Scotland, he adds these words, 'The K— of England desires that his friends would follow the directions of the duke of Hamilton, and not declare themselves till the duke has declared himself, when they may without danger follow his example.'...

From these circumstances I found out how matters were conducting[1], and was extremely surprised to find that what has happened almost cuts off the only resource the nation had left. I begged the earl of Errol to suppress the letter of the 1st of March, and I resolved to take advantage of that which desires the friends of the K— of England to regulate their conduct by the duke of Hamilton. I saw the nation ready to come to the last extremities to prevent the Union; that they only waited for a leader; that the duke of Hamilton wanted them not to think of the K—of England, by persuading them that the king [of France] neither had an inclination nor an ability to assist that prince; and the despair of the people augmenting every day, that the duke might flatter himself that they would at length address themselves to him. It appeared to me, that if he was not gained over by the court of London, these were his views, and he could have no other. I therefore resolved to act with a great deal of reserve till I had clearly discovered the inclinations of the people, and above

[1] As the London Edition is defective here, the Edinburgh version is followed.

all, of the Presbyterians; and if I found that they thought of the duke of Hamilton, I would enter into their measures, would act in concert with the duke, and persuade the nobility to join him in obedience to the orders of the K— of England, by persuading them that the duke acted only for the interest of that prince.

I discovered nothing of this my design to the high constable, knowing his attachment to the K— of England, and I wanted to keep myself at liberty to join either the party in favour of that prince, or of the duke of Hamilton, according as I found the nation disposed. I thought it would be safer for me to regulate myself by the disposition of the people, than by the offers of the duke of Hamilton, or by those of the friends of the K— of England; because the duke might have it in view to break the designs of the others by specious offers, which he could never execute; and the others, if they had any knowledge of the duke's designs, might act also in the same manner. I knew that the bulk of the nation was for the K— of England, but I was still ignorant of the intentions of the Presbyterians, and of the west-country people. I knew that these last were better armed than the rest, and I kept myself always ready to join with that party which they should espouse, as they would not stand in need of so many supplies, and are not so divided into different factions as the rest, and therefore it would be more easy to put them in motion at a small expence....

Having asked the character of the duke of Athol, the earl of Errol told me that the duke was about forty years of age; that he is very opinionated, but a man of great probity, and that his word is inviolable and may be depended upon; that he is haughty and passionate; that he is very powerful in several counties, and can raise 9 battalions among his vassals, of 600 men each, armed, regimented, and disciplined; that he had caused them to assemble and encamp every summer since the act of security had authorised the lords to arm and discipline their vassals; that he himself had seen them encamped the year before, and that the duke could arm a greater number; and that by the interest of his friends he is absolutely the most powerful lord in Scotland. I began then to think it was time to act, but not chusing to engage myself too much with the friends of the K— of England till I knew

thoroughly the intentions of the duke of Hamilton[1], I acquainted
the duke of Athol that I was coming into his neighbourhood,
and that I would see the other lords on my journey, so that he
would have full time to take measures with his friends....

At the same time, the better to manage the duke of Hamilton,
I dispatched a messenger to Edinburgh to Mr Hall, his confidant.
I expressed my surprize that he had not kept his word with me,
as the earl of Errol had neither brought me a letter from him,
nor a commission from the duke of Hamilton; that his conduct
did not correspond with what he had written to me at the
countess of Errol's; that I had orders to address myself principally
to the duke, who I knew was the soul of the whole affair;
therefore I desired that he would point me out the way how I
might see him in safety; that I had hitherto entered into no
measures with any one, nor would I, till I had his answer; that
I had some things to mention to him which would give him
satisfaction; that it was now in his power to cover himself with
immortal honour, and to render himself greater than any of his
ancestors; that I would remove all difficulties, and shew him
easy expedients that he did not think of; that if he neglected this
occasion, it would never return; that he would ruin not only his
country but himself, the English having been too much irritated
by him not to crush him; that I was going to set out on my
journey, and would on a certain day be with one of his friends,
whom I named, within a day's journey of Edinburgh, desiring
Mr Hall, who was there often, to be there that day, to shew my
letter to the duke of Hamilton, to rectify the mistake about the
letter from the K——, and to bring me the duke's answer. I assured
him that I was grieved to hear of his indisposition, and added
whatever I thought could express a hearty friendship and a
strong desire to satisfy him in every thing....

Having travelled all night, next morning I arrived at that
gentleman's where Mr Hall waited for me. He made me a
thousand compliments from the duke of Hamilton. He told me
that his illness had hindered him from sending me an answer by

[1] Lockhart attributes the Duke's caution rather to his interests in
England than to any hopes founded upon his royal descent. Cf.
Lockhart Papers [London, 1817], vol. i. 56.

the earl of Errol; that the duke begged of me to send him the letters which I had got for him; to inform him of the propositions which I had to make to him from the K——; to come directly to Edinburgh, and that he would do his utmost endeavours to see me.

Having been informed that the duke had no longer any credit with the friends of the K—— of England, from so many quarters, and by so many different persons, that I could no longer doubt of it, I had now only the hopes that he had still interest with the Presbyterians to intrigue with them about his own elevation to the throne, which in my first journey[1] I understood he had very much at heart; and I durst not open myself on that subject to Mr Hall, who is absolutely in the interest of the K—— of England, so that I was obliged to talk with him only in general terms.

I told him, that I was much afflicted on account of the illness of the duke of Hamilton; that I would willingly send him the letters that I had for him, by which he would see the little reason he had to complain of the king; but that I was not entrusted with any propositions, and had only come to receive those of the Scots; nevertheless, if any thing happened during the course of the negotiation in which I could serve him, he would find me most ready to give him all the satisfaction in my power; that I would willingly proceed to Edinburgh, if he would assure me that my journey should not be fruitless; but to go thither without being sure of seeing him would be too rash a step; that the city being at present very empty, it would be impossible for a stranger to be there without being remarked; that I despised the dangers to which my duty exposed me, but that it would be acting contrary to the rules of prudence to expose myself there needlessly; that he doubtless knew the mind of the duke of Hamilton as to this, and I begged him to tell it me without disguise.

He answered, that the duke of Hamilton earnestly desired to see me, but to tell me the truth, he did not believe that he could; that he kept his bed, and was always surrounded with his domestics; that the duchess his wife never left him; that he was transported to hear that the king had done him the honour to

[1] August 1705.

write to him, but that he had likewise expected a letter from the queen of England[1]; that as that princess had not written to him, he concluded that the scheme was not approved of by her, and that he had too much respect for her judgment to concern himself with an affair that she did not approve of; that he had suspected that I had no propositions to make to him; but that nevertheless I must begin with making propositions, otherwise no treaty could be concluded.

I answered, that I would not suffer myself to be so easily blinded; that the duke of Hamilton had recourse to very weak shifts; that he wanted only to find fault, and complained when he had all the reason in the world to think himself greatly honoured; that if the queen had written to him, he would have bethought himself of some other cause of discontent; that he well knew the K— of England had not written to him without consulting with the queen his mother; that I could not promise to go to Edinburgh to no purpose; that I had no time to waste; that he need not expect propositions from me, or that I would persuade him to take arms; that I had not charged myself with arguments on that subject; that he had been a long time solliciting succours; that I was disposed to promise him whatever supplies he wanted; that he had nothing to do, therefore, but to consider what plan to go upon, and what he was able to effect, as the succours would be regulated according to the state of the nation and its forces; that therefore it was his part to make proposals to me, and that after I had fully weighed them, I would do my utmost to satisfy him; that I had a very full authority to promise every thing that I thought necessary, and that I would not hesitate in agreeing to whatever I thought reasonable. I had reflected so fully upon the state and the forces of Scotland, that I was sure I could be able to answer all that they could allege to prove the necessity of great supplies; therefore I risked nothing in talking so boldly.

Mr Hall answered me, that I ought to know the Duke of Hamilton better than to scruple at these difficulties, which it was his custom to start on all occasions, though he afterwards thought no more of them; that he would relate to him my

[1] Mary of Modena, widow of James II and VII.

answer, and expected to find him very dry; that he had charged him to learn from me what succours the King would be pleased to grant to the Scots, and that he would soon return to me with the opinion of the Duke of Hamilton on that subject. I told him, that it was not yet time to talk of succours; that it was proper first to know perfectly the forces which the well-affected could raise, and the means they have to support them; and that after having reasoned on these points according to the rules of war, we might examine by the same rules what succours they would need; and that I believed he (Mr Hall) would not enter upon these particulars, they being out of his sphere; and that mean while I would tell him, that although the King had a great desire to assist the Scots, his Majesty did not pretend to make their cause his principal affair; that he was very willing to assist the Scots to make war, but that he was no way disposed to make war for them, and at his own expence; that however dry my answer was, his commission was still more so; and that I had no suspicion of so much coldness on the part of the Duke of Hamilton.

He then asked me if the King would not grant 10,000 men; I answered, No; and that I did not believe that they could be so unreasonable to ask them. However, said he, the Duke of Hamilton believes that it is the least that can be asked. You may tell the Duke of Hamilton, said I to him, that it is not usual to behave thus to a great King; demands ought to be supported by reasons given in with them; has he given you any? He confessed he had not received any. Upon which I told him, that I advised him not to ask the half; that perhaps, after examining every thing, it would be found that the Scots had no need of any foreign troops; that it would be needless to talk more of it, as he was not more fully instructed; and therefore I desired him to tell the Duke of Hamilton from me, that I had something very particular to say to him, which I would mention to nobody but himself; that I had so much respect for him, that I would wait yet four days before I entered into a negociation with the other lords, and that I would expect his answer at the Marquis of Drummond's[1]....

[1] James Drummond, later (1716) 2nd titular Duke of Perth.

Mr Hall returning to Edinburgh, I went the same day to
Lord Stormont at Scoon, who, having been informed in February,
by the Earl of Errol, that I was coming to Scotland, had been
more active than all the rest. He had made a progress through
all the south of Scotland, where he is very powerful, and having
also visited several of the chief men in the north of England, he
had returned to Scoon to meet me. I did not think proper to
stay there, being desirous to know what I had to expect from
the Duke of Hamilton before I engaged with the others. Lord
Stormont confirmed to me what the Laird [Ogilvy] of Boyn
and the Earl of Strathmore had told me of the Duke of Athol,
who having appointed a day with him for my return to Scoon,
and having agreed on the name I should take, and a pretence for
my continuing some time, I went to the Marquis of Drummond's,
where I arrived next day....

About this time, I received the answer of Mr Hall, mentioning
that he had found the Duke of Hamilton in a most distressed
condition, reduced to the last extremity, breathing with the
utmost difficulty, having had twenty-nine fits of the fever; that
the Duke was in despair that he could not see me; that he loved
and esteemed me; that he would willingly give his life to have
some discourse with me; that he made not the least doubt of my
friendship, therefore begged of me to excuse his not answering
the King's letter, nor that of the K— of England; that he would
do himself that honour with the first opportunity after he had
recovered his strength; that he would concur in all reasonable
measures for the restoration of the K— of England; but it was
his opinion that Prince ought not to risk himself without a considerable body of troops, and that he wished me a good voyage.

I was well informed that the Duke of Hamilton was not so
bad as Mr Hall would make me believe. I knew not what to
think of his way of acting: sometimes I imagined that he was
reconciled underhand to the court of London; and at other times
I believed that he only made so many difficulties that he might
be the more entreated. I thought therefore that I ought not to
make him too many advances; that if he had made his peace
with Queen Anne, I ought to conceal from him the state of our
affairs; and that if he wanted to make himself be entreated, I

ought to change my course, and by neglecting him, would make him court me.

I was quickly convinced that he did not act sincerely; for having learned that Mr Hall had written by the same messenger to two of his friends, I found means to get possession of the letters, in which he had written more openly. He says in the letters, that the Duke of Hamilton had thought that if he appeared too forward to accept of the succours of the King, that would put the K— of England under a necessity of coming over to Scotland, because the King would have just reason to be dissatisfied with that Prince if he refused to go thither when his subjects invited him and armed themselves to receive him; and fearing also that the King only made these advances to excuse himself from doing any thing else in favour of that Prince, the Duke had judged it proper, *in order to embarrass his Majesty* (these are his very words), to demand that the King should secure a considerable party in England, or that his Majesty should send a body of troops for the conquest of England, to act in conjunction with the Scottish army; that the Duke of Hamilton had it in his power to place the K— of England on the throne of Scotland without the assistance of France, although that Prince should bring no more than a single page with him; but in that case, the K— of England would depend too much upon his subjects.

I saw by these letters that the Duke of Hamilton sought underhand to break all the measures of the well-affected, and then to excuse himself to them by false pretences, which might lessen their confidence in the King's goodness and their attachment to France.

I was so incensed at this proceeding, that I would write no more either to the Duke of Hamilton or to Mr Hall; I said only by word of mouth to him who brought me the letter, that I had no answer to return. But upon reflecting that the Duke pretended to be able to put the K— of England upon the throne without the assistance of France, and that at the same time he endeavoured to hinder that Prince from coming over to Scotland, it came into my mind that he had still an intention of seizing the throne himself.

I was well assured that he would not have the least support
from the nobility and gentry. The Presbyterians then were his
only resource: and as I was not sufficiently informed of their
dispositions, I resolved forthwith to give my whole attention to
know them thoroughly, with the intention, that if I found them
still in his interest, to fall upon some means of renewing my
correspondence with the Duke. I dispatched a courier to the
Duchess of Gordon to excuse my going to Edinburgh. I represented to her, that since she so greatly distrusted the Duke of
Hamilton, it would not be proper for me to come so near him;
that he would infallibly learn that I was in the city, and that
from thence great inconveniencies would ensue. I therefore
begged of her to send me the particulars of what the chiefs of the
Presbyterians had proposed to her, and the same day I returned
to Lord Stormont's....She submitted to my arguments, and
dispatched to me a gentleman named Strachan, in whom the
chief of the Presbyterians had an entire confidence. Besides the
Duchess of Gordon's letter of credence, which was very ample,
he gave me a memorial written with the hand of the Laird of
Kersland[1], the most leading man among the Presbyterians, and
chief of one of the most considerable families in Scotland, of
which the following is a copy:

The Presbyterians are resolved never to agree to the Union,
because it hurts their consciences, and because they are persuaded
that it will bring an infinite number of calamities upon this nation,
and will render the Scots slaves to the English. They are ready to
declare unanimously for K— James, and only beg his Majesty that
he will never consent to the Union, and that he will secure and
protect the Protestant religion. The declaration with respect to religion
ought to be in general terms.

Those among the Presbyterians who are called Cameronians will
raise 5000 men of the best soldiers in the kingdom; and the other
Presbyterians will assemble 8000 more. They beg that the K— of
England would give them officers, especially general officers, and send
them powder, for they have arms already. Whenever his Br—
Majesty shall have granted the preceding demands, and shall have

[1] Ker of Kersland actually passed on to the Government information regarding Hooke's activities.

promised to follow his supplies in person to Scotland, they will take arms against the government, and will give such other assurances of their fidelity as shall be desired. Provided powder be sent them, they engage to defend themselves in their country with their own forces alone against all the strength of England for a year, till the arrival of their K— and the succours that he should bring with him. They leave it to that Prince to bring with him such a number of troops as he shall think proper. They believe, however, that he will not have occasion for a great number. They have a correspondence with the [Presbyterian] north of Ireland, and they are certain that the Scots who inhabit that province will declare for them....

Not doubting any longer of the designs of the Presbyterians, I now thought only of rendering the design more general, and of engaging in it the most considerable Lords of Scotland. The Duke of Athol being the principal among them, I waited his return with impatience; and he, finding that his journey would be longer than he expected, sent me two of his brothers, Lord James Murray and his brother [William], who, having married the heiress of the house of Nairn, was become Lord Nairn, and had taken the name and arms of that house. He would never take the oath of allegiance to King William or Queen Anne. They told me that the duke their brother was making a tour among his friends and his vassals, and had sent them before him to assure me of his zeal and of his good intentions....

After having talked a little together, they asked of me if I would not promise them 5000 men [from France]. I answered them...that the question was not whether the King could send 5000 men to Scotland, but whether they had need of them to deliver them from the yoke of the English; that they had not yet proved their want of them; and to put an end to the dispute, I would propose a difficulty which I believe they would find it very hard to answer; that the English had their eyes upon them, being well apprised of the general discontent of their nation; that as 5000 men could not be embarked without some bustle, on the first news of the preparations the English would not fail to suspect some commotion, and would immediately seize the leading men in Scotland, which would entirely break all their measures and make their design miscarry, without leaving them any hopes of their being able to resume it, since it was not an enterprize to be attempted twice.

I know not whether this reflection had any weight with them, or if they perceived that I sought pretences to avoid promising them any thing; but they instantly broke off the conferences and retired into another apartment....In taking leave of me, they told me that [they agreed] to lay aside the design of concluding a treaty, in hopes that his majesty would judge most properly of their wants....

The Duke of Athol arriving at his seat of Huntinghall, those who were at Scoon went to wait on him; and next day they shewed me a draught of [a] Memorial, in which they neither required a certain number of troops, nor a certain sum of money, but referred themselves absolutely to the King....When Lord Stormont went to him, he shewed him their Memorial finished. The Duke of Athol desired him to sign for him, and then added to it the last clause[1]....

A fair copy of the Memorial being written, Lord Stormont signed it first, and the Laird of Boyn afterwards. I told them that I could not refuse taking charge of their demands, even though I thought them too great, and that in my opinion they would have done better if they had not asked for so great a quantity of arms at once....

After taking leave of Lord Stormont...I paid a visit to the Marquis of Drummond. He and his friends had drawn up a Memorial, of which they gave me a copy: but when they had read that which I was charged with, they desired me to suppress theirs, and Lord Drummond and [Thomas Drummond] the Laird of Logie [-Almond] his relation signed mine in the name of the others, that is to say, of all the chieftains of the Highlanders of the west of Scotland.

Lord Kinnaird signed the Memorial the same day. He refused to see the names of those who had signed before him, saying, that what he did was from a principle of duty, and what he thought every honest man ought to do, and that he wanted not the authority nor the example of those who had preceded him.

The Laird of Abercairnie, chief of the family of Murray,

[1] Cf. infra, p. 26.

signed it for himself and for the Lords of Fintrie [David Graham] and of Newton [Sir Richard Newton]....

From Drummond I went to see the Earl of Strathmore, who signed for himself and for the Earls of Wigton and Lithgow, who had desired him to do so. He also did himself the honour of writing to the K——.

His brother [Patrick Lyon], the Laird of Auchterhouse, signed for himself and for the Laird of Carnwath, whom I mentioned before.

From hence I went to the Earl of Panmure's, brother-in-law to the Duke of Hamilton. He signed the Memorial, and gave me a letter for his Majesty, and another for the K—— of England. It was there that I first learnt the news of the victory of Almanza[1], which gave great joy to all Scotland.

I staid some days with the Laird of Pourie [Thomas Fotheringham], who signed for himself and for the whole shire of Angus, giving me a list of all the nobility of that shire, of whom he said he was certain.

From thence I went to the Duke of Gordon's in the depth of the North. He would not sign the Memorial, because one of the articles of it required the personal appearance of the K—— of England, and he could not prevail upon himself to think of exposing this Prince to the dangers of war, though he owned at the same time that his presence in Scotland would be worth ten thousand men to him. He was likewise not of the opinion of the others, in their demanding of his Majesty to send troops into England or Scotland. His Grace thought, that if the English should withdraw theirs from the Low Countries, there would not be any need of this new assistance, and that the King's forces would be more usefully employed against his enemies on that side. However, in his letter to his Majesty he approves of the Memorial, and he told me that he found it agreeable to the sentiments of all his friends with whom he had taken proper measures.

[1] Fought on April 25 [N.S.], 1707, it resulted in a victory for the French, under the Duke of Berwick, over the Earl of Galway and the Marquis Das Minas.

Going to see the Apostolical Vicar[1], I fell ill a second time at his house.

The Laird of Coxtoun [Alexis Innes] came to see me there. He is about forty-five years of age, has been in the army, and is rich and powerful between the rivers Spey and Ness in the north of Scotland. I had informed him of my arrival before I left the Earl of Errol's, and Mr Murray[2] had seen him since. He had visited all his shire, had conferred with the Stuarts, and finding the Memorial agreeable to the sentiments of those he had consulted, he signed it for himself, for the Earl of Murray, and for the Laird of Grant.

After recovering my health a little at the Apostolical Vicar's, I returned back to the Earl of Errol's castle. He had consulted his chief friends, and was not satisfied...that a treaty had not been made; because, said he, as the case now stands we are engaged, and the King does not promise us any thing. But, after knowing the reasons of the others, he approved them....He signed the Memorial for himself, for the Earls of Caithness, Eglinton, Aberdeen, and Buchan, for Lord Saltoun, and for the shires of Aberdeen and Merns.

The Great Marshal, being taken ill at Edinburgh, commissioned his cousin, the Laird of Keith, to sign for him, and wrote me word that he was not able to travel, but desired me to assure the King that he will be one of the first to join the K— of England upon his arrival. He has likewise promised twenty-eight field-pieces and two battering cannon, which are in his castle of [Dunnottar] in the east of Scotland.

Memorial of the Scottish Lords addressed to the King of France[3].

His Most Christian Majesty having been pleased to offer his protection to the kingdom of Scotland, in order to restore its lawful K—, and to secure to its nation its liberty, privileges, and independance: and his majesty having sent the honourable Colonel Hooke (who, besides his past services, has now again given fresh and signal proofs of his capacity, zeal, and fidelity for the service of the most

[1] Bishop Thomas J. Nicholson.
[2] Lieutenant-Colonel, of Abercarnie.
[3] *C. H. N.* 83.

Christian King, and of his Britannic Majesty) to confer with the Peers and other Nobility of this nation touching the measures that may be most conductive to so just and glorious an end.

We the underwritten Peers and Lords, having seen the full power given by his most Christian Majesty to the said Colonel, do in our own names, and in the name of the greatest part of this nation, whose dispositions are well known unto us, accept the protection and assistance of his most Christian Majesty with the utmost gratitude; and we take the liberty most humbly to lay before his said majesty the following representation of the present state of this nation, and of the things we stand in need of.

The greatest part of Scotland has always been well-disposed for the service of its lawful K— ever since the revolution, as his most Christian Majesty has often been informed by some among us. But this good disposition is now become universal. The shires of the west, which used to be the most disaffected, are now very zealous for the service of their lawful K—. We have desired Colonel Hooke to inform his most Christian Majesty of the motives of this happy change.

To reap the benefit of so favourable a disposition and of so happy a conjuncture, the presence of the K— our Sovereign will be absolutely necessary; the people being unwilling to take arms without being sure of having him at their head. We have desired Colonel Hooke to represent to his Majesty the reasons of this demand.

The whole nation will rise upon the arrival of its K—: He will become master of Scotland without any opposition, and the present government will be intirely abolished.

Out of [the numbers that will rise]¹ we will draw 25,000 foot, and 5000 horse and dragoons; and with this army we will march strait into England: We, and the other Peers and Chiefs, will assemble all our men, each in his respective shire.

The general rendezvous of the troops on the north of the river Tay shall be at Perth: Those of the western shires shall assemble at Stirling; and those of the south and east at Dumfries and at Duns.

Those that shall be nearest the place where the K— of England shall land shall repair to him.

We have computed the number of men which will be furnished by each of the shires that we are best acquainted with; and we have desired Colonel Hooke to inform his most Christian Majesty thereof.

¹ The London edition has 'Out of this great number of men.'

For the subsistence of these troops there will be found in our granaries the harvests of two years; so that a crown will purchase as much flour as will keep a man two months. There will be commissaries in each shire, to lay up the corn in the magazines in such places as shall be thought most proper, and Commissaries-General, who will take care to supply the army with provisions wherever it shall march.

The same commissaries will furnish it with meat, beer, and brandy, of which there is great plenty all over the kingdom.

There is woollen-cloth enough in the country to cloath a greater number of troops, and the Peers and other Lords will take care to furnish it.

There is great quantity of linen, shoes, and bonnets for the soldiers. They will be furnished in the same manner as the woollen-cloths. Of hats there are but few[1].

The same Commissaries will furnish carriages for the provisions, of which the country abounds.

The inclinations of all these shires (excepting those of the west) for the K— of England have been so well known and so public at all times since the Revolution, that the government has taken care to disarm them frequently; so that we are in great want of arms and ammunition.

The Highlanders are pretty well armed after their manner.

The shires of the west are pretty well armed.

The Peers and Nobility have some arms.

There is no great plenty of belts and pouches, but there are materials enough to make them.

The few cannons, mortars, bombs, grenades, &c., that are in the kingdom, are in the hands of the government.

No great plenty will be found of hatchets, pick-axes, and other instruments for throwing up the earth: but there are materials for making them.

Commissaries will be appointed to furnish cattle for the conveyance of the provisions, artillery, and carriages, the country being plentifully provided therewith.

There are some experienced officers, but their number is not great.

With respect to money, the state of this nation is very deplorable. Besides that the English have employed all sorts of artifices to draw it

---

[1] 'The natives wear bonnets instead of hats.'—Hooke's note.

out of the kingdom, the expedition of Darien has cost large sums: our merchants have exported a great deal: we have had five years of famine, during which we were obliged to send our money into England and to Ireland to purchase provisions; and the constant residence of our Peers and Nobility at London has drained us of all the rest. What our nation can contribute towards the war is therefore reduced to these two heads: the public revenue, which amounts to one hundred thousand five hundred pounds Sterling a year; and what the Nobility will furnish in provisions, cloaths, &c., the quantities and proportions of which will be settled upon the arrival of the K— of England. Having thus set forth the state of the nation, we most humbly represent to his most Christian Majesty as follows:

That it may please his most Christian Majesty to cause the K— our Sovereign to be accompanied by such a number of troops as shall be judged sufficient to secure his person against any sudden attempts of the troops now on foot in Scotland, being about two thousand men, which may be joined by three or four English regiments now quartered upon our frontiers.

It would be presumption in us to specify the number: but we most humbly represent to his Majesty, that the number ought to be regulated according to the place where the K— of England shall land. If his Majesty lands north of the river Tay, a small number will suffice for his security, because he will be joined in a few days by considerable numbers of his subjects: he will be covered by the river Tay and the firth of Forth, and all the shires behind him are faithful to his interests.

But if, on the contrary, his Majesty lands upon the south-west or south coast, he will want a large body of troops, on account of the proximity of the forces of the English and of their regular troops. We believe that eight thousand men will be sufficient.

But with respect to the number of troops, we readily agree to whatever shall be settled between the two Kings; being persuaded that the tenderness of the most Christian King for the person of our Sovereign falls no way short of that of his faithful subjects.

We also beseech his Majesty to honour this nation with a General, to command in chief under our Sovereign, of distinguished rank, that the first men of Scotland may be obliged to obey him without difficulty; and to cause him to be accompanied by such General Officers as the two Kings shall judge proper.

The Peers and other Lords, with their friends, desire to command the troops they shall raise, in quality of Colonels, Lieutenant-Colonels, Captains, and Ensigns : but we want Majors, Lieutenants, and Serjeants to discipline them.

And if our enemies withdraw their troops from foreign countries to employ them against us, we hope that his most Christian Majesty will send some of his over to our assistance.

The great scarcity of money in this country obliges us to beseech his most Christian Majesty to assist us with an hundred thousand pistoles, to enable us to march strait into England. We stand also in need of a regular monthly subsidy during the war : but we submit, in that article, to whatever shall be agreed upon by the two Kings.

We likewise beseech his most Christian Majesty to send with the K— our Sovereign arms for twenty-five thousand foot and five thousand horse or dragoons, to arm our troops, and to be kept in reserve, together with powder and balls in proportion, and also some pieces of artillery, bombs, grenades, &c., with officers of artillery, engineers, and cannoneers. We submit also in this to whatever shall be settled between the two Kings.

We have desired Colonel Hooke to represent to his most Christian Majesty the time we judge most proper for this expedition, as also the several places of landing, and those for erecting magazines, with our reasons for each : and we most humbly beseech his Majesty to choose that which he shall like best.

And whereas several of this nation, and a great number of the English, have forgot their duty towards their Sovereign, we take the Liberty to acquaint his most Christian Majesty, that we have represented to our K— what we think it is necessary his Majesty should do to pacify the minds of his people, and to oblige the most obstinate to return to their duty, with respect to the security of the Protestant Religion, and other things which it will be necessary for him to grant to the Protestants. We most humbly thank his most Christian Majesty for the hopes he has given us by Colonel Hooke, of having our privileges restored in France, and of seeing our K— and this nation included in the future peace : and we beseech his Majesty to settle this affair with the K— our Sovereign.

We have fully informed Colonel Hooke of several other things, which we have desired him to represent to his most Christian Majesty.

And, in the pursuit of this great design, we are resolved mutually to bind ourselves by the strictest and most sacred ties, to assist one another in this common cause, to forget all family differences, and to concur sincerely and with all our hearts, without jealousy or distrust, like men of honour, in so just and glorious an enterprise. In testimony whereof we have signed these presents, the seventh day of the month of May, of the year one thousand seven hundred and seven.

(Signed) ERROL.	N. MORAY.
PANMURE.	N. KEITH.
STORMONT.	DRUMMOND.
KINNAIRD.	THO. FOTHERINGHAM.
JAMES OGILVIE.	ALEX. INNES.

Hooke[1] had no sooner finished his Negotiations than he took his leave of his Friends, assuring them that the K—g should be in Scotland by the next August, and went in a French Ship which waited upon him on the North Coast of France, where he arrived in May 1707, and having given an account of his Ambassy and the Reception he met with, Triumphed no little over the Earl of Midleton, whom and his Friends in Scotland he accused of backwardness to serve the King.

In the mean time every body expected to have heard of the Designs being put in Execution; but some Weeks before the Month of August (the time appointed for making the Attempt) Notice was sent that it could not be done then; and thereafter several Diets were prefixed which took as little effect, and it was next to a Miracle that so long delay and so many off puts did not bring all to Light, and occasion, either then or at least afterwards, when the Attempt was made and miscarried, the ruin of many People; for as I said before, the Design was known to so many People, and so much discoursed of in common Conversation, that it was strange Witnesses and Proofs should be wanting to have hanged any Man. But such was the Loyalty and Affection of the People to the King, that tho' the Government knew there had been a Correspondence with France, yet could they not procure any certain Intelligence, nor afterwards the least accusation against any one of the many who they knew were deeply dip'd and concern'd in it.

But to proceed, after several times had been appointed for

[1] *L. M.* 358.

making the Attempt, and nevertheless no appearance of its being
Executed, People began to think that the French King's Affairs
being somewhat retrieved by the Battle of Almanza, which
happened during the time Hooke was in Scotland, he was
resolved to reserve this Design in favour of the King's to another
occasion; and this proceeded from reflecting on Hooks Behaviour
here, and Jealousy, I'm afraid too well grounded, that the
French King only minded our King in so far as his own Interest
led him, and made use of him as a Tool to promote and be
subservient to his own private Designs[1].

None were more of this Opinion than the Duke of H[amilto]n;
so that having waited, without seeing any Reason to believe the
French King was in earnest, till the end of January 1708, his
Affairs in England requiring his Presence, he set out about that
time from Kinniel to Lancaster....But on the third Morning
after he set out, as he was preparing to move on from Sir David
Murray of Stenhope's House, where he had been all Night, an
Express from Captain [Harry] Straton overtook him, intimating,
That by the Post which came in the Night before, he had
received Letters with an account that at last the Expedition was
resolv'd on, and would be Executed betwixt [then] and the
middle of March. Mr Lockhart of Carnwath having convey'd
his Grace so far, he shew'd him Captain Straton's Letter, and
seem'd extreamly puzled how to behave; but after some Consideration resolved to proceed on his Journey; for, said he to
Mr Lockhart, the Design cannot be long a Secreet, since the
Preparations for it will be publick to all the World; and if I,

[1] On August 2, 1707, the Duke of Hamilton urges that the
Chevalier 'come soon, otherwise the opportunity will be lost.' The
Duke of Gordon writes to Chamillart on August 9, 'We are in great
consternation here at not hearing from you.' The Laird of Kersland
writes to the same on August 16 and 20, 'Once more, do not lose
time; for if you do, you lose every thing.' 'For God's sake! What
are you thinking of?' writes the Duchess of Gordon, '...Come when
you please, and to what port you please, you will be well received;
but if you do not come soon, or if you do not send us speedily an
assurance of assistance, the party will be broken and it will be too
late.'—*C.H.N.* 112, 114, 115.

after I am come so far on my Journey with my Family, do all
of a sudden return back, every Body will conclude it is with a
Design to join the King, and so I shall be exposed to the Malice
of my Enemies, and be certainly clapt up in Prison and sent to
England; whereas, if I go on, perhaps they may think I am not
very forward in hazarding, and have stept out of the way on
purpose, and an Express can be easily at me in two or three
Days; I shall be always ready, and am able to force my way thro'
England to Scotland; besides, the People of Scotland are all
ready enough to join the King at the Instant he Lands, and I
do not know but I may do him better Service by being in the
North of England to excite his Friends there to appear for him.
Mr Lockhart having little to say against these Reasons, his
Grace desir'd him to communicate the same to Captain Straton
and his Friends, and that they should send off an Express to him
as soon as they had reason to believe that the King was ready to
Sail, and another as soon as he was Landed; and he concerted
with Mr Lockhart, that upon the K—g's Landing he should
instantly repair to the Shire of Lanerk (where both their chief
Interests lay) to raise and lead their Friends, and such as would
take Arms to meet the Duke at Dumfries, where he promised
to meet him, and where he was sure to be joined with a great
number of Horse and Foot, both from that Country and the
Western Borders of England, and would instantly Proclaim the
King there, and thus be in Condition to defend the Borders of
[Scotland] against any Attempt from England until a Scots
Army was formed, the Parliament convened, and the King's
Affairs settled. Thus they two parted, and you shall see by and
by, his Grace would have Executed what he then proposed.

It is beyond my reach to determine the Cause of this sudden
Change in the French King's Councils; some were pleased to
say that it was long e'er he could be prevailed upon to make the
Attempt; others again, that he all along design'd it; but the
time of its being accomplished was kept a mighty Secret as long
as possible from any body but his own Ministers, because of the
Divisions that were at the Court of St Germains, and the
Intelligence that was found to have gone too often from thence
to England. It won't be much out of the way to leave them for

some time in France busie in making Preparations for the
Design, and have under Consideration what probability the King
had to expect Success.

In the first place then, he was sure to be made welcome in
Scotland, to have his right asserted by the Parliament, and an
Army of Thirty or Forty Thousand Men (picked out of the
many Thousands that would have offer'd their Service) raised,
the Nobility, Gentry, and many of the Commons being prepared
to receive him, and having provided themselves with good
Horses. The regular Troops wanted Ammunition and other
Warlike Stores, and did not exceed Two Thousand Five Hundred
Men, of whom at least 2000 would infallibly have joyned with
him, nay, the very Guards done Duty on his Person the first
Night he had Landed; all the Garrisons were unprovided and
must have yielded at the first Summons; the Equivalent Money
which came down the preceeding Summer from England was
still in the Country, and a good part of it in the Castle of Edinburgh, and would have helped well to carry on the War. A
Fleet of Dutch Ships had some time before run a Ground on the
Coast of Angus, wherein was a vast quantity of Powder, Cannon,
and small Arms, and a great sum of Money, all which the
Gentlemen in that Country would have secured: In short, all
things concurred to render the Design successful in Scotland.

In England the regular Troops were scarcely five Thousand
Men, and those for the most part newly raised, the opposite
Parties and Factions so numerous, and Jealousies and Animosities
so great, that it might reasonably be expected (as it actually
happen'd) all would be in the greatest Confusion imaginable,
for every Party suspected the other was privy to the Design; so
that in all appearance every body would have succombed, or if
any resistance had been made, the Scots would have given such
a Diversion to the English Arms, That France had a fair
Opportunity of reducing Holland, and by that means breaking
the Confederacy, and then the hardest part was over. It would
appear odd that England should be thus catch'd Napping, when,
as I told you before, they knew what Temper Scotland was in;
and that their had been trafficking with France was no secret;
for besides that the design was too much devulged at home, The

Duke of Hamilton was assured by a certain General Officer, That during the last Campaign, the Duke of Marlborough had Information of the whole Project from a Person belonging to the Earl of Melfort. Whether the English did not believe that the French King would have prosecuted the Measures, or as some think, that the Duke of M[arlboroug]h and the Earl of Go[dolp]hin were Privy and had Consented to it, or Content it should go on, resolving e'er it ended to provide for their own security, or what other Reason to Assign for England's being so unprovided is what I can't determine[1]. But certain it was, that England was no ways in a readiness to oppose such a Storm; and its more as probable, if the King had but once set his foot on the Scots Shore, all his Subjects would have soon submitted, the fatal Union been dissolv'd, and himself restor'd to his Crowns[2].

The King's part was to hasten over to Scotland, to bring Money, Arms, and Ammunition for the Men he could raise, where, upon his Landing, to March strait to Edinburgh, there to Proclaim himself King of Scotland, declare the Union Void and Null, emitt a Declaration or Manifesto promising to Maintain and Govern his Subjects of both Kingdoms by the Established Laws thereof, Calling a New and Free Parliament, to whom should be referr'd the determination of all religious Affairs, and further providing for the Security of both Civil and Religious Concerns; Lastly, requiring all his good Subjects to assist him on his design of recovering his own and the Nations Rights and Priveledges, and as soon as the Parliament had adjusted Affairs and form'd an Army, to March without delay into England. These then being the Grounds whereupon the King was to form his Design, let us return to where we left off.

[1] Cf. Mathieson, *op. cit.* 284.

[2] How unprepared Scotland was to meet the impending expedition appears from statistics furnished in *An Account of the late Scotch Invasion, with true copies of authentick Papers* [n. p. 1709]. The pamphlet includes a forcible speech by Lord Haversham in the House of Lords on the matter; information as to the condition of the Scottish fortresses; and various letters of David Earl of Leven and Melville, then Commander-in-Chief in Scotland, in support of Haversham's allegations.

No sooner did the French begin to make their Preparations at Dunkirk than all the World save Scotland was amazed! England was Confounded, and Holland affraid of their own Terretories: But upon the King's coming thither in Person, the design was clearly discover'd in Scotland, nothing was to be heard but Prayers for a Lucky Voyage; and when the time drew near, most People of note slip'd privately out of Edinburgh to the Country, to prepare themselves for joyning the King. In England the Consternation was General, the Publick Credit gave wa[y] to so great a degree that their came such a Demand of Money upon the Bank, that had the News of Sir George Bing's having Chased the French off the Scots Coast come a Day later, it had broke and been shut up, and with it the Credit of the Government, which alone was a sufficient Compensation for all the Expence the French were at.

However, it being high time to provide against the Storm, Major General Cadogan shipped in Holland Ten British Battalions to be ready to, and which actually did, Sail for Tinmouth as soon as they were Inform'd the French Fleet was Sailed. Among these Troops were the Earl of Orkney's Regiment and the Scots Fuziliers, who declar'd they would never draw their Swords against their Country; but before these Troops could have come to Scotland the first Brush had been over, and all things in a readiness to have given them a warm reception; neither could the Force which were order'd to march from England (most of them being in the Southern parts of it) and from Ireland have come in time to prevent Scotland's being in Arms and Drawn together to support their King and Country, and in that Case it would have been no easy matter to have disappointed them; for as the Quarrel was just, so were all Men bent to hazard the utmost in defence of it: But that on which England depended most was the Fleet, and indeed it is incredible how soon a mighty one was fitted out, which prov'd too strong for the French, and the only means to frustrate the design and undertaking; though had not several cross Accidents happen'd, the French might have Landed, notwithstanding the English Fleet.

As soon as the French Fleet was ready to Sail, the King

Dispatched Mr Charles Fleming (Brother to the Earl of Wigton) to acquaint his Friends in Scotland thereof, and with him he sent several Copies of a Paper containing Instructions to his Subjects how they were to behave, particularly desiring them not to stir till they were sure he was Landed, and that then they should secure all the Money, Horses, Arms, and Provisions that were in the hands of such as were not well affected to him, and even their Persons if possible, and Mr Fleming was to Cause provide Pilots to meet him at the Mouth of the Firth of Forth and Guide his Fleet up the same, being resolv'd to Land on the South side thereof, at or about Dunbar.

Having[1] received an order from the K— my master, on the 28th of February [N.S.], 1708, to set out for Scotland, I left St Germain on the 29th, charged with instructions which his M—y judged necessary for the principal Lords of that kingdom, and was pleased to trust me with. I left Paris the 1st of March, and I arrived at Dunkirk on the 3rd, where the absence of Mr Canan[2], whom I was ordered to carry with me to conduct me, hindered my embarking till the 6th, when Mr Arnott arrived from Paris to be transported to Scotland, with some instructions of the K— my master, lest any misfortune should happen to me. Count Forbin, and M. de Guay, intendant of the marine, judged it proper to send us both off the same evening in different frigates. I went on board the *Cigalle*, commanded by M. Lotton, which had formerly on two different occasions sailed from Dunkirk [on the like service].

Having arrived [March 2, O.S.] within two leagues of the land, I went on board a fishing-boat that I might not be suspected, and landed at the castle of Slaines, belonging to the Earl of Errol, who received the news I brought him, after which he had sighed so long, with all the joy that might be expected from a man who had given all the proofs of most extraordinary zeal for the service, being greater than could be required from one less zealous than himself, he having exposed himself and his family to almost inevitable ruin by receiving into his house all envoys who have been sent to Scotland these four or five years

[1] *C.H.N.* 178. Charles Fleming's narrative.
[2] Colonel Alexander Cannon, who served under Dundee in 1689.

past, the vessels which have been sent thither sailing always directly to his castle. He also furnished to all, without exception, money and horses necessary to keep up a correspondence throughout the kingdom, and even hired vessels for some persons, which has cost him large sums and greatly indebted that family.

The Earl of Errol, having read the K——'s instructions which I put into his hands, instantly dispatched a messenger to Mr [James] Malcolm [of Grange], a gentleman of known fidelity, and who lived very near the mouth of the Firth of Edinburgh, with orders to have a boat ready and pilots to go on board the first vessel that should give the signal agreed on[1]. This Mr Malcolm punctually executed, having been on board the *Proteus*, the only vessel that entered the Firth[2], for which he has been obliged to keep himself concealed ever since. The same express of the Earl of Errol went afterwards, by his orders, along the coasts of Fife and Lothian, to give notice to the well-affected to have boats and pilots ready, which was so faithfully executed by them, that many of them have been imprisoned on this account.

Upon my arrival, he also sent to the Earl Marshal, who, living at no great distance, came the same evening, when I gave him the instructions I had for him. He immediately took the necessary measures for giving notice to his friends in that country, and for going to the county of Marr, where he is hereditary great bailiff; and next day he accordingly went thither. As I was ordered to follow the measures which should be prescribed to me by the Lord High Constable and Earl Marshal, in giving notice to the chiefs of the country, and delivering to them the instructions of the K—— my master which I had for them, they desired me on the 4th to write to Mr Nic[h]olson, Catholick bishop of that kingdom, to inform him of the present state of affairs, that he might give notice to the Catholicks of the North to hold themselves in readiness. I wrote likewise, by their orders, to the Duchess of Gordon upon the same subject, which she communicated to the Marquis of Huntly her son, who was then in the North, that he might make every thing ready in the counties of Inverness, Ross, and Lochabar, in which counties he has great interest.

[1] *Infra*, p. 43.   [2] *Infra*, p. 261.

I likewise gave notice to the Laird of Coxtoun, who is well known to the K— for his fidelity and the services which he rendered him in the late war. Having seen the Chevalier Keith[1] and Colonel Gidun, and the Earl of Errol having engaged to give notice to Major-General Buchan, on [March 3] I left Slaines, which is in the county of Aberdeen. That shire and all those northward from it were very zealous for the interests of the K—. I passed the shire of Marr without stopping, as the Earl Marshal had engaged to inform them of what was necessary

On the [5]th I arrived at Lord Strathmore's in Angus, and gave him the instructions of the K—. He was transported to see affairs in so great forwardness, and sent to some of the chief gentry in order to take the necessary measures at that juncture. He also sent to Lord Panmure, but he was at Edinburgh on particular business of his own. The K— is always sure of him, he having never consented to take the oaths to the present government. The same evening I arrived at Lord Nairne's, in the county of Perth, who expressed great zeal for the service of the K—; and as I had a letter of the Earl of Errol for him, that he might inform me of the most proper measures to see his brother the Marquis of Athol, he undertook to conduct me to him. We found that Lord in such a temper as we could wish. For five months before, he had all his vassals ready to take arms upon the first news of the K—'s arrival. He is very powerful, both in the number of his own vassals, and of others who are bound to join him. He asked of me several times, and with great earnestness, the name of the General who was to command them. I found him, and all the other chiefs whom I saw, fully persuaded that it was the Duke of Berwick; for they could not imagine that he could be recalled from Spain for any other purpose, as he was a subject of his B—c M—y. They had conceived so great an esteem for him, that I durst not venture to tell them that he was not to be employed in the expedition; but told them, that before his arrival at court that could not be determined.

Lord Nairne afterwards conducted me to Lord Broadalbin's, who not only engaged to cause his vassals, who are very numerous, to join the K—, but also to keep the Argyleshire men, who are

[1] Later (1712) 10th Earl Marischal.

looked upon as the most disaffected, so in awe that the K—
should meet with no opposition from them. He read the K—'s
instructions, which I gave him, with great joy. From thence I
went to Castle-Drummond, where I found the Marquis of
Drummond and his brother [Lord John], sons of the Duke of
Perth. They received the good news that I brought them with
great joy; and the Marquis immediately sent to give notice to
several chiefs of the Highlanders, who have a confidence in him,
to hold themselves in readiness, and took also the necessary
measures to inform the other chiefs of that country. I next day
went to Stirlingshire to Lord Kilsyth's, who was then at Edinburgh, as was also my brother the Earl of Wigtoun, who lives
very near that place, though in another shire. The people of
Stirlingshire are very unanimous for the K—'s service, and had
united under the command of the Earl of Linlithgow. On
[March 11] I went to [William Cochrane] the Laird of Kil-
maronock's in Dumbartonshire. He is very zealous in the K—'s
interest, and sent to the Earl of Dundonald, his nephew, to
inform him of the state of affairs. I remained here some days,
expecting with impatience the news of the K—'s arrival.

By[1] this time the Publick Letters were full of the French
Preparations to invade Scotland; nay, the French King had
solemnly taken Leave of the King, and wishing him a prosperous
Voyage, concluded with a Wish, *That he might never see him
again*; and had ordered his Ambassadors at Foreign Courts to
notifie his Design to the Princes at whose Courts they resided.

This[2] gave me considerable surprise. I knew the situation in
Scotland, and realised clearly that there was no hope of success
in that quarter. It is true that Queen Anne had recently brought
about the union of England and Scotland under a single Parliament, and that the innovation had caused a good deal of discontent, whence it might appear that those who were opposed
to the measure would not fail to rise in favour of James III. But
none the less, there seemed very little prospect of a revolution
in his favour. And besides, the Minister [of Marine] did not
mention any port [in Scotland] which was in a condition to
receive us, and I could not refrain from telling him...that the

[1] *L.M.* 370.   [2] *M.C.F.* 239.

project of invasion was entirely without grounds of encouragement; that Scotland was calm and tranquil; that not a single district had risen in arms; that we could not count on any port where our Fleet might anchor, or where the King of England and his troops could disembark in safety; and finally, that to land six thousand Men without an assured means of retreat was, in fact, to sacrifice them and to send them to certain destruction.

M. de Pontchartrain replied, 'You are too ready to raise objections; it should suffice you to know the King's wishes. His Ministers, no doubt, are better informed than yourself. And besides, have I not already told you that the discontented [in Scotland] only await the arrival of our fleet to declare themselves openly? Dismiss your doubts therefore, and think rather of justifying the good opinion we have of you.' 'Sir,' said I, 'I am zealous for the interests of my Master, and I cannot see him sacrificing six thousand men, who might be better employed elsewhere, without raising my voice in protest; for, if they disembark in Scotland, you may consider them, I assure you, as already lost.'...

[Meanwhile] the Intendant of Dunkirk, in accordance with the instructions he had received from the Minister, had already arrived at Court. Thereupon, the Board met, and after a consultation to which I was not admitted, arranged a scheme for the transport of the force which they proposed to despatch to Scotland[1]. They computed that fifteen transports would be required, each of which could carry three hundred men. To these fifteen transports they proposed to add five men-of-war, each of which could convey three hundred Men. Thereby, said they, we have all that we require for our six thousand Men, and twenty Ships will suffice....

[M. de Pontchartrain], having sent for me, informed me.... 'The King is providing 6000 men to accompany the King of England to Scotland where a considerable number of his subjects only awaits his arrival to declare for him. His Majesty has selected you to escort the Prince and his troops. You will there-

[1] The regiments ordered for service in the expedition were those of Bearn, Auxerre, Agen, Luxembourg, Beaufermé, Boulogne, and the Irish corps.—*C. H. N.* 131.

fore proceed at once to Dunkirk and prepare the necessary
transports.'...

The entire scheme appeared to me so ridiculous, that for-
getting to whom I was speaking, and giving the rein to my
tongue[1], I asked, 'Who is the ignoramus responsible for this
arrangement?' Somewhat astonished, the Minister enquired
wherein I found it defective. 'In everything,' said I; 'for, in
the first place, some allowance should have been made for the
fact, that since Dunkirk lies between Holland and England, the
enemy may be upon us any moment. And in the second place,
the transports are cumbrous and badly constructed, and therefore
quite unfit for an expedition of this sort, in which speed is
essential if we are to prevent the enemy's scouts from coming up
with us....What we should do is, to secure and arm the smartest
privateers at Dunkirk, and though they will carry fewer soldiers
than the transports, we can take more of them with us. With
such vessels we shall sail much quicker, and if we encounter
contrary winds, we can bring-to without drifting from our
course; while, if the enemy come up with us in superior numbers,
we shall be in a better position to escape.' The Minister paid
some attention to my suggestions, and told me to arrange the
details of the scheme....

On the eve of my departure for Dunkirk, I waited on the
King to take my leave. 'M. le Comte,' said His Majesty, 'you
realise the importance of your Commission; I hope that you
will acquit yourself worthily in it.' 'Sire,' I answered, 'you do
me great honour; but if your Majesty would grant me a few
moments, I would venture to represent certain matters in regard
to the commission with which I am charged.' The King, whom
the Minister had informed of the objections which I had already
urged, replied, 'M. de Forbin, I wish you a successful voyage;
I am busy and cannot listen to you now.'

The next day I set out, and having arrived at Dunkirk, I set
myself with all possible diligence to equip thirty Privateers and
five Men-of-War. There were many difficulties in the way, but
at length I surmounted them. To allay the curiosity of the public,
who were discussing the object of so considerable an armament,

[1] 'Me laissant aller à toute la vivacité d'un Provençal.'

and already penetrated its secret, I gave out that MM. de
Tourouvère, de Nangis, and Girardin were equipping the vessels
for their own use.

At length [1708] everything was ready, so far, at least, as I
was concerned, and we awaited only our sailors and soldiers in
order to embark. The latter arrived first[1]. I was informed that
they were at St Omer, a day's march from Dunkirk. We were
still without our sailors, however; and I feared that the arrival
of six thousand Men, added to the fact that our large flotilla lay
under the very nose of the enemy, would cause fresh speculations,
the more so since the whole of France was getting wind of the
project, owing to the movement towards Dunkirk of all the
English and Irish in the Kingdom.

To prevent such a contingency, I took with me M. Duguay,
Intendant of the Port, and M. Beauharnais, Intendant of Naval
Armaments, and went to the Comte de Gacé, who, having been
appointed to command the troops, had arrived [at Dunkirk] two
days before, to represent to him the inconvenience that would
ensue if the six thousand men arrived before all was ready for
their departure.

The Comte de Gacé agreed with me, and, recognising that
the troops ought to delay their arrival until the very eve of our
departure, ordered them to remain at St Omer in the meanwhile.
A few days later our sailors arrived; the ships put out into the
Roads; the soldiers were summoned, and all went on board.

The King of England arrived two days after. Whether from
fatigue or some other cause, he fell ill of measles and for two
days was in a fever. The delay which his illness caused to the
sailing of our Fleet allowed the enemy time to reconnoitre our
position. Thirty-eight English Men-of-War anchored off Gravelines[2], two leagues from Dunkirk. Having viewed them closely
myself and made out that they were actually men-of-war, I sent
a letter to Court, pointing out that the enemy's strength was too
superior to ours to allow us to set sail under their observation;
that to endeavour to do so would mean the total loss of the

[1] They appear to have been ordered to repair to Dunkirk by the
end of February.

[2] Commanded by Sir George Byng.

expedition; that the enemy, being ready to follow us, would not fail to seize the opportunity to attack us, and since we had no port of safety in Scotland, it was obvious that they had but to attack us in order to work their will upon us; and that in my opinion we ought to dismiss our forces and postpone the expedition to a more fitting opportunity.

But nobody in Dunkirk agreed with me. Several prattling individuals, ignorant, or perhaps with interested motives, declared positively that the ships we saw were only merchantmen which had been hastily assembled and sent to sea, in the hope that haply they might prevent, or at least delay the sailing of our fleet. They blamed me for raising difficulties, and made countless suggestions in which their secret motives were apparent.

In answer to the letters which I sent to Court there came back an order to dismiss the expedition. The grumblers raised their voices louder than ever, and when the enemy retired to an anchorage in the Downs at some twelve leagues' distance from Dunkirk, expressed themselves in a tone even more disagreeable than they had already employed.

Several who were anxious for the departure of our fleet wrote to Court and to the Queen of England, and made lying representations to both. These new letters altered the decision already arrived at. The Queen was at Versailles and once more importuned the King. He granted her request, and I received concise orders to conform myself to the wishes of the King of England and to obey him implicitly.

The troops were still on board, and the King of England had recovered his health. A favourable wind was all that we required to set sail. We were still waiting for it when the Comte de Gacé, who had been promised a Marshal's Baton as soon as the King of England started, perturbed at our many delays, and afraid lest his hopes should be destroyed or their fulfilment postponed if we did not start, set himself to induce the King to go on board, so that, as he said, His Majesty might be ready to sail with the first favourable breeze.

The King, influenced by these representations, summoned me to him and declared his intention of taking up his quarters on board ship. I pointed out to him that as neither wind nor tide

was favourable for our departure, it hardly appeared necessary
for His Majesty to embark thus early. I begged him to trust
in me, and assured him that so soon as the opportunity arrived,
whether in the day-time or at night, I would take such measures
as should not delay our departure a moment.

Next day the King returned to the charge, having been
pressed again upon the matter in the interval, and told me he
was determined to take up his quarters on board. This renewed
attack embarrassed me. I told him that there was no immediate
necessity for him to do so, but that it was for him to give his
orders, and for me to obey, though I washed my hands of all
responsibility.

From the intrigues of those who pressed the King so strongly
to embark I saw, that beyond their own private interests, they
were anxious to foist upon the Department of Marine the whole
responsibility for the enterprise.

I was by no means blind to the jealousy which existed between
the Ministers of War and Marine. The emissaries of the former
hastened the embarkation of the troops in order that, if the
expedition proved abortive after the King and the Generals were
on board, the Minister of War might be able to charge the failure
to the dilatoriness of the Department of Marine, and to represent
to the King, 'Sire, I have done all that devolved upon me. The
troops with their Generals have embarked, and I have punctually
executed Your Majesty's orders. If the project has not succeeded,
the fault is attributable solely to the Admiralty.'

To spare M. de Pontchartrain, whose interests I still had at
heart, though I was not without grounds for complaint against
him, I called on the Comte de Gacé, to whom I represented how
premature it was for the King to embark, seeing that wind and
tide were not favourable. My remonstrance had little effect
upon him, and it was in vain that I pointed out the many risks
which so unwise a step might entail upon the whole expedition.
He only met my objections with vague and unsatisfactory replies.

At length, angry at receiving stubborn answers, I lost patience,
and said with emphasis, 'Monsieur, you are anxious to induce
the King of England to embark before the proper time. Be
careful, and rest assured that you deceive neither the Minister

of Marine nor myself. The King must embark only when wind and tide are favourable. If you persist, I obey. But mark this, you will all certainly be drowned. As for me, I risk nothing. I can swim, and shall come to no harm.'

I hazarded this threat in the hope that it might intimidate the Comte. But his desire to pay court to the Minister of War, and the promise of a Marshal's baton, which he had never dreamed of winning so soon, rendered all my efforts useless. The King of England and all the General Officers went on board[1], and I was obliged to set sail[2].

I was risking the whole expedition, since they would have it so, and was forced to anchor among the shoals [3]. That very night a gale of wind put the whole fleet in peril. The King, young as he was, faced the danger with a courage and coolness beyond his years; but his suite were thoroughly frightened.

The Comte de Gacé, who had been proclaimed the previous evening on board my ship as Marshal of France, under the title of Maréchal de Matignon, was not a bit less frightened than the English. All of them were exceedingly[4] sea-sick, and begged me to put back into the Roads[5].

It gave me considerable satisfaction to see them so very unwell, having fulfilled their desire to put out to sea. 'I can do nothing,' I told them, 'the wine's drawn and you must drink it. Suffer, feel as ill as you please; I'm quite comfortable, and don't pity you at all. You have your wish. Why are you dissatisfied?'

Three of our best ships were nearly lost; they broke their cables and were saved only by a miracle[6]. Two days later, the

[1] The Chevalier was on board Forbin's ship, the *Maroe.—C. H. N.* 151.

[2] On March 6 [O.S.], at six in the evening. The flotilla consisted of five men-of-war, two others fitted as transports, and twenty-one frigates.—*Ibid.* 152.

[3] Off Nieuport.—*Ibid.* 152.

[4] 'Tous vomissoient jusqu' aux larmes.'

[5] The gale continued until ten o'clock at night on the 8th.—*C. H. N.* 152.

[6] The three ships were, the *Proteus, Guerrier,* and *Barrentin.* They carried six hundred troops.—*Letter of the Maréchal de Matignon.—*

wind becoming favourable, we set sail[1], and on the third day were off the Coast of Scotland, in sight of land. Our Pilots had made an error of six leagues in their bearings. They altered our course, and the wind and tide becoming contrary, we anchored [on March 12] at night-fall at the mouth of the Edinburgh River, about three leagues from land[2].

In vain we made signals[3], lit fires, and fired our cannon;

C. H. N. 159. Their loss was serious, since the whole expedition numbered only five thousand one hundred troops, and carried ten thousand muskets, one thousand pistols, and one thousand 'musketoons and carbines, without any saddles.'—*Ibid.* 152. The *Proteus* was one of the two men-of-war fitted up as a transport. She followed the squadron on the 9th; arrived at the Forth, in advance of Forbin, on the 12th; succeeded in escaping when Byng's squadron came in sight, and returned to Dunkirk on the 20th of March.—*C. H. N.* 140.

[1] At ten o'clock at night on Monday, March 8.—*C. H. N.* 152. Before they sailed, 'after several deliberations as to the place in the North of Scotland where Mr Hoocke wanted them to land, or the firth of Edinburgh, the latter opinion prevailed by the advice of [Lord Charles] Middleton, and the harbour of Bruntisland was fixed upon for the landing place. From thence it was proposed to send a detachment to take possession of Sterling, where there is a bridge over the Forth.'—*C. H. N.* 153.

[2] 'After having sailed from Monday [the 8th] at 10 at night to Tuesday [the 9th] at 6 in the morning, we were forced to lie to till 10, to wait for the vessels that had fallen behind. The rest of that day and all night we proceeded with a brisk gale, when his B. M—y became very sick. We continued our voyage on the [10th] and [11th] but the following night, fearing lest we should pass beyond the mouth of the firth of Edinburgh, we judged proper to lie to. On Friday the [12th] we discovered the coast of Scotland; but having proceeded too far north, we were obliged to return southwards to enter the river of Edinburgh.'—*M. d'Andrezel's Account* (*C. H. N.* 153). They anchored near the Isle of May.—*Ibid.*

[3] Forbin sent a frigate up the river flying an English flag, with orders to fire '20 canon,' the pre-arranged signal.—*M. d'Andrezel's Account.* (*C. H. N.* 153.)

nobody appeared. On the stroke of midnight I was informed
that five cannon-shot had been heard from the south. I had not
taken off my clothes since we sailed from Dunkirk, and rising
hastily, I concluded that the five cannon-shot must be the signal
of the enemy, who had followed our fleet.

I proved right in my conjecture; for at day-break [on Saturday,
March 13] we discovered the English Fleet anchored at four
leagues distance from us. The sight of them caused me considerable uneasiness. We were shut in in a sort of bay, with a cape to
be doubled before we could gain the open sea.

I saw at once that considerable coolness was necessary if we
were to extricate ourselves from our critical position. Rapidly
making all sail, I bore down on the enemy as though I designed
to attack him. The English ships were under sail, and seeing me
manœuvre as though I was coming up to them, they put themselves in battle-order and so lost a good deal of way. Profiting by
their lack of vigilance, I signalled to the fleet to clap on all sail
and follow me, and changing my direction, thought only of
getting away as fast as possible.

While I was thus engaged, the Englishmen on board my ship
began to murmur, complaining openly that I was running away
for no reason, and that the ships we had seen were only a Danish
fleet which visited Edinburgh every year to take in a cargo of
coal[1].

I thought it well to put a stop to these statements by a closer
examination of the enemy. I detached a swift frigate therefore,
which was sailing near me, and ordered her commander to
approach as near as he could to the English Fleet, and if it
proved to be a Merchant Fleet, to fire a couple of shot and bring-
to, and if it was, as I surmised, the English Fleet, to fire five
shots and make all sail to rejoin me.

Meanwhile, to lose no time, I was still pressing on towards
the cape, with the object of doubling it and gaining the open.
The enemy gave chase, and had I had those heavy transports,
as had been at first arranged, we must infallibly have been lost.

[1] A fleet of Dutch East-Indiamen appears to have been in the
Forth at the time, waiting for a convoy to proceed to Holland.—
C. H. N. 143.

That I succeeded in saving the expedition was due to no other
cause than, that having swift privateers recently docked, we soon
gained considerably upon our pursuers.

A single Ship of the Enemy managed to come near us, though
she had to sail her hardest to do so. To avoid her I was obliged
to change my course somewhat[1]. The Ship, seemingly determined to single out mine (apparently in order to have the honour
of fighting the King of England), fired a broadside into M. de
Tourouvère, whose ship [the *Auguste*] was following in my
wake. It is almost inconceivable how much the sight of that
single vessel, some four leagues ahead of her consorts, alarmed
the English on board my ship. They gave themselves up for lost,
and their alarm caused me considerable satisfaction.

While they were in this condition, the frigate which I had
sent to reconnoitre the enemy returned. She reported that she
had counted thirty-eight Men-of-War, and among them more
than ten three-deckers. 'You are joking,' said I to the officer
in a bantering tone. 'They are merchantmen, and they come to
Edinburgh every year to take in coal.'

The English, getting more and more alarmed, proposed to
the King that he should go on board the frigate which had
returned from reconnoitring, and should land at a Castle on the
sea-coast belonging to a Lord of whose fidelity the King was
well-assured[2].

The King mentioned the proposal to me. 'Sire,' I replied,
'you are quite safe here and your enemies can do you no harm.
That vessel which is pursuing us, to the alarm of all these
Gentlemen, is not formidable, and, were Your Majesty not on
board, would soon be sent to the right-about. But I will take all
necessary measures, and soon we shall be far away from all
pursuit.'

The King was entirely satisfied by my assurance; but the
English, whose terror increased in proportion as the enemy drew
near, importuned the King afresh, magnifying the peril in which,
they said, I was placing him, and with such success that the
King requested me to provide him a Boat in which to transfer

[1] 'Faire vent-arrière.'
[2] Slains Castle, the seat of the Earl of Errol.

himself to another Vessel, as had been suggested to him. Upon that I told him that there was no risk if he remained where he was. But he replied, that he wished to be obeyed and not reasoned with.

'Sire,' I replied, 'Your Majesty shall at once be obeyed'; and I ordered the master-pilot to let down a Boat. I signed to him at the same time, however, to do nothing further. Then turning to the King, 'Sire,' said I, 'may I request Your Majesty to withdraw to your cabin; I have something of importance to communicate to you.'

'What do you wish to say to me?' said the King when we had entered his cabin.

'Sire,' I replied, 'Your Majesty will readily understand, that having received most particular orders to guard your person, I should have been the first to propose your transferring yourself to another vessel were I not assured that you run no risk by remaining in mine. I beg of you to have confidence in me, and to reject the bad advice which is being given you on all sides. I will act with the utmost caution, and should it be necessary for Your Majesty to transfer yourself to another ship, I undertake to inform you at the proper time.'

The King, who had reluctantly acceded to the importunity of the English, was quite satisfied; but the whistling of cannon-shot so much augmented the fears of those cowards, that they returned to the charge, and represented to the King the danger to which my rashness was exposing him, and their anxiety lest it were already too late for him to extricate himself from it. They again urged him to land at the Castle which they had named, and so successfully convinced him that no other course was open to him, that the King told me he would have the boat prepared at once and without argument.

'Sire,' I answered—I am naturally hasty and impatient—'I have already had the honour to assure Your Majesty that you are perfectly safe here. I have received orders from the King my master to take such precautions for your safety as I should for his own, and I will never consent to Your Majesty leaving this ship to expose yourself in a Castle far away from succour, where Your Majesty may to-morrow be delivered up to your enemies.

I am charged with your safety, and my head will answer for any harm that may befall you. I beg you, therefore, to trust me implicitly and to listen to no one else. Those who venture to give you other advice than this are either traitors or cowards.' An English lord, who was standing near the King, joined in. 'Sire,' said he, 'M. le Comte understands his business better than we do. He answers on his head for your safety, and you must trust him.'

My firmness in refusing to allow the King to land silenced his other advisers. But observing that the enemy ship, aided by the course she had so far been keeping, was still gaining upon us, I said to the King, 'Sire, it is now clear that that vessel is giving her attention solely to us, since she has passed-by several others of our ships which she could have engaged. I must consider whether there is any risk to Your Majesty in remaining on board. Up to this point the enemy has had an advantage over us in the course she has been sailing. But now she is on the same tack as ourselves, less than half-an-hour will decide. If we out-sail her there is no cause for anxiety, and we need but continue our course. But if she is the better sailer, Your Majesty will go on board that frigate close at hand, and then, being relieved of anxiety regarding Your Majesty's person, I will accost that importunate fellow, and render good account of him within an hour. Meanwhile a boat shall be got ready, and do you be good enough to select those whom you wish to accompany you, that they may be ready should the necessity arise.'

The King selected his Confessor, Lord Perth, the Maréchal de Matignon, and Lord [Charles] Middleton[1]. I begged those gentlemen to curb their impatience, and assured them that if His Majesty was compelled to leave the ship, the English ship would not long continue to cause them any anxiety.

After watching her for a few minutes, I saw that she was making little head-way, and that I had already gained upon her considerably. I communicated the news to the King. 'Sire,' I said, 'we shall shortly have left that ship behind us, and Your Majesty can remain where you are.'

The result soon justified my opinion; for the Enemy, despair-

[1] Son of the Earl of Middleton.

ing of overtaking us, hove to, intercepted the Chevalier de
Nangis [in the *Salisbury*][1], and attacked him. Seeing myself no
longer pursued, I despatched four swift Frigates to instruct the
rest of the Fleet to crowd on all sail at night-fall, and to steer
East-North-East.

[On[2] the morning of the 14th] I had some discourse with Mr
Forbin, to know of him whether, as we could not land at the
firth of Edinburgh, we might not attempt a landing at some
other place. He proposed to me Inverness, a port in the north of
Scotland, and we immediately went together and mentioned our
proposal to the K. of England, who received it with joy, and told
us that we need only consult together about the proper means,
and that he would follow what we determined upon. As we had
no pilots on board who knew that harbour, the Count de Forbin
sent the Laird of Boyne[3] in search of some at Buchanness. All
the [14th] the wind favoured our course to the north of Scotland;
but at 10 at night, a contrary wind arose, which continuing very
strong all next day, Mr Forbin said that it was time to represent
to the K— the inconvenience of continuing that course, which
would inevitably occasion the dispersion of the rest of our fleet,
and the scattered ships would run a great risk either of falling
into the enemy's hands, or of being run aground, in case they
were pursued, or even of wanting provisions. The impossibility
of the Laird of Boyne's getting on shore, and consequently of
bringing us pilots, the uncertainty and risks of landing at a port
we were unacquainted with, and where the enemy might again
surprize us, with other risks and difficulties, being represented
by Mr Forbin to the K. of England, in presence of the Duke of
Perth, Lord Middleton, Mr [Richard] Hamilton, Lord Galway,
and Messrs Beauharnois and Andrezel, the K. of England, with
the unanimous approbation of all these gentlemen, determined
to return to Dunkirk, where, on account of the calms and
contrary winds, we did not arrive till to-day[4]. I am very much

[1] The *Salisbury* struck her colours.—*C. H. N.* 147.

[2] *C.H.N.* 160. From a letter of the Maréchal de Matignon,
dated 'Dunkirk, 7th April [N.S.], 1708.'

[3] On board the *Americain.*—*C. H. N.* 150.

[4] March 27 [April 7 N.S.]. M. d'Andrezel gives the following

afflicted, Sir, not to have a better account to give you, and to
have seen all our hopes blasted by so unsurmountable difficulties. I beg of you to be so good as to make the King acquainted
with the excess of my grief on this occasion, and believe me to be
perfectly, &c.

Upon my landing with the King, I find that the *Salisbury*, on
board of which was M. le Marquis de Levy with 400 men[1], is
missing, and we do not yet know what has become of the three
other small privateers. Mr de Bernieres has informed you that
he had landed the troops as they arrived, and had sent them into
quarters, where they will need some repose. I shall immediately
order on shore those that we have brought, and shall wait your
orders as to the destination of them and the general officers. We
were only nine ships in company when we arrived here [Dunkirk].

You[2] have heard the Reasons for the not Landing alledged
by the Marishal of Montignon in his Letter to Mons. Chamillard;
but these will appear too frivolous: And yet consider the Want
of Resolution and Firmness that has of late appeared in the
French Councils, and 'tis not improbable, that having mist of
the first Aim of Landing in the Firth, and being afraid of the

account of the return voyage :—'These reasons, and our apprehension
of wanting provisions, obliged us on the [15th] to direct our course
for Dunkirk. We fell in with six Dutch vessels, which Mr Forbin
would have attacked, and judged that he would have taken, if he had
not been charged with the person of the K. of England and the
troops and money of the King. The [16th, 17th] and [18th] we made
but little way, by reason of the calms and contrary winds. The [17th]
two frigates sent back from Dunkirk joined the squadron, escorted by
four men-of-war....On the [18th] the advice-boat, which had landed
in Scotland two Scots men, rejoined the fleet, and all the news they
brought was, that when they had landed the gentlemen, they were
ordered to sail off. Since that time the weather has been so contrary,
that all we could do was to arrive on the [27th] in the road of Dunkirk, with four vessels and five frigates. We hope the rest are arrived
or will arrive forthwith in the harbour of that city.'—*C. H. N.* 155.

¹ Besides various officers, the ships carried five companies of the
Bearn regiment.—*C. H. N.* 146.

² *L. M.* 375.

English Fleet's falling upon them, they might be at a stand and despair of succeeding. But is it not strange they should have undertaken such an Expedition, and not reflected upon and been provided with Orders for all Accidents that might happen? and was [it] so extraordinary a Thing that they could not foresee that the English Fleet (which was then at Sea) might have endeavoured to prevent the Landing in the Firth, and yet on such an Emergency leave all to the Admiral's own Disposal! But since, as I mentioned before, the King was so pressing to have Landed on the North, I'm apt to believe Fourbin had secret Orders from his Master which he did not communicate to the King. And therefore I can't altogether condemn those who are of Opinion that the French King did never design the King should Land; for being fully perswaded and satisfied that the Scots were zealously bent to rise in Arms, he might think that upon his Fleet's Arrival on the Coast they'd have appeared; and having once set the Island by the Ears together, and kindled a Civil War, he might spare his Men and Money, and reserve the King in his Power to serve him on another Occasion: Else, say they, Why did he not send such a Number of Forces as was capitulated? for the Treaters demanded six or seven thousand, and others ten thousand, which was promised, and yet they were but betwixt four and five thousand, and those none of the best; neither was the Sum of Money, nor Quantity of Arms, and other Warlike Stores, near so great as was demanded and agreed to. And since he had been at so much Charges in equipping this Expedition, and made such a Noise of it all the World over, Why did they not Land in the North or West, where they could meet with no Opposition! 'Tis true indeed, the South Side of the Firth was the Place advised and most proper (tho' other Places, both in the North and West, had been spoke of too), because the North Country was secure against any Attempts, and well inclined to serve the King; and the Landing on the South Side of the Firth gained them Edinburgh, and opened a Communication betwixt the North and the South, and the West of Scotland and North of England; but sure the difference 'twixt West, South, and North was not so great as, if any one failed, the whole Design was frustrated.

But not to insist further on the French King's secret Designs (which are all Misteries to us), this is certain, that had the French managed their Affairs right, they might have landed even in the Firth; for had they Sailed their course directly from Newport Pits, they might have reached it a Day sooner than they did; but in place thereof, tho' they knew the English Fleet was in quest of them, and that England and all the World knew of their Design, stood out so far to the North Seas, for fear, as they since alledged, of allarming England, that the first sight they had of Scotland was near Thirty Miles to the North of Aberdeen[1], and so, tho' they had the start by near a day of S[ir] George Bing, yet he arriv'd in the Firth in a few Hours after them, and one of their Ships[2] which proved leaky and was obliged to return to Dunkirk, and remained there two Days after they sail'd, reached the Firth several Hours before them; and if it was true, as I have been inform'd, that the French King's Orders to Fourbin were, That provided he could Land on any Place on the South of the Firth, rather than lose the opportunity, he allowed him to destroy his Ships and join his Seamen to the Land Forces, Why did they drop their Anchors at the Mouth of the Firth, and lose half a Day and a whole Night[3]? For had he sail'd on, he might have reached the Windings in the Head of the Firth before the English Fleet could have come up to the Firth, and lain some time concealed from them, who, we saw, knew not where the French were, but droped their Anchors too; but supposing the English had discovered them, next Day they 'd at least got so many Hours Sailing of them, that before they could have come up, their great Ships might have been unloaded, and the lesser ones run into Creeks and shallow Places (which abound there), where the English big Ships could not have come at them; lastly, it was unaccountable in them to come from Dunkirk, where were abundance of Scots Seamen who would have been glad of the occasion, and not bring a Pilot who

[1] Cf. Forbin's statement *supra*, p. 43.   [2] The *Proteus*.

[3] M. de Bernières in a letter of March 30 [N.S.] explains that the tide was ebbing at daybreak on the 13th, and that Forbin was compelled to wait until noon. In the interval, Byng's squadron appeared.—*C. H. N.* 138.

knew the Coast with them, the loss of which they found when they arrived there, and were obliged to take in some Fishermen for that purpose off of Mont[r]ose. I know some have attributed their not Landing to the D[uke] of P[ert]h, whose Heart, they say, failed him when it came to the push; but for my part, I cannot conceive how this Opinion or Instruction could have that weight in the managing a Matter of such Importance; again, it has been said that the E[arl] M[arischa]l omitted to answer the signal of a Ship which was sent by Agreement to the Coast near his House, to learn intelligence from him of the State of Affairs. 'Tis true, indeed, his Lordship failed on his part, but can it be thought that the vigorous Execution of the Project could stop on so slight a Disappointment? Besides, Mr Malcolm of Grange did actually go Aboard that Ship which I told you came after the French out of Dunkirk and arrived in the Firth before the Fleet, and informed them of all that was needful: But to leave these Speculations with this Animadversion, That the French might have Landed if they had pleased or managed their Affairs right, and that time must discover the true Reason of their not Landing, of which (by the by) none of the Court of St Germains, tho' often wrote to on this Subject, will give any return, which makes it the more Misterious.

The[1] K——'s return to Dunkirk, which was known by the public papers, threw the whole country into a consternation that cannot be expressed. I had been a witness of the good disposition of the great part of the kingdom through which I had travelled, and I was well informed of the good intentions of the rest of the nobility and gentry of the country. Never was seen so universal a joy at Edinburgh as that which appeared in every body's countenance for three or four days before the K——'s arrival. The loyal subjects thronged together, and those of the government durst not appear in public. They had no confidence in the regular troops, knowing that the best part, both of the officers and soldiers, were well affected to the K——. Besides, there was neither powder nor ammunition in the castle of Edinburgh, nor in that of Stirling; and they knew that all the gentry would revolt from the government the moment the K—— landed. So

[1] *C. H. N.* 183. Charles Fleming's narrative.

that it was believed, that on the K——'s arrival, those who adhered to the government would retire towards Berwick. But when it was known by the Gazettes that the K—— was returned to Dunkirk, the consternation was so great, that every body appeared distracted. They had received orders, after the instructions that I had given them, not to take arms openly, or appear n the field till the landing of the K——. The French fleet had retired without their receiving any order from the K—— how they were to act, and they had no chief or person who could take upon him to give them orders.

[Meanwhile,][1] as soon as certain Accounts of the French being ready to Sail came to Edinburgh, Mr John Hamilton, Son to Mr Hamilton of Wishaw, was dispatched to the Duke of Hamilton, and having reached Ashton in Lancashire in three Days, gave his Grace an Account of the joyful News, whereupon he made all things ready, and sat up three Nights expecting every Moment the other Express with the account of the King's being actually Landed, in which Case he was resolv'd with about Forty Horses to have rid Night and Day, and forced his way from the Messenger (his Grace being put in Messengers Hands upon the first account of the Invasion, by Orders of the Council of England) and thro' the Country till he had reached Scotland, which no doubt he might and would have accomplished; but alas, the first News he had was of the sad Disappointment.

It is too Melancholy a Subject to insist upon the Grief their disasterous Expedition raised in the Hearts of all true Scots Men; the Reader may easily conceive it was very great, since thereon depended the Nation's Freedom from Oppression and Slavery.

On the other hand, the Revolutioners [*i.e.* the Whigs] were not able to bear the good Fortune, but Triumphed over all they thought inclined towards the K——g against the Union. Immediately the Castles of Sterling and Edinburgh, and all the Prisons in Edinburgh, were crammed full of Nobility and Gentry: At first, no doubt, the Government expected to have had Proof enough to have brought several of them to Punishment[2], but

[1] *L. M.* 381.

[2] A verdict of 'not proven' was returned in the case of such as were put upon their trial for appearing in arms.

failing, blessed be God, in that, the next use they made of them was to advance their Politicks; for no sooner did any Person who was not of their Party pretend to stand a Candidate to be chosen a Parliament Man at the Elections, which were to be next Summer, but was clapped up in Prison, or threatened with it if he did not desist; and by these means they carried, generally speaking, whom they pleased. But to return to the Prisoners: after they had been in Custody for some Weeks, Orders came from London to send them up thither, which was accordingly done, being divided in three Classes, and sent up three several times, led in Triumph under a strong Guard, and exposed to the Raillery and Impertinence of the English Mob; and now it appeared to what a fine Market Scotland had brought her Hogs, her Nobility and Gentry being led in Chains from one end of the Island to the other, merely on account of Suspition and without any Accusation or Proof against them.

Whilst this was a doing, the Duke of Hamilton, being likewise brought up Prisoner to London, and taking the Advantage of the Discords betwixt the Treasurer and the Whigs, struck up with the latter, and prevailed with them to obtain not only his, but all the other Prisoners Liberation (excepting the Sterlingshire Gentlemen[1], who were sent home again to undergo their Tryal) upon their finding Bail to appear again against a certain Day (which was likewise soon remitted) and engaging to join with them (the Whigs) and their friends in Scotland, viz. (the Squadron) in the Election of the Peers for the Parliament of Great Britain, which having accordingly done, several of the Court Party were thrown out; this certainly was one of the nicest steps the Duke of Hamilton ever made, and had he not hit upon this favourable Juncture and managed it with great Address, I am afraid some Heads had paid for it; at best they had undergone a long Confinement, so that to his Grace alone the Thanks for that Deliverance was owing.

Having thus finished the Account I designed to give of the

[1] These, 'having, as they thought, receiv'd certain Intelligence that the King was Landed, mounted their Horses, and advanced in a good body towards Edinburgh from the Shire of Sterling, but being quickly inform'd of the bad News, returned home again.'—*L. M.* 380.

Scots Affairs, I may appositely conclude with the Words of
Æneas when he begun his Melancholy Story,

> Quis talia fando
> Myrmidonum, Dolopumve, aut duri Miles Ulisses,
> Temperet a Lachrymis?

and surely the Consideration of Scotland's present Circumstances
must be grievous to any that will but take a short view of the
State from which that Kingdom is fallen, and what it was before
England Usurped such a Dominion over it.

CHAPTER II

SHERIFFMUIR, 1715

[On[1] the 3rd of August 1713], about an hour after [the dissolution of Queen Anne's last Parliament], I[2] mett General [James] Stanhope walking all alone and very humdrum in Westminster-hall. I askt him what the matter was with him, for he seem'd to be out of humour when ev'ry other body was glad to get into the countrey? He answered, that he thought all true Brittains had reason to be out of humour. I reply'd, that I thought myself a Brittain true enough, and yet was in a very good humour. Why, said he, then it seems you have not consider'd the Queen's speech. Yes, said I, I have, and was pleas'd with it, for I think she spoke like herself. That's true, answer'd he, for from what she said I look upon our liberties as good as gone. I wish with all my soul it were so, said I. Why, returnd he, do ye declare openly for the Pretender? The Pretender, said I; I was not so much as thinking of him; but as you Englishmen have made slaves of us Scotsmen, I wou'd be glad to see you reduc'd to the same state, and then we shou'd be both on an equal footing, which you know in other cases is thought necessary for making the Union more compleat. Well, said he, 'tis no jest, you'l get your Pretender, and you'l repent it, I dare answer for it, e'er long; and with that he went off in a prodigious fury. The truth is, this gentleman was not the only person; for all, both Whigs and Tories, lookt upon the King's restauration as determin'd by the Queen and her councils, and were anxious to see the success of such an important affair and the event of so critical a juncture....

That the Queen did of a long time design her [half-]brothers restauration, I do not in the least question, but was prevaild with to postpone and delay it, partly by her own timorous nature, partly by the divisions and discord of her Ministry, and

[1] L. P. 479.   [2] George Lockhart.

partly by the tricks, intrigues and pretences of the Lord Oxford, in whom for a long time she plac'd entire confidence, and cou'd scarce at last be perswaded that he did not deserve it. [But] it pleasd God, by the Queens death [on the 1st of August, 1714] to blast all our hopes and expectations.

And indeed, on a review of the causes of the many disappointments of all the designs in favour of the prince and his father, it wou'd seem that Providence, as a punishment to these nations, wrought against them. For they were more occasion'd by the immediate interposition and visible hand of God than the power and contrivance of their enemies. Not to mention the winds, which alone hinderd the late King James from making his descent from La Hogue [1692], when he brought a good army alongst with him, and had many friends ready in Brittain to join and declare for him, nor how the same cause stopt the present King in Newport Pits [1708] and afforded therby time and opportunity for the English fleet to come up and prevent his landing in Scotland, when it was more than probable his attempt wou'd have succeeded;...and now, the Queen, when so many years work and the effects of so many consultations and contrivances were just ready to be executed, was remov'd, and the nation left in a state of the utmost confusion. And it will not be far out of the road to take notice, that about a year afterwards [September 1, 1715] the French King [Louis XIV] died, and by his death rendered abortive what was then, with such a prospect of success, contrivd and ready to be executed for the Kings restauration.

At[1] the death of Queen Ann, tho' I[2] was young, 17 years old, I was capable of judging a little of the state of the Kingdome of Scotland, and of the inclinations of the people. The long course of prosperity which her reign had been attended with, together with the hopes that she in her lifetime, or at least at her death, would settle the succession on her [half-]brother, had kept the Jacobits (who are the prevailing party in that Kingdome) not only from giving her any disturbance from the time of the miscarriage of the descent which was designed from Dunkirk [in 1708], but even made them [till the[3]] end of her reign

[1] K.M. 1.   [2] James Keith.   [3] A lacuna in the text.

[willing to be partn¹]irs in the gover[nment. But so¹] soon they
saw their [hopes put¹] off by her death, a forreign familly placed
on the throne, and those who had made the fatal union of the
two crowns, and who wou'd naturally sustain it, again in power,
they resolved, in conjunction with those of the same party in
England, to endeavour to shake off the double yoak, and free
themselves from slavery and usurpation by the restoration of
King James the 3d, son to King James the 2d, and in this they
hoped to be assisted by those [Tories] who had been employed
by the late Queen in the later end of her reign (when she
certainly had a warm side for that party), and who were now
so obnoxious to the present Government and King [George I]
for entring into these measures, as well as for making the peace
of Utrecht [1713], that some of them were forced to fly out of
the Kingdome soon after her death, for fear of being exposed
and abandoned to the fury of the Whigs; and those who stay'd
in it resolved to find their safety in that of their country, by
boldly opposing the late come Prince [George I]², and raising
what force they cou'd draw together in favour of his competitor.

The chief of these in England was the Duke of Ormond,
who had been Generalissimo of the forces at the death of the
late Queen, and in Scotland the Earl of Mar, late Secretary of
State, but who had been both dismissed from their employements
on the arrival of King George, to make place for the contrary
faction, who now ruled without rivals....

To these two the Jacobits adressed themselves on the death
of the Queen, but particularly to the Duke of Ormonde, who
was then Captain-General of the British forces, but had much
more credit with the people then he had with the troopes, who,
by the negligence of the Earl of Oxford (then High-Treasurer),
were still composed of the same Whig officers who had served
under the Duke of Marleborough....The Duke, finding himself
not sure of the army, delayed entering into the measures which
were proposed to him immediatly after the Queen's death, and
an accident which shortly after happen'd convinced him that he

¹ A lacuna in the text.
² Anne died on August 1, 1714. George landed at Greenwich on
September 18 following.

cou'd stay no longer in England with safety, but must go seek
the protection of some forreign Prince[1], who wou'd help the
party with arms and money, at least, if not with men....And
thus the rest of the year 1714 continued quiet enough, tho' not
without signs that next year wou'd not be so....

The Duke of Ormond being now out of the Kingdome, the
King's friends applied themselves particularly to the Duke of
Marr, especial the Scots, who tho' not so numerous as the
English, were not inconsiderable on many accounts: first, because
of the body of Highlanders which, on the first occasion, cou'd
be drawn together, and if well commanded were able to have
made themselves masters of the wholle kingdome of Scotland;
and, secondly, on account of the many sea ports they were
masters of, by which succours might come from abroad; and
indeed the English resolved to make use of those advantages:
they push'd on the Scots (who wanted no spur) to the attempt,
giving them all the fair promises imaginable of help howsoon
they shou'd take arms; and how well they performed it shall be
afterwards discover'd. They concerted with the Duke of Marr
that he shou'd immediatly go to Scotland, and there declare
publickly for King James, and that howsoon they heard of his
being [proclaimed they[2]] wou'd declare for [him. Meanwhile[2]]
to enable him [Mar] to prosecute his design, they gave him
7000 pound sterling to carry with him.

Wherefore[3], on the 2d of August [1715], or as some say the
1st, in the Evening, his Lordship, in the Dress of a private
Person, embark'd with Major General [George] Hamilton,
Colonel [John] Hay, and two Servants, on board of a Collier in
the Thames, and arriving in two or three Days at Newcastle,
hired there a Vessel belonging to one Spence, which set him
and his Company on Shore in the Ely, from whence he got over
to Creil in the Shire of Fife. Soon after his landing he was
attended by Sir Alexander Areskine, Lord Lyon, and others of
his Friends in Fife, to whom he made known the Design of his
coming, and then went forward to Kinoul, where he staid on

[1] Ormonde fled to France in July 1715, driven by fear that his
impeachment, already voted, would be followed by imprisonment.
[2] A lacuna in the text.   [3] *R.* 187.

Wednesday the 17th, and on the 18th he passed the River Tay, about two Miles from Perth, with 40 Horse on his way to the North. Next Day he sent Letters to all the Jacobites round the Country, inviting them to meet him in haste at Brae-Mar, where he arrived on Saturday the 20th of August[1].

There is no room to doubt that he had before-hand concerted Measures with them, and that they were previously advised of his coming before he arrived in Scotland: For, on Saturday the 6th of August, their Friends at Edinburgh were apprized of it; and early next Morning, Captain John Dalzel, a half-pay Officer, who, in View of this Rebellion, had thrown up his Commission to the Earl of Orkney, was sent out to give the Alarm to his Brother, the Earl of Carnwath, then at Elliock, where he arrived that Night, and early next Morning Expresses were sent to the Earl of Nithsdale, the Viscount of Kenmure, and others of their Friends in those Parts....Accordingly, in a few Days after he [Mar] arrived at Brae-Mar, he was there attended by a great Number of Gentlemen of the best Quality and Interest of all his Party: And particularly at their Great Council, which was held about August 26, there appeared the Marquis of Huntley, eldest Son to the Duke of Gordon; the Marquis of Tullibardine, eldest Son to the Duke of Athol; the Earls of Nithsdale, Mareschal, Traquair, Errol, Southesk, Carnwath, Seaforth, Linlithgow, and several others; the Viscounts of Kilsyth, Kenmure, Kingston, and Stormount; the Lords Rollo, Duffus, Drummond, Strathallan, Ogilvie, and Nairn, with a good many Gentlemen of Interest in the Highlands, amongst whom were the two Generals Hamilton and [Alexander] Gordon, [Colin Campbell of] Glenderule, [Lyon of] Auldbair, [Patrick Lyon of] Auchterhouse, Glengary[2], and others from the Clans[3].

[1] Some say he went by Dundee; but here I have followed the Report of the Spies whom our Friends in those Parts had sent to observe his Motions at that time, and whereof an Account was sent up to Court, Aug. 26th.—Rae's note.

[2] Alexander Macdonald or Macdonell.

[3] This List is to be found in the *Annals*, vol. II, p. 25, and *Compleat History of the late Rebellion* (Lond. 1716), p. 13, tho' I doubt if some of them were there.—Rae's note.

Having thus got his Friends together, he address'd himself to them in a public Speech, full of Invectives against the Protestant Succession in general, and against King George in particular; wherein, to gloss his Actions with a seeming Reflection as of Sorrow for what was past, he told them, 'That tho' he had been instrumental in forwarding the Union of the two Kingdoms in the Reign of Queen Anne, yet now his Eyes were open'd and he could see his Error, and would therefore do what lay in his Power to make them again a free People, and that they should enjoy their ancient Liberties, which were by that cursed Union (as he call'd it) delivered up into the Hands of the English...and to establish upon the Throne of these Realms the Chevalier St George (the Pretender), who, he said, had the only undoubted Right to the Crown, [and] had promis'd to hear their Grievances, and would redress their Wrongs. And hereupon excited them all to take arms for the said Chevalier, whom he stil'd King James the VIIIth, and told them, that for his own Part, he was resolved to set up his Standard, and to summon all the fencible Men of his own Tenants, and with them to hazard his Life in the Cause. He encouraged them likewise by giving them Assurance, that there would be a general Rising in England on the same Account; That they should certainly have a powerfull Assistance from France and from other Parts, from whence their King, as he call'd him, had already had large Supplies and Promises of more; that Thousands were in League and Covenant with him and with one another to rise and depose King George and establish the said Chevalier....'

With these and other such Arguments, which he proposed unto them with a popular Air, he at length prevailed upon them to embrace his Project....However, the Noblemen and Gentlemen did not immediately after this Meeting draw together their Men, but went every Man back to his own Estate to take their Measures for appearing in Arms when they should hear again from the Earl of Mar, who remain'd, in the mean time, in his own Country with some few Attendants only. These Noblemen and Gentlemen, being returned home, began to draw together their Servants and Dependants in all the Places where they had Interest, making several Pretences for doing so, but did not discover the real Design till things were in readiness to break out. And indeed it was but a few Days after, that the Earl of Mar summon'd them all, at least such as were near at hand, to a general Meeting at Aboyne in Aberdeenshire, on the third of September, in order to concert farther Measures for their appearing in Arms. And having there directed the drawing together their Forces without any loss of time, he returned to Brae-Mar, and...set up the Pretender's Standard at Brae-Mar on the sixth of September 1715, and there proclaim'd him King of Scotland, England, France, and Ireland, &c. 'Tis reported, that when this Standard was first erected, the Ball on the Top of it fell off, which the superstitious Highlanders were very much concern'd at, taking it as an Omen of the bad Success of the Cause for which they were then appearing, and indeed the Event has proven that it was no less. Thereafter they went to a small Town named Kirkmichael, where, having proclaim'd the Pretender and summon'd the People to attend his Standard, they staid some few Days, and then proceeded to Moulin, another small Town in the Shire of Perth, where they likewise proclaim'd him, and rested some short time, gathering their Forces, and where, by the coming in of others of their Party, their Number was considerably increas'd....

In the mean time, while the Rebels were forming their bloody Project, and, not without Grounds, conceived great Hopes of a powerful Assistance from Lewis XIV, the then French King, it pleased God, by a merciful Providence, for us to remove him out of this World [Sept. 1, 1715][1].

It 's[2] to be thought that the certaintie of the French King's death, which was brought us before anie act of hostilitie begun, would have disconcerted my Lord Mar, who had founded his own plan, as well as his arguments, on the assistance that was to be sent from France....But his Lordship of Mar's views, being of another nature, opiniated their persisting, assureing positivelie, that to his certaine knowledge the Duke of Orleans, who, he

[1] He...left his Kingdoms to his Great Grandson Lewis, born the 15th of February 1710, and was now but five Years and eight Months old, and the Regency to his Nephew, Philip Duke of Orleans.—Rae's note.   [2] *S. M.* 31.

said, was a young prince full of fire and no worse inclined to serve the King, would push that affair with more vigour than the old King, whose death was the happiest thing could happne to us.

After the meeting of Aboyn [September 3], Mar returned to Indercauld's[1] house, who, because his vassall for a small part of his estate...he [Mar] commanded to get the Fercharsons, his Clan, together in armes to obey his orders. This gentleman, tho' as zealous as anie, but haveing had more occasion to know his Lordship then others, did not amuse himself with what his Lordship said, refused to stir till the King's landing, and the meantime, being unwilling to make noise or struggle, left his house to Mar and retired to Aberdeen. He applied himself next to Inderie[2], another of his vassalls, and the second man of that Clan, who, not haveing so much to loose as the other, was disposed to rise with the first, but would have nothing to doe with Mar, in spite of the intreaties of all his friends, till the Marquise of Huntlie, to whome he offered his service, persuaded him to submit to obey my Lord Mar....His Lordship haveing thus gained him, offered him the command of all his men, thinking by his means to raise the whole Clan Ferchasone; but to no purpose, for neither he [n]or his Lordship had influence enough to bringe out above a hundred, or a few more, out of Brae Mar. By this time the Earle of Linlithgow and Viscount of Kilseyth...came and joyned him [Mar]. The first of those Lords spoke a good dale of his interest, tho' it never appeared amongst us....The other had no pretensions to that...so it may be believed his equipage was very small, and his attendants verie few to be helpfull to us, which consisted onlie of tuo servants....

[1] Farquharson of Invercauld had great possessions in the head of Braemar, which, lying within the lordship so called, were held by him of the Earl of Mar, and so he was his feudal vassal. But as a chief of his own tribe, the Clan Ianla, he was of course independent of his feudal superior. Invercauld took arms afterwards, and became Colonel of a regiment of his own name, when he was taken at Preston.—Sir Walter Scott's note.

[2] John Farquharson of Inverei, descended from a younger son of Finlay Mor Farquharson of Invercauld.—Sir Walter Scott's note.

However, this was sounded in our ears and through the whole countrie, that tuo Peers, with great numbers, had alreadie joyned Mar; and the news of armes and officers being come was repeated on all occasions. These, and a great many as groundless reports, wrought so much on those of the east and north parts of the countie of Fife, that they sent to tell me they were goeing off. They got over the Tay, most of them at little blind ferries, and were not in all fortie. Some skult in the borders of the Highlands for some time, there being no fourage where Mar was, and a few of them joyned him. [Walkinshaw of] Barafield, a gentleman from the west, whose domestick affairs being in disorder, engaged earlier than was to be expected of a man of his sense...got orders to waite of the Earle of Strathmore, a younge gentleman of eighteen years old, who had the most good qualities and feuest vices of any younge man I ever saw: the business was to get him to proclaim the King at Dundee and Forfar...while Alexander Maitland[1], uncle to Southesque...was to push Southesque his nephew...to proclaime at Montrose, another royall burrough, in the countie of Angus....

In the mean time, the Marquise of Tullibardine, a modest, good-natured younge gentleman...with the assistance of his brothers, Lord Charles and Lord George[2] Murrays, and their uncle, Lord Nairne, was endeavouring to bring over the Athole men, who were naturallie well inclined to the cause, but were afraid of their master, the Duke of Athole, and desired that at least that regarde should be had to him, that he should be spoke to.

Mar...sent Lieut.-Colonel [John] Hay, his brother-in-law, to offer him from the King the command of the armie under the Duke of Berwick, requireing of him to get his men together, and proclaime the King in thrie days. The Duke ansuered, It was strange, if the King designed him anie commission, he had not sent it directlie to himself....I won't pretend to determine that the Duke of Athole would have joyned; but I can say... that Mar did not treat him as a man of that consequence ought to be, and, for his own ends, did not want he should joyn; which

[1] Son of the third Earl of Lauderdale, and brother to Mary, Countess of Southesk.—Sir Walter Scott's note.
[2] Prince Charles's General in the '45.

is proven further by his sending Collonell Hay to him, the man on earth the most unacceptable to him....It 's certaine, he was of that consequence that he 'd [have] done more in one day in raiseing the Highlands than Mar did in tuo months, and had been master of the Bridge of Striveling before the Gouvernment could [have] takne their precautions....

[Mar] being informed that Strathmore and Southesque were readie to proclaime...expresses were sent to all the Low Countrie about, affirming that eight thousand men had alreadie joyned my Lord Mar; upon which, Strathmore and Southesque, with the gentlemen of Angus, proclaimed in the three towns alreadie mentioned.

The more the number hookt in by these methods increased, the greater the ferment grew....By their help the Earle of Panmure, who hitherto had resisted all with steadieness...thought he was too longe of proclaiming the King in Brechin, a royall burrough in his nighbourhood, and accordingly did it without further hesitation.

But it must be owned the Gouvernment contributed most to Mar's project, by the Act of the Brittish Parliament made at that time[1]; which being put in execution speedilie after it past, fiftie of the most active or most considerable Lords and Gentlemen were cited, some to render themselves in fifteen days, and others in fortie, according to the distance they lived from Edinbourgh, under the pain of forfaulture of their liferent escheat. All those were buoy'd up to the last day of their citations by the great pains Mar and his emissaries took to make them expect the King daylie, or, at least, the Duke of Berwick, with great secours from France; and no bodie, in that great ferment of spirits and great expectation, careing to give bad exemple by delivering up himself first, they were at last all caught in the same noose, their time being elapsed and no place left to repent. ...But it 's certaine most were undetermined even to the last minute....

Those of the Whig partie in the toun of Pearth keept the Tories still under, haveing disarmed them more by the authoritie

---

[1] The *Act for Encouraging Loyalty in Scotland* received the royal assent on August 30, 1715.—*R*. 208.

of the Magistrats, who were Whigs, then by their superioritie or number, but were not a little alarmed at the report of my Lord Mar's haveing got so many men together....They addressed themselves to the Duke of Athole, the onlie man of their nighbourhood who was able to assist them, or who they had the least reason to trust, and not haveing ane intire trust in him neither, or doubting his Highlandmen, I can't tell whether, they would take no more than tuo hundred. And on the other hand, they sent to the Earle of Rothes, Sherrife and Lord Lieutenant of the countie of Fife, begging his aide with the posse-comitatus....He had not been wanting before to promise them his assistance, and was at pains enough to make good his promise, and issued out ane order for all the fensible men of the Countie to meet him at a place called Cashmoor. The gentlemen took no notice of his orders, nor did the commons, except those who the ministers forced to goe to the place of rendevouse, to the number of fifeteen hundred mob, and all that their outmost diligence could perform. But...the unluckie choice of a place called moor[1] appeared ominous, and that, with the flying report of the Highlandmen's haveing made themselves masters of Pearth, made them throw doun their armes and run, notwithstanding the trouble that Rothes and his ministers gave themselves to stop them. In the meantime, the storie of Pearth being takne was not without foundation; for the Torie burgers, who were considerable in that place, being animated with the neus of my Lord Mar's being so stronge, begun to caball; and after feeling the tuo hundred Highlandmen's pulses, or at least their pulses who commanded them, sent to Liutennant-Coll. [John] Hay, son to my Lord Kinnoule, in their nighbourhood, to let him know, that if he could get anie number of men together and come to their assistance, they would revolt and deliver him up the toun, since there was nothing to be feared from the Highlandmen.

He assembled most of the gentlemen of the countie of Fife who were skulking in Pearthshire, who made the greatest part of the cavalcade, and with a very few of those of Pearthshire who joyned, they made up fortie horse....Noe sooner Collonell Hay appeared [September 18] with the fortie horse on the other

[1] Sinclair remarks that it called up reminiscences of Tippermuir.

side the Tay then the Torie burgers, who expected them, revolted, seised the boats in the sight of the other partie and Magistrats, who drew up under armes but durst not stir for fear of the Highlandmen, while their adversaries were bringing the gentlemen over the river, which is there about tuo hundred yards broad. The Whigs made no difficultie in delivering up their armes, which were given to the Tories, and some of them road post to Edinbourgh to inform the Gouvernment; all of those, as we were told, assureing positivelie there were some thousand Highlandmen got into Pearth.

By so manie concurrent accidents did Pearth fall in the hands of our people, without his Lordship of Mar's knouledge, which if we had not got possession of, his whole designe must have proven abortive, for there was no other place where ane armie could [have] been formed.

In[1] the Mean Time, while the Rebels were gathering in the North, a Conspiracy was formed to surprize the Castle of Edinburgh[2], on the Eighth of September 1715, betwixt 11 and 12 at Night, by mounting the Walls on the West side of the Castle, not far from the Sally-Port, by Ladders made of Ropes provided for that Purpose by Direction of the Lord Drummond, a Papist, which were to be pull'd up by Lines to be let down from within, and fixed to a large Piece of Wood and fastened with Anchors within the Castle-Wall by some Soldiers of the Garrison, whom one Mr Arthur, formerly an Ensign in the Castle, and afterwards in the Scotch-Guards, had engaged in this Conspiracy, by giving them Money and Promise of Preferment. The principal Traitor, William Ainsley, a Serjeant, who hath since been hang'd[3] for his Villany, had the Promise of a Lieutenant's Place, and James Thomson and John Holland, two single Centinels, had received, the one 8 Guineas and the other 4, with the Promise of a better Reward if the Design should succeed. And it hath since appear'd by their own Confession, That the Numbers engaged in this Attempt were about Eighty besides Officers, whereof about the one half were Highlanders

[1] R. 198.
[2] An account of this plot is also in S. M. 29–31.
[3] December, 1716.

...[and] That the Lord Drummond was to be Governor of the Castle, as being the Contriver of the Design, and that upon the Success of it, the Conspirators were to fire three Rounds of the Artillery in the Castle, which, by the Communication of Fires to be kindled at convenient Distances, was to be a Signal to the Earl of Mar immediatly to march towards Edinburgh with his Rebel Forces, to make themselves Masters of that important City and Castle.

This dangerous Design, tho' kept Secret among the Conspirators till but a short Time before it was to have taken effect, was happily prevented by the Care and Vigilance of that worthy Gentleman, Sir Adam Cockburn of Ormistoun, Lord Justice Clerk. 'Tis reported that Mr Arthur had communicate the Matter to his Brother, Doctor Arthur[1], a Physician in Edinburgh, whom he had but then engaged into the Jacobite Measures, and that this Gentleman having appear'd very melancholy all that Day before the Attempt was to be made, on the Thoughts of the sudden Revolution that was at hand, his Lady importuned him till she got into the Secret, and that Evening, about ten o'Clock, sent a Servant with an unsigned Letter to my Lord Justice Clerk. But whether his Lordship had his Intelligence from this or some other Hand...so soon as he came to the Knowledge of it, he sent an Express to Lieutenant Colonel [James] Stuart [Stewart], Deputy Governour of the Castle: And that it was but a little before that my Lord had the Information appears in that the Gates were shut, and it was near Eleven o'Clock when the Person that carried it came up, who, being challeng'd by the Centries, was let in when he had told them he had an Express for the Governor. Whether he had dropt anything of the Secret to the Port-Guard, or they had only Suspicion of some more than ordinary Danger which brought an Express at that Hour of the Night, I know not; however, they instantly planted their Men in three several Posts, viz. The North and South Flankers and the fore Wall of the Low Guard, in order to make the best Defence they could.

By this Time the Conspirators rendezvouz'd at the Foot of the Castle-Wall with all things ready for the Attempt, and

[1] His relation of the attempt is in the *Stuart Papers*, iii, 550.

Thomson and Holland were waiting to assist them within. The Governor having received the above Express, it is said he ordered the Officers under him to double their Guards and make diligent Rounds; but it seems that he either went to Bed, or otherwise fail'd of his Duty, and acted not vigorously enough upon this Occasion, or suitable to the Danger; for which he was deprived of his Post, and in a short Time after committed Prisoner in the Tolbooth of Edinburgh. But to return to the Story of the Castle; the Garrison being thus alarmed, and as Lieutenant [Francis] Lindsey with a Party was marching down to the Sally-Port, where the Attempt was designed to be made, the above-mentioned Traitors had let down a Rope, which being fixed to the Top of one of the Ladders, they were actually pulling it up in order to fix it for the Assailants to mount; but observing the Approach of the Party[1], they threw over the Ropes, and so let the Ladders fall: Upon which, the Centries having heard the Noise, one of them fired, and the Conspirators fled and dispersed. But a Party of the Town-Guard, which, at the Request of my Lord Justice Clerk, the Lord Provost had sent out with Major James Aikman to patrol about the Castle, coming up upon this Alarm, they found one Captain M'lean, formerly an Officer of King James the Seventh, sprawling on the Ground and bruised by a Fall from the Precipice, whom they secured, with Alexander Ramsey and George Boswel, Writers in Edinburgh, and one Lesly, formerly Page to the Dutchess of Gordon. They likewise found the Ladder, with a Dozen of Firelocks and Carabines, which the Conspirators had thrown away in order to make their Escape the better.

And thus by the good Providence of God their Design was happily frustrated, which, if it had succeeded, would certainly [have] been of very ill Consequence to his Majesty's Affairs in Scotland: For by that Means the Rebels had not only been Masters of the Castle, the strongest Fort in the Nation, with Abundance of Arms and Ammunition to furnish those who

---

[1] 'The sentrie perceaveing the rounds comeing about, called down to them, "God damn you all! you have ruined both yourselves and me! Here comes the round I have been telling you of this hour, I can serve you no longer."'—*S. M.* 31.

would fight for the Pretender, and vast Sums of Money to pay them, but could also [have] commanded the City of Edinburgh, and kept a Communication betwixt their Friends in the North and those in the South. And beside, the Royal Army would [have] been hereby deprived of Military Stores, which they afterwards found necessary, to oppose this Rebellion.

His[1] Majesty, having Intelligence of the Motions of the Tories in Scotland, had on or before the nineteenth of August appointed the Lords Lieutenants for the several Shires, with Orders for raising the Militia there, and using all suitable Endeavours to preserve the publick Peace in that Part of Great Britain....

The Regiments of the Earls of Forfar and Orrery, with that of Lieutenant-General [John] Hill[2], being recalled from Ireland, were arrived at Edinburgh by the 24th of August; and about that Time, Orders were given to Major General Wightman[3], who was then upon the Spot, forthwith to march with all the Regular Troops that could be spared; to form a Camp in the Park of Stirling, as well to secure that important Castle as the Bridge over Forth, the chief Pass by which the Rebels at that Season of the Year could pretend to penetrate into the Southern Parts of Scotland; and to quarter the Half-pay Officers in such a Manner over the Country as that they might be in readiness to encourage, exercise, and command the Militia on any Emergence. The General accordingly ordered the Half-pay Officers to their proper Posts, and went up himself to Stirling with a Part of these Troops, and marked out a Camp for them: And on the 28th he was follow'd by five Companies of the Earl of Forfar's Regiment, who were then in Leith, and next Day, by the Royal Regiment of Scots Grey-Horses, commanded by the Earl of Portmore, and a Detachment of Lord Shannon's

[1] R. 205.

[2] Royal Irish Dragoons. For the identification of the regiments engaged at Sheriffmuir cf. *infra*, p. 118.

[3] General [Thomas] Whetham, then Commander-in-Chief in Scotland, having received the Orders from Court, sent General [Joseph] Wightman to mark out the Camp; and the Army encamped at Stirling the 29th of August, 1715.—Rae's note.

Regiment of Foot, with two Pieces of Cannon and six Waggons loaden with Ammunition. The Day after, General Whetham went thither also, and in two or three Days returned to Edinburgh: And in a short Time after Decamped from Holy-Roodhouse, and the Remainder of the Lord Shannon's Regiment of Foot, and what other Troops he had there, march'd up to Stirling on the 8th of September to joyn the Camp. This was a just and necessary Step of the Government to prevent the Rebels securing that Post to themselves....And besides, this was the most secure Situation for the Royal Army, which was then but weak: For at first they had no more than four Regiments of Foot upon the Reduc'd Establishment, which was of 257 Men to a Regiment, and four Regiments of Dragoons, of under 200 Men to a Regiment: So that at first, the Forces posted at Stirling were not much above 1500 Men. This Post being secured, the Government immediately apply'd it self to encrease the Forces, and ordered the Regiment of Dragoons belonging to the Earl of Stair, with two Regiments of Foot which lay in the North of England, to march thither with all Expedition. The Regiment of Dragoons of Evans, with the two Regiments of Foot of [Jasper] Clayton and Wightman, that were gone over to Ireland, were likewise recall'd; but it was a long Time after 'ere they could join the Camp, as we may hear in its place.

At the same Time, Letters were sent over to Holland to quicken the coming of the 6000 Men, which by the Treaty of Guarantee the Dutch were to send; and though they had accordingly order'd the Scotch Batalions in their Service to move towards the Coasts to be in readiness to embark for Great Britain if Occasion required, and two of them were on their March from Maestricht to Ipres by the 10th of September, N.S.; But upon the repeated Assurances the French Ambassador had given them on the Part of his Court, That the French King had not the least Thoughts of breaking the Treaty of Utrecht by sending the Pretender to England, they suspended their Naval Armament, and delayed sending over their Forces till they were again demanded.

The[1] Duke of Argyle, who before was Commander in Chief

[1] R. 218.

of all the Land Forces in Scotland, was now made General of
His Majesty's Army....His Grace having waited on the King
on the Eighth of September at Night to receive his final Instructions, on the Ninth he set out for Scotland, and was followed
soon after by his Grace the Duke of Roxburgh; the Marquisses
of Annandale and Tweedale; the Earls of Selkirk, Loudoun,
Rothes, Haddington, Ilay, and Forfar; the Lords Torphihen
and Beilhaven; Sir David Dalrymple, His Majesty's Advocate,
Sir William Johnston of Westerhall, and others of our Nobility
and Gentry who were then attending the Parliament....

About the same Time, the Earl of Sutherland had offered his
Service to go raise the Highland Clans in the most Northern
Shires of Scotland, of which he was lately made Lord Lieutenant;
his Offer was kindly accepted, and...His Lordship Landed at
Leith on the 21st of September and...sail'd to the Northward
about four Days after. But of the Conduct of the Earl of Sutherland and His Majesty's good Friends in the North we shall hear
by it self[1].

His Grace the Duke of Argyle, attended by several Persons
of Note, arriv'd at Edinburgh on [September] the 14th at Night.
Next Day he went up to the Castle and view'd the Garrison,
Fortifications, and Magazines: And...the Day after, his Grace
set out for the Camp at Stirling, accompany'd by his Grace the
Duke of Roxburgh, the Earl of Haddington, Colonel Middleton[2],
and several other Officers and Gentlemen of Distinction. Soon
after he arriv'd at the Camp he review'd the Army, which did
not then exceed 1840 Men, the Regiments of Carpenter and
Ker included.

In[3] the meantime, Mar got younge Strathmore, who was
very alerte, to raise tuo hundred Low Countrie men and march
to Pearth with such armes as they had, all more for shew and
countenance then use. Those were no sooner got into toun than
all were satisfied they were stronge enough; and a report being
spread of the Duke of Argyle's comeing to attack them, they
resolved to stand it with the tools they had, and the few pounds

[1] *Infra*, p. 171.
[2] Of Seaton, Co. Aberdeen. M.P. for Aberdeen Burghs.
[3] *S. M.* 40.

of pouder they pickt up in the toun, which I don't believe were above five or six.

The Duke of Argyle...had gone to Striveling some days before, where he found...no hopes of the possibilitie of recovering Pearth by any detachment he could make from Stirveling out of that handful he had there....

All this past in a week after takeing of the toun; and notwithstanding my Lord Mar had proclaimed some weeks before, he was not as yet in a capacitie to assist or reinforce us with any detachment, tho' they gave him out to be four or five thousand men stronge...and to give him his due, was doeing all he could to raise the Athole-men and everie bodie else; and by all his letters was makeing us expect him everie day with a great armie; and order'd that no horse should come up to him, because there was no fourage....At last, after all this great expectation, Struan Robertson[1] came to us with tuo hundred and fiftie Highland-men....

At this time the Earle of Southesque came to Pearth with about thirtie horse from Angus, and a hundred and fiftie Low Countrie foot....

My Lord Panmure came next into toun, with a hundred Highlandmen and tuo hundred Low Countrie men. Auchter-house, uncle to Strathmore and to the Earle of Aboyn, brought in the Aboyn men. My Lord Nairne and his son brought in their own men and some of the Duke of Athole's Highlandmen; and now they were in all a great many men, but no such thing as order....Tho' so many men were got together, there was no monie to pay them, except what everie one gave his own people out of his private purse, which could not subsist longe. I, happning to meet with Mr Hary Maule[2], fell into regrateing the unluckie state we were in for want of armes, pouder, and monie. He said then, very ingenuouslie, That never men were so idlie brought in for their lives and fortunes as we were.

But lyes, the life of our affair, were spread with more industrie than ever, of pouder, armes, and monies being sent us. Some of our gentlemen, who had thought that they had takne monie

[1] Alexander Robertson of Struan, thirteenth Laird; died 1749.
[2] Titular Earl of Panmure (1723).

enough with them to doe their busieness, or who came out in such haste that they had no time to provide, were goeing daylie home to get new supplies. I used to tell them, to no purpose, that some of them would be kidnapt; amongst others, Sir Thomas Bruce [of Kinross], a gentleman of very good estate, was oblidged to goe home some such [an] errand...and was takne by a partie of dragoons which my Lord Rothes brought with him, and from thence was carried to Leslie House[1]....

My Lord Mar begun at last to move towards us [at Perth][2], haveing succeeded in raiseing almost all the Athole and Tullibardine men by the means of Tullibardine, Lord Charles and Lord George Murrays, the Duke's three sons, and one hundred of the Mar-men, by the help of Inderei, for the others would take no notice of him so longe as Indercald would not engage. On his marche he was joyned by my Lord Drummond and those who followed him, who, not being Highlandmen, would not rise till the others came to force them out[3].

Generall Hamiltone came into Pearth tuo or three days before my Lord Mar, and the troopes with him, to regulate the quarters and prepare magazines of meale and fourage, which seem'd needless till then, nobodie thinking of it....He was not ane hour in toun when he askt for me....He told me I was to be sent over to the Lothiens, with a thousand men under my command to raise those gentlemen who were for us in the southern counties, and from that to marche into England....I must own I was not fond of that commission, and suspected my Lord Mar had pitched on me rather to put me out of the way then out of friendship; yet I thought I could not in honour refuse it, and, if proposed to me after, would have gone[4], provided

[1] Rothes prevented a party of Jacobites from proclaiming the Chevalier at Kinross on September 26. He captured Bruce there.—*R.* 232.

[2] From Moulin, through Logie Rait and Dunkeld.—*Ibid.* 219.

[3] At Logie Rait Mar's force was but one thousand well-armed men. But at Dunkeld, besides fourteen hundred of the Atholl men, he was joined 'by 500 of the Earl of Broadalbin's Men, commanded by Campbel of Glenderule, Campbel of Glenlyon, and John Campbel his Chamberlain, and several others.'—*R.* 219.

[4] The commission was entrusted to Mackintosh of Borlum.

I had seen armes, pouder, and ball, without which I had flatlie denied.

From what Generall Hamiltone had told me, I formed a very bad idea of the state of our affairs, for it shewed me clearlie that my Lord Mar's system, of England's riseing on the first account of our being up in armes, must [have] been false; as well as his telling us that it was desired by the English that we should rise first, to draw all the troopes our way, and by that deversion untie their hands, and give them ane opportunitie of formeing into bodies; when no sooner he had got a few of us together than he was meditateing to send a thousand of us to England, which must weakne us so much, that he'd never thought of it if he had the least hopes of England's riseing without it, since, contrarie to the pretended concert, it would rather keep the troopes in England then draw them our way....

My Lord Mar comeing at last to Pearth [on September 28] with those he had got together in the Highlands, we were drawn out to the North Inch to receave him, and from that time did he daylie take more and more upon him to act like our Generall, and did all of himself, without consulting anie bodie, as if he had been another Moses, meek and spotless, and without a blemish, sent from Heaven with a divine commission to relieve us miserable wretches out of bondage: so mean an opinion had he of all of us present, and so great was ours to be of him, that 'Illi summum rerum judicium a Deo datum: nobis sola obsequii gloria relicta videretur.' (Tacit.)

'Tis[1] not to be forgot, That the very same Day the Earl of Mar came to Perth, Mr James Murray, second Son to the Viscount of Stormont (who, in the Month of April before, had gone over to the Pretender) arriv'd incognito at Edinburgh from France, by way of England, and crossing the Firth at Newhaven above Leith, he got over to Fife, and thence to the Camp at Perth. His Arrival gave another Occasion of great Rejoicings among the Rebels: For having deliver'd to the Earl of Mar the Letters he had brought him from the Pretender, and produc'd such Authorities as made it appear that he himself was appointed Secretary of State for the Affairs of Scotland, he gave

[1] R. 221.

them Assurances of a speedy and powerful Assistance from France, and of their pretended King's Resolution to come to them in Person[1]. And indeed, if the Pretender's Affairs abroad had continued in the same flourishing Condition as when Mr Murray left the Court of St Germains, 'tis probable the Rebels here might quickly have seen the Performance of these Assurances.

For, about that Time, the Pretender's Friends had procur'd him no less than Twelve large Ships of War, with several Frigats of good Force, and were openly loading on them vast Quantities of Ammunition, Small Arms, a Train of Artillery, Mortars, Shells, Bullets, with Generals, Officers, Soldiers, and Volunteers in Abundance, in the Ports of Havre de Grace, St Maloes, and other Places on the Coasts of France.

But[2] to return to Pearth. His Lordship [of Mar] was not longe there when the Highlandmen begun to mutinie for want of pay....Southesque gave five hundred pound to help to supplie the present wants with great frankness, and Panmure followed his exemple and gave as much. A Councill of Finance was instantlie establisht to fall on ways and means to raise monie, and it was determined to levie eight months cess in these Low-Countrie counties we were masters of....Mr Francois Steuart, brother to the Earle of Murray[3], was made thresaurer, and a committee was establisht for providing the armie with fourage and meale. Tho' orders were given out to form into regiments, everie one did as they pleased. My Lord Drummond, who had got six hundred men together under his name, tho' a great part of them belonged to Lord Strothallan, Logie[4], and his other

---

[1] It was also reported that he brought from the Pretender a Patent, creating the Earl of Mar a Duke, by the Stile of the Duke of Mar, Marquis of Stirling, and Earl of Alloway: And tho' there was little more said about it, yet the Relation seems justify'd by this, That in some of the Papers Printed at Perth, he is stil'd the Duke of Mar.—Rae's note.   [2] *S. M.* 72.

[3] He was fourth son of Alexander, sixth Earl of Moray, and, by the death of his brothers, succeeded to the dignity himself in 1736, and carried on the line of the family.—Sir Walter Scott's note.

[4] Thomas Drummond of Logie-Almond.

nighbours...formed them in three battalions, contrarie to everie bodies advice, who told him they 'd make one good, but could not make three....

My Lord Drummond was not now content to be a great prince at home, but must come into a forraigne service and be made Liutennant-General of the Horse, which was the command of the whole gentlemen; whether it was that he was the man of the best familie, or because of his distinguisht prudence, for he had ane equall pretension to both, I can't tell....Houever ...Will Drummond...brought alonge with him [from France] the King's commission to my Lord Drummond to command the horse....

Tho' we were onlie four squadrons of horse in Pearth, we could not agree about the post of honour, and in this, as well as in all other things in the whole course of our affair, it would appear that those who had the least title to any thing expected most. All the others took it ill that Linlithgow, whose squadrone was weak and mostlie composed of Stirveling-shire gentlemen, which was the youngest countie, should carrie the Royall Standard....Fife and Pearthshire differ'd in their ranking; for tho' it was advanced Fife gave the first vote in all the Scots Parliements, after the Peers, yet Perthshire had always protested against it....

My Lord Tullibardine, Lord Charles and Lord George Murrays formed each of them regiments out of the Athole men and those of Tullibardine, as did their uncle, Lord Nairne, some stronger, and some weaker, as they could get those men to follow them. My Lord Ogilvie, son to the Earle of Earlie, a very younge gentleman, and representative of a verie noble familie, and who was said to be of the first who was engaged, formed a regiment out of the Ki[rr]iemure and Glenprossen men, and made Sir James Kinloch[1], who joyn'd him with his following, his Lieut.-Collonell. Steuart of Indernitie[2] did the same

---

[1] Sir James Kinloch of that Ilk, in Perthshire. His father, Sir David Kinloch, was created a Baronet by James II. He died 1744.—Sir Walter Scott's note.

[2] John Stewart of Invernitie, descended from a cadet of the family of Stewart of Grantully. The instance in the text is one amongst many

with the Garntillie men who folloued him. We of the horse
were order'd to divide each squadrone in three companies, and
name our officers for each company....As to the Captains,
Liutenants, and Cornets, after tuo day's dispute we at last
named them, tho' I can't say to everie bodies satisfaction....
Southesque had Strathmore to compeat with him for the command of the gentlemen of Angus. My Lord Rollo and Collonell
[John] Hay, who, supported by my Lord Mar because his
brother-in-law, brought it tuice to a vote of the gentlemen of
the Pearthshire squadrone which of them should command, and
[Hay] lost it as oftne, in spite of Mar's influence. Linlithgow
would [have] had as little to keep him in countenance as a great
many other Lords whose names I need not mention, if Mar had
not given him the Royal Standard[1], which brought him a command out of all sorts of people, and made up but a weak squadrone
at best. In my command of the Fife gentlemen I had no rivall,
even tho' I made my court to Mar first and last but very ill, by
telling my opinion of him very plainlie; nor was it in his pouer
to stir up a rivall against me, even tho' he gave a commission of
Collonell to Major [Henry] Balfour, a gentleman under my
command, tuo months before any other publick commission was
given....

While everie one was building castles in the air, and makeing
themselves great men, most of our armes were good for nothing;
there was no methode fallne on, nor was the least care takne to
repair those old rustie brokne piceis, which, it seems, were to be
carried about more for ornament than use, tho' gunsmiths were
not wanting; but this was either because he who took upon him
the command expected no pouder from the beginning, or because
what was everie bodies business was no bodies.

of the policy exercised by the more prudent Jacobites in these uncertain
times. The Chief or Representative of a great family staid at home and
professed submission, while it often happened that some cadet or younger
brother possessed influence enough to bring out his followers and clan.
Thus *lands and tenements* committed no treason.—Sir Walter Scott's note.

[1] It was carried by Edmonston of Newton, exiled for aiding and
abetting Graham of Inchbraco in the slaughter of John, Master of Rollo,
8th May 1691.—Sir Walter Scott's note.

The noise of the Duke of Berwick's landing did now decrease daylie, as if there were no more need of him, my Lord Mar being now fixt....

My Lord Mar's great and onlie business was now to put Huntlie, Marishall, and Seaforth in mind of their promises, and press them...to joyn him with all speed; the same care was takne of the Clans, as they then begun to call them, Clan Ronald, Glengarie[1], Lochiell[2], and Steuart of Apin; who got their orders to marche into Argyleshire, under the command of Generall Gordone, to disarme the one half of the Duke of Argyle's following, and bring off the other, who, it was said, were willing to joyn us. Tho' none of all those were at that time stirring, yea, some did not move for some months afterwards, we were made believe, day after day, that those who were to joyn us were at hand, and that the others were on their marche back from Argyleshire towards us, haveing succeeded.

Mar[3], after comeing into Pearth, did nothing all this while but write; and, as if all had depended on his writeing, nobodie moved in any one thing; there was not a word spoke of fortie-fieing the town, nor the least care takne of sending for pouder to any place; we did not want gunsmiths, and yet none of them was imployed in mending our old armes. Whoever spoke of those things, which I did oftne, was giveing himself airs; for we lived very well, and as longe as meat, drink, and monie was not wanting, what was the need of anie more; most of us were goeing home everie day for our diversion, and to get a fresh

---

[1] Alexander Macdonell, Baron of Glengary, called the Black. He made a great figure in that stormy period, and carried the Royal Standard at the Battle of Killiecrankie. He died in 1724.—Sir Walter Scott's note.

[2] John Cameron of Lochiel, son of the renowned Sir Evan Dhu, of whom tradition records such extraordinary [feats]. Sir Evan was still alive in the 1715, but incapable, from his great age, of taking the field. Donald Cameron of Lochiel, son of John, and grandson of Sir Evan, united all the accomplishments of a gentleman and scholar with the courage and high spirit of a Highland Chief. He is the hero of Thomas Campbell's poem entitled 'Lochiel.'—Sir Walter Scott's note.

[3] S. M. 92.

supplie of the readie. In that we folloued strictlie the rule of the gospell, for we never thought of to-morrow. If it escaped any extravagant fellow to say that more troops were comeing to joyn the Duke of Argyle from England or Ireland, he was lookt on as a visionare; or if any seemed to think that these few troops he had would fight, there was no doubt he was a couard and despair'd of our success; which, I 'm shure, they could not [have] been so positive of in their circumstances but by believing no bodie would fight against them, which they said confidentlie; but so soon as men have nothing reasonable to trust to, they seldom faile to please themselves with phantoms, and a drouning man cautches hold of everie straw.

Of manie of those Lords and Chiefs of Clans who had first engaged so franklie at Aboyne, few seemed as yet to remember their promise, except Glengarie, who—it 's hard to say whither he has more of the bear, the lyon, or the fox in him, for he is at least as ruff and cunning as he 's bold—finding his nighbours backward, to encourage them, got his men together, and marched into the Braes of Glenorchie, where he continued eight days before any bodie joyned him. Captain of Clanronald and Sir John M'Lean were the nixt who raised their men; for Locheill and Stuart of Apine would by no means marche into Argyleshire; no more would those who my Lord Bredalbaine had promised, I believe not being as yet determined to rise, nor being willing to disoblidge the Duke of Argyle; houever, they pretended they 'd doe any thing but be imployed that way, and continued at home, while Generall Gordon marched on to execute his orders. How little he did there, and how much time they loosed, being fooled by my Lord Isla, I shall tell you in the proper place[1].

We[2] shall now leave the Rebels gathering at Perth and give some further Account of the Royal Army....The Duke of Argyle when he arriv'd at Edinburgh, being advis'd of the great Disproportion between the Regular Troops and the Rebels' Army...sent [a] Letter to the City of Glasgow....In Compliance therewith, the Loyal City sent three Battalions of their best Men, well arm'd, from Glasgow to Stirling: The First upon

[1] *Infra*, p. 98.   [2] *R.* 223.

the 17th, the Second upon the 18th, and the Third upon the 19th of September...having prevail'd with the honourable Colonel Blackader[1] to accept the Office of Colonel in Conjunction with the Lord Provost....

Expresses were sent to all the well-affected Gentlemen and People in the West and other adjacent Places to signify to them, that his Grace [of Argyll] thought it absolutely necessary for His Majesty's Service that all their fencible Men should assemble in Arms at Glasgow. To which Place they flocked accordingly in a few Days after, in great Numbers[2], well arm'd and accoutred, ready to march as his Grace should direct them....

The Earl of Ilay, in pursuance of his firm Zeal for the present Establishment of the Protestant Succession, had been all this while exerting his Vigilance to the utmost at Edinburgh, in dispersing and seizing all he could meet with that were known to be disaffected to his Majesty's Person and Government, and, but some short Time before this, had the good Fortune to baffle an Attempt that was made by about 200 armed Jacobites to seize the Town Guard and put the City in Confusion, by getting hold of Burnet of Carlops and some others of the Ring-leaders at the Place of Rendezvous but a few Hours before the Plot was to be put in Execution: And now his Lordship was sent to Argyle-shire to assemble the Vassals of his Brother the Duke of Argyle, and the other well-affected People in those Parts, for His Majesty's Service, to prevent the rising of the Rebels in the West-Highlands, and secure the Town of Inverary: For which End, Colonel Alexander Campbel of Finah [Finart] had been sent thither some few Weeks before, to act in Concert with the other Deputy Lieutenants of Argyleshire.

It[3] was about this time that we sent out our first command [from Perth] to sieze the armes at Bruntisland. But before I goe further, I must take leave to tell, than ane old friend of mine

[1] Cf. *The Life and Diary of Lieut.-Col. J. Blackader*, by Andrew Chrichton [Edin. 1824], chap. xix, for the Colonel's account of his service with this regiment.

[2] For instance; Hamilton, tho' but a small Town, sent 70 Volunteers to Glasgow....And Strevan sent 60....And other Towns Proportionally. —Rae's note.   [3] *S. M. 95.*

and my familie's, with whome we had longe dealing, being a merchant, called me out to the South Inch of Pearth by six of the clock of a Sunday morning [October 21]....He told me, He had rid the whole night to let me know that there was a small ship in the harbour of Bruntisland, loaded with armes and ammunition for the Earle of Sutherland². I ask't him, If he knew any thing of the number? He said, They were at least three thousand. It 's easie to judge I was transported with the news, tho'...not being altogether so well with my Lord Mar, was at a loss how to behave in it. But on second thoughts, [I] resolved to goe straight to him....I found him in bed, and told him my storie, and at same time gave him the caracter of my friend....I went after that to Hardie's³ without anie conclusion; and, a little after my friend went away, I was sent for by my Lord Mar about eleven of the clock. He askt me, How I would bring off those armes in case I were commanded? I said, I knew no other way than that which I had told him alreadie; onlie added, that what armes were to be brought alonge must be done by the baggage-horse of the armie...and whoever went must marche out by five in the evening, to make sure of the ship before she could get out of the harbour; and, above all, the ports were to be all shut before four, to hinder intelligence, and before any bodie was commanded or the marche spoke of. Mar said, I was in the right, and without saying more I went to dine.

Ane hour after, I was called for again, and ane order was given me in writeing....I had almost forgot to tell that he who brought the information had told, it was absolutelie necessarie we should be at Bruntisland by tuelve of the clock at night at furthest if we dessigned to succeed, that being the time of full sea, and the ship being to saile that tide. I told my Lord Mar, We might run some risque in the back-comeing, since we were to pass within ten miles of Stirveling, both in goeing and comeing back, and that we might loose so much time at Bruntisland as

¹ R. 234.
² The arms had been despatched from Edinburgh Castle for the Earl's use in the North of Scotland. The master of the vessel put into Burntisland to see his wife and family there.—*Ibid.* 234.
³ A vintner in Perth.

[would] give the dragoons, which was the onlie thing I had to feare, time to cut us off, since we were not to be above fourscore horse...and [I] put him in mind of a hundred foot being necessarie to be left in the Castle of Bruntisland, to take care of those armes we left, in case we could not bring all off. This he went into against his will, and said, He 'd send five hundred foot after us, and post Indernitie at Kinross. Accordingly I set out by five of the clock with fourscore horse....We seized severall small boats the minute we came into toun [Burntisland], and after placeing a few sentries about the toun...we forced some toun's men to goe alonge with ours to bringe in the ship, which was seized with no difficultie; but the wind being contrarie, it was hard enough to get the ship brought into the harbour....At last, those boats brought in the ship by maine force against the contrarie wind, and those aboard of ours, being seamen, did their dutie very well. I stood in the water to the middle of the leg and, with my oun hands, receaved all the armes from the ship's side, and found, to my great grief, but three hundred, wanting one; we found a bag of flints and tuo little barrels of ball, and tuo or three barrels of pouder, about a hundred pound each, and some cartridge boxes....We seized the armes of a big ship which lay in the harbour, which were about tuentie-five firelocks, and with them a barrell of pouder, and at sametime, the armes of the Toun Guarde, about thirtie....We got back to Pearth before five of the clock, and marched nere to fourtie Scots miles in tuentie-four hours.

As[1] the Seizing this Ship and Arms gave some Reputation to the Earl of Mar, so their Success in that Undertaking encouraged the Rebels to invade the Province of Fife, which they did, not many Days after, with a Detachment of 4000 Men in several Bodies, who, ranging over the Country, seiz'd all the Arms they could find, to make some Amends for the Disappointments of those they expected from France, which were stop'd...at Havre de Grace. They likewise took Possession of the Towns of Kirkcaldy, Kinghorn, Brunt-Island, Dysart, Weemse, and several other Towns, and so became Masters of the whole North Shore of the Firth of Leith, in Sight of the City of Edinburgh....

[1] R. 234.

The Rebels were now Masters of all the Eastern Coasts of Scotland, from Brunt-Island to Murray Firth, which extends to above 160 Miles on the Shore: And on the West side, the Isle of Sky, the Lewise, and all the Hebrides were their own; being the Estates, generally speaking, of the Earl of Seaforth, Sir Donald M'donald[1], and others of the Clans who were in their Interest: So that from the Mouth of the Water of Lochie to Faro Head, all the Coast of Locquhaber and Ross, even to the North West Point of Britain, was in their Possession. In a Word, they were possess'd of all that Part of the Kingdom of Scotland which lies on the North Side of the River Forth, excepting the remote Counties of Caithness, Strathnaver, and Sutherland, beyond Inverness, And that Part of Argileshire which runs North-West into Lorn and up to Locquhaber, where Fort-William continued in the Possession of his Majesty's Troops....

In the mean Time, the Northern Clans were upon their March to join the Earl of Mar: And on the 5th of October [Lachlan Mackintosh] the Laird of Macintosh, who is Chief of a numerous Clan of that Name in the Shire of Inverness, arrived at Perth with 500 stout Men well arm'd[2]. As Brigadier M'Intosh of Borlam had perswaded his Chief and his Men (who were always for the Revolution interest) to engage in these pernicious and rebellious Measures, so he placed himself at their Head and formed them into a Regiment, which was reckoned the best the Earl of Mar had. On the 6th he was joined by the Marquis of Huntley with 500 Horse and 2000 Foot, and next Day, by the Earl Marischal with 300 Horse and 500 Foot[3]: But the Earl of Seaforth was yet left behind for fear of the Earl

[1] Of Sleat....Chief of that part of the Sept [Macdonald] who acknowledge descent from Donald Gorme.—Sir Walter Scott's note, in *S. M.* 193.

[2] Farquharson of Invercauld arrived with him.—*Ibid.* 103.

[3] Sinclair asserts that those whom the Earl brought to Perth 'were not then fourscore,' and that they were very badly mounted. Huntly, he says, brought one hundred and sixty horse and fourteen hundred foot. The dates of their arrival at Perth he gives as, the Earl Marischal on October 8; Huntly on October 9.—*Ibid.* 123, 157, 158.

of Sutherland's invading his Country, but soon after attended the Pretender's Standard at Perth with 800 Horse and 3000 Foot[1]. By this Time their Army amounted to 12,600 Men, and being afterwards joined by General Gordon and the Western Clans, to the Number of 100 Horse and 4000 Foot, but a short Time before the Battle, made in all 16,700 Men[2]. This was the whole Strength of their Army, and these, except about 3000 which were in Garrisons dispers'd, and the Detachment [under Mackintosh of Borlum] that went to the South, were all in a Body at the Battle of Dumblain or Sheriff-Muir, of which we will hear in its Place.

It[3] was now thought the proper time to put the dessigned project of passing the Frith in execution. Generall Hamiltone haveing told my Lord Mar of his communicateing that secret to me[4], his Lordship was pleased to send for me, and askt, before Generall Hamilton and Mr Malcome, who were the onlie present, What number of boats I thought could be got together on the coast, and in what places? I said...all I could tell him was, That what boats were of use were to be found from Wemyss to Creile, in the touns and villages all alonge that coast; that there was a great many of them, but could not tell their number.... Then he begun to speak of haveing all those boats sent up to Bruntisland, where, on my haveing formerlie told him the castle was stronge, he had put a guarrisone to keep our communication with the countie and coast of Fife. I told his Lordship, He was to consider that bringing all those boats together to Bruntisland was a double mouvement, and that the men-of-war, who were in station all over the Frith, would see them and bear up to them, as they did to the least small boat alone; besides...tho' there were no men-of-war in the case, their very goeing off from Bruntisland would have a bad effect; for after haveing alarm'd the Duke of Argyle with the first mouvement of

[1] *Infra*, p. 115.
[2] This total is certainly much in excess of the actual numbers. Sinclair gives Mar about six thousand foot and about six hundred horse after Huntly's arrival on October 9.—*S. M.* 157.
[3] *S. M.* 104.   [4] *Supra*, p. 74.

bringing the boats there, it would give him time to take his precautions....

I took freedom to ask his Lordship, Where he designed they should land on the other side, in case he proposed some advantage by their goeing off from Bruntisland which was not to be got from another porte? He said, They were to land on the Lothien coast, at any place to which they found the wind fairest, and then either marche to Haddintoun or the Cittadell of Leith. I said, They might doe the same from the place where the boats lay then...[and] in the end told his Lordship That I was no sailer, but I doubted of the whole project....Mar said I was to goe in a day or tuo on command to Fife....

In that time he made Mackintosh with his Clan, and the Fercharson's, my Lord Nairne and Lord Charles Murray with the Athole men, Earle of Strathmore with his regiment of Low Countriemen, and Logie Drummond with my Lord Drummond's men and his own, defilée by Kinross, corp after corp, to Bruntisland, to the number of tuo thousand tuo hundred. When he had thus disposed things, he called me, and gave me [my] orders[1] under his hand and seale [dated October 5]....

I marched straight to Couper, where that night [October 6] I proclaim'd the King....After comeing to Couper I had given out that I was to goe back to Pearth by Dundee; and...to make that take the better, I ridd half a mile towards Dundee, and falling in after into the St Andrews road, got there by break of day, and took some few horses on the road or near it.

So soon as we got there we proclaimed, and at the same time searched all the suspected houses for armes and horses. We succeeded as ill there as at Couper, and got onlie a few broken rustie muskets....Haveing severall touns to proclaim in, I thought it was a little too earlie to refresh there, for the King's health must be drunk in everie one of them, otherwise the ceremonie was null and voide.

We marched from that to Creile, and...came to Creile

[1] Sinclair's orders were, to collect arms and money and to proclaim the Chevalier in Cupar and in the coast towns of Fife, from St Andrews to Dysart, and thence to return to Perth. The enterprise was designed to prepare for Mackintosh's passage of the Forth.

[October 7] before tuelve, and proclaimed the King that moment; the few rustie armes of that poor honest toun were delivered with no pain....Before I marched from Creile I askt Hary Craufurd if he could get as many boats as could transport tuo thousand men over the Frith; and how soon they could be got; and how he thought that project would succeed, in case the men-of-war should get the least hint or fall in with them? He said, The project would doe, and he did not doubt but as many boats could be got, but that it would take at least three days to get all readie. He desired more time to think of it, and said he 'd come that night to Pittenweem, where we were to be, and speak further about it....

I marched from that [Crail] to Kilrinnie, Anstruther Easter, Anstruther Wester, and Pittenweem; and after proclaimeing in all those royall burroughs, and makeing search for armes and amunition, according to my intelligence in all those places, I got nothing worth the nameing, except some bars of lead, which, being weightie, I left the one half in safe hands to be sent for, and took the other half alonge with me. That night I took up my quarters in the Abbay of Pittenweem, which, being nere the toun, afforded us all we wanted....

I had not slept ane hour, when I receaved a letter from my Lord Mar, which I shall insert from his originall....

I desire, upon sight hereof, that you 'll send all the barks and boats that can possiblie be had to Bruntisland, without looseing a moment of time, the troops of Bruntisland haveing orders to embarke there; and I have order'd all the Troops here [at Perth] to marche to-morrow morning [October 8] towards Stirveling, which will make your joyning us again the more easie....

After receaving my Lord Mar's letter, I wrote him an answer, giveing an account of everie thing I had done in my march, and letting him know that Mr Craufurd had assured me that the transport was practicable, and that he 'd doe what he could to get them boats soon readie, but it was not to be done in less than three days....

By seven of the clock [on October 8] I receaved a letter from Mackintosh of Borlome from Bruntisland, who now begun to be call'd Brigadeer Mackintosh. His letter assured me that a great bodie of both foot and horse of the enemie was alreadie in Dumfermling, and that they were to march towards him as soon as the moon rise, and for that reason most earnestlie desired I should joyn him with all possible diligence....

I...wrote back to Mackintosh of Borlome, telling him I had no orders to obey him; and tho' I had, if his intelligence was true, it would be impossible to joyn him, since I believed he must be attackt before his letter came to me; nor, were I with him, could those under my command be of any use to him.

Haveing thus reason'd, I...had no more to doe but to proclaim in Ely, Leven, and Wemyss....I got on horseback after eight, and haveing sent severalls best known in the countrie out to reconnoitre on all the roads, I continued my route four miles up the coast, and...changed my route nere Durie, and marched northward cross the countrie, nere Melville House, where I resolved to take up my quarters that night [October 8]....But Major Balfour, to whom my Lord Mar had given the conjunct command, tho' he did not pretend to determine me, yet presst hard before the whole command, that being onlie nine miles from Pearth, we should marche that night to it...to which I consented, haveing no reason to give why I should not. And haveing day enough, fed our horses and halted there above an hour, and march'd, as we did all alonge, in order and at leasure, the shortest way thro' the hills of the north of Fife, and got to Pearth before it grew dark....

I found all our armie draun up before the toun of Pearth, and it was then my Lord Mar's first and onlie commission [from the Chevalier] was read[1]....

Some days after my returneing to Pearth, Mackintosh was order'd to leave Bruntisland and march with those under his command to Creile, Anstruthers, and all those touns where the boats lay, and to embarque in these places, and saile straight over the Frith to whatever port the wind blew fairest; and left some men in Bruntisland Castle, as he was commanded, to amuse the men-of-war who had been cannonadeing him there for tuo days together without doeing the least harm; Mr Craufurd and some

[1] On October 6, Mar received his commission from the Chevalier.— *R.* 433.

others, who were let into the secret, haveing prepar'd the boats and made that affair prettie easie.

The[1] Earl of Mar, to prevent all Suspicion of their Design to embark on the East Shore of Fife, and to draw off the Ships from the Mouth of the Firth, caus'd another Body of Men to march openly to Brunt-Island, who got several Boats together and made a Feint of embarking there. The small Ships of War, which were cruizing in the Firth to observe their Motions, had, with the Custom-house Smacks, brought several of their Boats to Leith, pursuant to the Order of the Duke of Argyle; and now[2], having Notice of their daring Attempt to embark at Brunt-Island, they mann'd out their Boats in order to attack them, and slipping their Cables, stood over to that Shore to second their Boats, and to cannonade the Boats in the Harbour, as also the Town of Brunt-Island, in case they made any Resistance; but the Rebels, having raised a Battery and planted some Cannon on the Out-part of the Harbour, fired many Shots at the Ships, and the Ships at them, though without any Damage on either Side.

Nor did this Piece of Policy fail them in the Management of their grand Design: For while some of them amus'd the King's Ships near Brunt-Island, as if they would cross above Leith, their main Body, consisting of 2500 Men under the Conduct of Brigadier-General M'intosh of Borlam (as they were pleased to call him), came down to the Shore under Cover of the Night in order to embark at Pittenweem, Creil, the Ely, and other Ports on that Coast.

On Wednesday, the 12th of October at Night, some of them embarked, and others next Night, in open Boats, taking their Course directly to the South Shore of the Firth, which is there about 16 or 17 Miles broad; His Majesty's Ships in the Firth, either espying them from their Top-Masts, or having Notice of their Design, weigh'd Anchor on the Top of the Flood, and set sail to intercept them; but, the Wind not being fair, they were not able to come Time enough to prevent their Passage: Yet one Boat was taken with 40 Men, who were made Prisoners in Leith, and their Officers were committed to Edinburgh Castle.

[1] R. 258.   [2] October 11.

Others were forced back to the Fife Side again; amongst whom, the Lord Strathmore and his Lieutenant Colonel Walkingshaw of Barrowfield; and a great many Men were forced into the Isle of May, where they staid till the next Night, and then got back to Creil on the Shore of Fife, and, in a few Days after, they joined the Earl of Mar at Perth[1]. The rest of this Detachment design'd for this Descent upon Lothian, being in Number about 1600 Men[2], landed in the Night time at North-Berwick, Aberlady, Gallon, and other Places, about 12 Miles East of Edinburgh....

As soon as John Campbel, then Lord Provost of Edinburgh ...had Notice of their Landing, he ordered the City Guards, the Train'd Bands, New Levies, and Associate Volunteers to the respective Posts assign'd them, for Defence of the City and to prevent Disturbance within it. The Associate Volunteers had the Nether-bow Port, the Gate next to the Rebels, assign'd them as their Post, which they guarded with great Care and Diligence for ten Days' Time....

The Lord Provost having further Intelligence by the Spies he had abroad that the Highlanders were in Haddingtoun on Thursday Night [October 13], and supposing they might take their Rout towards Edinburgh, on Friday the 14th in the Morning, about the very same Time they began their March, his Lordship sent an Express to the Duke of Argyle, advising him of the Rebels being at Haddingtoun the Night before, desiring his Grace to send a Detachment of the regular Troops to the Support and Assistance of the Loyal Citizens. The Duke, having received the Express, and without loss of Time perceiving the dangerous Consequences of their seizing Edinburgh, did that same Day, about Noon, mount 200 Foot on Country Horses for the greater Expedition, and with 300 chosen Dragoons

[1] Strathmore's men numbered nearly three hundred. Mackintosh was blamed for having embarked without leaving clear directions to the others. Sinclair states that Strathmore was confined to the Island of May for eight days.—*S. M.* 128.

[2] A large number of Mackintosh's force did not embark at all. Sinclair states that only eleven hundred landed in Lothian.—*Ibid.* 128, 129.

marched, or rather posted, to the Relief of Edinburgh, and about Ten at Night came opportunely to the West-Port when the Rebels were not far from the East. Soon after, his Grace entered the City, to the unspeakable Joy of the loyal Inhabitants where he was joined by the Horse Militia of Lothian and the Mers, with a good many Volunteers, both Horse and Foot, who with the Marquis of Tweedale, the Lord Belhaven, &c., had retired into Edinburgh on the Approach of the Rebels.

The Rebels were advanced as far as Jock's Lodge, not a Mile from the Royal Palace of Holyrood-House, in a full March to the City, when my Lord Duke arrived; but finding no Numbers come out to join them, and being informed as well of the Posture of the Citizens as of the Approach of the Duke of Argyle...they halted, and calling a short Council, resolved to go down to Leith; so they speedily turn'd to the Right and marched to Leith, which, being an open Place, they entered without any Resistance; and after they had made themselves Masters of the Guard, they opened the Gates of the Tolbooth, and set at Liberty their Men that were taken in the Boat as they were crossing the Firth: Then, entering the Custom-House, they seized a considerable Quantity of Brandy and other Provisions. Thereafter they marched over the Bridge and lodged themselves in the old Citadel, a square Fort with Four Demi-Bastions, built in the Usurper's Time, with a large dry Ditch about it, never entirely demolish'd, only the Gates defac'd, the Ramparts still remaining untouched, as firm and high as ever, with a good many convenient Houses built within it by the Inhabitants of Leith and Edinburgh for the Benefit of the Air, as a Summer's Retreat. In this Fort, such as it was, they posted themselves and began to fortify; and first, they went on Board the Ships in the Harbour and seized several Pieces of Cannon, with Powder and Ball and what else was proper for their own Defence; and next, they planted some Cannon at all the Ports and upon the Ramparts, and barricaded the most accessable Places with Beams, Planks, Carts fill'd with Earth and Stone, and other Materials. Thus it stood with the Rebels, who had got themselves into the most convenient Situation that could be imagined for their Purpose, where they had Time and Leisure in Safety to contrive their Escape: For, considering who was now close at their Heals, it was fit to lay all other Projects aside.

On Saturday[1] Morning early, the Duke of Argyle[2]...march'd directly towards the Citadel; and having posted the Dragoons as near the North-East Side as he could with Safety from the Enemy's Fire, and the Foot on the South-East, he himself, with the Generals [William] Evans and Wightman, Colonel [Charles] Deburgay, &c., went down betwixt the Fort and the Sea, to reconnoitre where or in what Part it might be most conveniently attacked: His Grace having summoned the Rebels to lay down their Arms and surrender, upon Pain of High Treason, declaring withal, that if they obliged him to bring Cannon to force them, and they killed any of his Men in resisting, he would give them no Quarter, He received a resolute Answer from a Highland Laird called Kinackin, who told the Duke, That as to surrendering, they laughed at it; and as to bringing Cannon and assaulting them, they were ready for him; that they would neither take nor give any Quarter with him; and if he thought he was able to force them, he might try his Hand. And thereafter, having asked the Sentiments of the Gentlemen, they unanimously gave it as their Opinion, that as things then stood it was impracticable to attack it, considering that the Enemy were within strong Walls, near to double the Number of the Besiegers, well supplied with Cannon and small Arms; when his Grace had neither Cannon, Mortar, Gunner, nor Bombardier (being all at Stirling) to make Way for an Assault, or to force them out of their strong Entrenchments.

The Duke himself added, that being now about 200 Paces from it (where, be the by, the Enemy's Ball were grazing among their Horses Feet), before he could come at the Foot of the Wall, or to either of the two baricaded Places, he might in all probability receive five Fires, which, at a modest Computa-

[1] October 15.
[2] 'Tis not to be forgot, that some of the Ministers of Edinburgh, as they had appeared in Arms in the City to animate their People to act vigorously in Defence of that Important Place, so now they came along in this Expedition, in Rank and File, like common Soldiers, with Firelocks and Bayonets.—Rae's note.

tion, might cut off half of his Men, and be as far from his Purpose as ever....And thus, the Duke being unwilling to expose the brave Gentlemen Volunteers...and the few Regular Troops he had...His Grace retired to Edinburgh in the Evening, to cause the necessary Preparations to be made to attempt the dislodging of the Rebels next Day.

Mackintosh[1], after being invested in the Citadell of Leith, or on the approach of the enemie, had found means to send tuo letters to my Lord Mar[2]. We, in the mean time, knowing nothing of this, were order'd to march by break of day next morning [October 16], and drew up without the toun [Perth], where we continued three hours....

His Lordship of Mar came out about ten of the clock; orders were instantlie sent alonge the line that all Noblemen, Heads of Clans, and Commanders of Corps should repair that moment to a house in the front; which accordinglie being done, care was takne to put out all others, and the doors shut. My Lord, with a most dejected countenance and a sad voice, told us, He was sorrie to give us the bad neus of Mackintoshes being invested in the Citadell of Leith, and that his goeing there, contrarie to his Lordship's last orders, would in all appearance prove a fatall mistake to him; and next read us tuo dismall letters, where Mackintosh, appearing disheartned, said that a few hours would determine his fate, in these words, but that he 'd doe his best; tho' he mentioned the preparations of cannon and bombs with terrour, which, he said, would soon doe his work. My Lord Mar said, He gave him over for lost, and did not see that we could help him in the least, except by makeing a feint towards Stirveling, to bring the Duke of Argyle back, and even that appear'd to him unnecessarie, believing him alreadie takne....Generall Hamilton said, That makeing a feint towards Stirveling might doe good and could doe no harm, and in all events it ought to be done. No bodie saying one worde, the marche was determin'd, and we marched off the ground that moment to Auchterardoch....

[1] *S. M.* 130.
[2] Mackintosh despatched a boat from Leith, and discharged a 'Cannon after her,' to make the Men of War imagine her an Enemy to the Rebels.'—*P. H.* 12.

We cantoon'd that night at Auchterarduch and about it, where we came very late, which occasion'd great difficultie in getting quarters, and march'd next morning [October 17], and halted towards night at Arduch, and drew up there for some time, both foot and horse, where it was believed we were to ly in the fields that night. But all of a suddain, I received an order to follow the other horse, who begun to file off; we marched at a great trot, in a heavie rain, in the dark, and came to Dumblain betwixt eight and nine....

We continued there till tuelve of the clock [next day, October 18] in the bitterest cold that I ever felt; at last his Lordship of Dummond...was designeing to marche back, when he reflected that he had forgot to proclaime the King at Dumblaine, haveing had so great matters to mind, and returned to the toun with a few gentlemen and did it....

Then we marched back and cantoon'd in and about Auchterarduch, where the foot joy'nd us from Arduch. How, in that wide cantoonment, we missed the haveing many of our horses and men takne or cut off, I can't account for; onlie that regular troops make but bad partizans, and above all the English, who have been least used of anie to the *petite guerre*[1].

[Meanwhile,][2] the Rebels [at Leith] seeing that there was no longer Expectation of Encouragement from their Friends in Edinburgh, and being likewise informed that the Duke of Argyle was making Preparations to attack them with Artillery, that same Night [October 15], about nine a Clock, they abandoned the Citadel of Leith in the deepest Silence, taking the Advantage of the low Ebb of the Tide, and march'd off by the Head of the Pier on the Sands Eastward, to cover their Retreat, and so went to Seaton-House, a strong old Castle, about seven Miles from Edinburgh belonging to the Earl of Wintoun; leaving behind them about 40 Men (who had made too free

---

[1] Mar's account of this march upon Stirling is in a letter to Thomas Forster, in *S. M.* 146; *R.* 291. Thence it appears, that but for news of Argyll's having been reinforced, and the impossibility of joining hands with Gordon and the Clans, Mar contemplated a general advance against Argyll, and no mere feint to draw off the Duke from Mackintosh.

[2] *R.* 264.

with the Brandy which they found in the Custom-House) with
some Baggage and Ammunition, besides some Stragglers that
lagg'd behind in their March, which were taken by a Detachment under the Command of Colonel Debourgay....About two
in the Morning they arriv'd at Seaton House, where they were
join'd by some of their Friends, who, having cross'd the Firth
farther East, had not landed so soon, nor been able to come up
to them on their March to Leith.

The Duke having got Notice that Morning[1] that the Rebels
had deserted the Citadel of Leith and were got into fresh
Quarters at Seaton, he sent an Express to Sterling for four
Gunners and two Bombardiers of the small train that was there
with the Army; and in the mean time, ordered two Pieces of
small Cannon and two Mortars to be got ready in Edinburgh
Castle in order to dislodge them: But the Rebels, before they
retired from Leith, having sent over a Boat with an Express to
the Earl of Mar to acquaint him with their Proceedings and
Circumstances, the Earl, to withdraw the Duke of Argyle from
attempting any thing against them, gave out that he would pass
the Forth with his Army, either at Stirling [or] near the Bridge
of Down; and in Order thereunto, they began their March....
Which being notify'd to Lieutenant General Whetham, who
commanded at Stirling in the Duke's Absence, Upon Sunday
Night and Monday Morning [October 16 and 17] he sent three
Expresses to my Lord Argyle with certain Intelligence, That
the Rebels, to the Number of 10,000 Men, were upon a full
March from Perth towards Stirling. The last of these Expresses
bore, That their Vaunt Guard and 4000 of their best Men were
to be at Dumblain that Night....

Upon these Advices, the Duke, having left 100 Dragoons
and 150 Foot under the Command of Colonel [the Hon.
William] Ker, Major General Wightman, &c., together with
the Militia and Gentlemen Volunteers, under the Command of
their proper Officers, for the Security of the City of Edinburgh
and to carry on the Seige of Seaton House, he mounted, with
200 Dragoons and 50 of the Foot, on Monday the 17th about
Noon, and arriv'd at Stirling about 8 at Night; at which time

[1] Sunday, October 16.

it was confirm'd by many of the Inhabitants of the Town of
Dumblain, and by several Countrymen who had been chas'd
from their Dwellings upon the Approach of the Rebels, that
their whole Army was to be at Dumblain next Morning,
resolving to take the Advantage of his Grace's Absence, and to
cross the Forth either at Stirling or near it. But as his Grace's
Return gave new Life and Vigour to his formerly disponding
Army, who now thought no Numbers too many for them, so
it struck a Damp upon the Spirits of the Rebels at Dumblain,
who being soon after apprized of it by Letters from two of the
Jacobite Inhabitants of Stirling, they stood to their Arms all
Night, and early next Morning [October 18] retir'd and made
a sudden Retreat back to Perth.

But to return to the Highlanders under the Command of
Brigadier M'Intosh. As soon as they were got into Seaton House,
they entrenched the Avenues and fortified the Gates, so as they
were not in Danger of any Surprize: And the Duke of Argyle
...at the same time when he sent for the Gunners from Stirling,
he sent out a Detachment of Dragoons with a Party of the
Volunteer Horse to alarm them; but so soon as they appear'd
near Preston Pans, a Party of the Highlanders march'd out of
the Castle and formed themselves in order to receive them: The
Party from Edinburgh, finding that their Situation and Posture
was such as nothing could be attempted without more Forces,
retir'd and returned to Edinburgh that Night, and the Rebels
likewise retir'd into their Garrison. And on Monday the 17th
(when the Duke went to Stirling) the Lord Torphichen, with
the 200 Dragoons which his Grace had left, and the Earl of
Rothes with 300 Gentlemen Volunteers, marched from Edinburgh to Seaton House; but finding the Rebels so strongly
entrench'd within the Gates, that it was impossible to dislodge
or reduce them without Artillery to batter the House, they
returned that Night *re infecta*, after they had exchanged some
Shots with the Rebels (as one[1] says) and the Rebels with them,
without any Damage on either Side.

While the Rebels continued there, they sent out Parties who
brought them in great Plenty of Cows, Sheep, Meal, and other

[1] *P.H.* 18.

Provisions, and gave out that they design'd to fortify there and make Seaton a Magazine while they rais'd an Army, as well from the Borders and West Parts of Scotland, as from Edinburgh and the Country about. But having on the 18th received Letters from the Earl of Mar, in Answer to theirs from Leith, with Orders to March towards England, and at the same Time an Express from Mr Forster[1] inviting them to meet him at Coldstream or Kelso; On Wednesday the 19th, early in the Morning, they marched from Seaton and arrived that Night at Longformachus, about 17 long Miles from thence. As they march'd by Hermistoun[2] House, the Seat of Dr Sinclair, their Brigadier M'Intosh, in Resentment of the Doctor's Conduct at Keith[3], gave Orders to plunder and burn it; but Mr William Miller of Mugdrum, Major of his Regiment, and Mr Meinzies of Woodend having dissuaded the Brigadier from raising Fire so soon, the Burning of this House was prevented; yet, the other Part of the Order was put in Execution by the Lord Nairn, who caused his Highlanders to plunder it of every thing valuable which they could carry with them.

As soon as Major General Wightman had received Intelligence of their Motion from Seaton, he marched from Edinburgh with 80 Dragoons, 50 Militia, and some Volunteers to attack them in the Rear: And having put 50 of the Foot into Seaton House (where they recovered much of the Spoil which the Rebels had left behind) and order'd the Court Walls thereof to be demolished, that it might not be a Refuge to others of the Rebels who might possibly come over the Firth, or to M'Intosh and his Men, in case they should return to that Place, he return'd in the Evening with several Prisoners who had lagg'd behind. Besides those, several others deserted during this Day's March, who were afterwards taken up by the Country and sent into

---

[1] Thomas Forster, leader of the Northumberland Jacobites.

[2] Herdmandston, four miles south-west of Haddington.

[3] Doctor Sinclair had surrounded the house of Hepburn of Keith, whom he suspected of an intention to join the Jacobites in arms. Shots were exchanged and Hepburn's younger son was killed. 'This was the first Blood spilt in the Rebellion.'—*P. H.* 19.

Edinburgh and Glasgow, where they were kept Prisoners till the Rebellion was over.

The Gentlemen...who were assembl'd at Kelso[1], being inform'd of the Rebels their March, and finding they could not defend the Place against so great a Force, did on Thursday the 20th abandon it, most of them going for Edinburgh, and carrying all the Arms with them. That same Day, M'Intosh and his Men set out from Longformachus and marched to Duns. Next Day [October 21] they drew up in Battalia while the Pretender was proclaimed, and then retired again to their Quarters. And having collected the Publick Revenues there, they set out on Saturday the 22d for Kelso, where they arriv'd that Evening, as we shall hear anon[2].

Having[3] thus far treated of the late Rebellion...it may not be improper to acquaint the Reader with the State of the Rebellion in the West-Highlands, and the prudent Conduct of the Earl of Ilay and his Majesty's other good Friends at Inverary, and in some other Parts of Argyleshire; which was of very great Importance to his Majesty's Service at this dangerous and critical Juncture.

The Duke of Argyle having about the middle of September sent Orders to Colonel Alexander Campbel of Finab [Finart], who then had the Command of an Independent Company, to repair to Inverary and bring together the Militia of Argyleshire as soon as possible, and to send an Escort for Arms and Ammunition his Grace had sent to Glasgow for the use of the said Shire, that they might be in Condition to prevent the rising of the disaffected Clans, or keep them from joining the Earl of Mar: In Obedience thereto, the Deputy Lieutenants immediately enter'd upon Measures for raising the Militia; but about the

---

[1] Sir William Bennet and others were sent by Argyll from Stirling on October 11 and reached Kelso on the 13th to put that shire into a posture of defence.—*R.* 255.

[2] On the same day, October 22, the Northumberland and Nithsdale Jacobites, under Forster and the Earl of Kenmure, reached Kelso. Thereafter, the three forces combined in the march into England which ended with their surrender at Preston on November 13. That episode is treated in chap. III.   [3] *R.* 283.

20th of that Month, before any great Progress could be made therein, Glengary and Glenmorristoun came to Abahalider in the Braes of Glenorchy with about 500 Men, on purpose to Raise the Body of the Shire in Favour of the Pretender, founding their Hopes upon the Design they had form'd of taking his Majesties Friends unprepar'd, and the Divisions they fancied were then amongst them. They had concerted that the whole of the Clans should join Glengary, that they should first seize Inverary, where they expected to meet with no Opposition, and that with all their Strength, together with the Men they proposed to raise in Argyleshire, they should march to the Plains of Buchannan, where the Earl of Mar was to join them by the first of October[1]: From thence they resolved to take their Rout by Glasgow into England, not doubting that their proclaiming the Pretender at Inverary and Glasgow would give some Reputation to their Undertaking: But the Duke of Argyle's Orders had reached his Friends in those Parts, Time enough to enable them to get such a Number of Men together as Glengary did not find it convenient to attack them, though he continued in that Station till Clanronnald came to Strathphillen.

For Colonel Campbel was appriz'd of their Design by one of the Clans: And at the same Time, the Deputy Lieutenants conceived it was the best Service could be done to the Government to divide and bring off the Clans and detain them as long in Argyleshire as possible, thereby to gain Time, that the Troops expected from Ireland might arrive to join the Duke of Argyle at Stirling before the Clans could join the Earl of Mar at Perth....

In this Sentiment they were confirm'd by the Orders which Colonel Campbel then receiv'd from his Grace, to use his utmost Endeavours with Lochiel, or any other of the Clans or their Friends, to influence them to remain dutiful in their Allegiance to his Majesty's Service; allowing him, in his Name, as having Power from His Majesty, to offer them, in that Event, Safety and Protection. The same Night he received that Letter, he had a Message from Sir Duncan Campbel of Lochnell, Cameron of Lochiel, and [Robert] Stuart of Appin, acquainting him, That

[1] About a fortnight before Mar's advance towards Dunblane in support of Mackintosh.

if he could promise them the Duke's Friendship, they would, as soon as they could get their Men together, march them to Inverary, and join his Men who were then in Arms for the King, and they themselves would go to Stirling to wait on his Grace[1]. Upon which, Colonel Campbel communicated to their Messengers the Assurances his Grace had empowr'd him to give them, and likewise acquainted Glengary by a Letter that he might expect his Majesty's Pardon if he deserv'd it, and sent Alexander Campbel of Barcalden[2] to the Earl of Broadalbine[3] to dissuade him from entering into their Measures, and failing of that, to persuade his People to continue in their Duty to his Majesty. Some few Days after, he receiv'd the like Message from some other of the Chiefs of the Clans, and returned an Answer to the same Effect.

In return to the Notice he had given to Lochnel, Lochiel, Appin, and others, they advis'd him that they had appointed to meet at a Place call'd the Sui in order to go to Stirling, and that Cameron of Lochiel, in his Way thither, was to wait on the Earl of Broadalbine in order to persuade him into the same Measures....But about the End of September, the Colonel received another Message from Sir Duncan Campbel and Appin, acquainting him that Lochiel had miss'd the Earl of Broadalbine at his own House, and had gone to Loggarett to wait on him, where he was with the Earl of Mar, which they look'd upon as a Breach of their Concert, and that therefore they were resolved to go to Stirling without him; which Resolution the Colonel approved of. Next Day, Sir Duncan Campbel came to Inverary

---

[1] Mar's project of directing the Clans into Argyllshire against the Campbells, with the object, it was declared, of 'revengeing private quarrells on the Duke of Argyle,' was the cause of the unwillingness of Lochiel and of Stewart of Appin to engage at this point.—*S. M.* 144, 157.

[2] Barcaldine, in Ardchattan, Argyllshire.

[3] He joined Mar at Perth before Sheriffmuir. 'His extraordinarie caracter and dress made everie bodie run to see him, as if he had been a spectacle,' writes Sinclair; 'He was the merriest grave man I ever saw.' Upon his suggestion, Mar sent for a printing press from Aberdeen to provide the army with news.—*S. M.* 185.

and acquainted him that Stuart of Appin seem'd rather resolv'd to be unactive than to go to Stirling; therefore he thought, as the Days of his Citation were running[1], it was his Duty and interest not to wait for him. The Colonel persuaded him rather to expect Lochiel's Return to the Country, if possible to keep him and Appin to their first Resolution; which he did accordingly, and inform'd the Duke of Argyle of the Occasion of his Delay in coming to Stirling, but afterwards finding them[2] determin'd to go in to the Rebellion, he left them and repaired to Stirling.

About the 6th of October, the Earl of Ilay was sent by the Duke, his Brother, to Inverary, as above[3], to command the Loyal Posse of that Country at the earnest Desire of that People, who requested that one of the Stock of that Family would come to head them. About the same Time, M'Donald, Captain of Clanronnald, with about 700 Men, came to Strathphillen in Perthshire, where Glengary, who some Time before was rein-forc'd with 300 of the M'gregours and Glenco-Men, together inforc'd with the Rebels formerly with him, join'd him.

The[4] Clan-Gregiour is a race of men so utterly infamous for thieving, depredation, and murder, that after many acts of the councel of Scotland against them, at length, in the reign of King Charles I, the Parliament made a strict Act suppressing the very name. Upon the Restauration, viz. in the year 1661, when the reins were given to all licentiousness, and loyalty, as it was then call'd, was thought sufficient to compound for all wickedness, that act was rescinded. But, upon the late happy Revolution, when the nation began to recover her senses, some horrid barbarities having been committed by that execrable crew, under the leading of one Robert Roy Mc gregiour, yet living, and at this present in arms against His Majesty K. George, The Parliament under K. William and Q. Mary annulled the said Act rescissory, and revived the former penal Act against them.

This Act is still continuing in force; but upon hopes given them, as 'tis said, by the E. of Mar, of having that brand of

---

[1] He was among those cited, under the *Act for Encouraging Loyalty in Scotland*, to appear at Edinburgh. The Act had received the royal assent on August 30.—*R.* 211.

[2] Lochiel and Appin.   [3] P. 81.   [4] *L. L. E.* 3.

infamy taken of 'em and getting their name restor'd on condition they would appear for the Pretender, about the end of
September last [1715] they broke out into open rebellion under
the conduct of Gregor Mc gregiour of Glengyle, nephew to the
above mention'd Rob. Roy Mc gregiour, and in a considerable
body made an excursion upon their neighbours, especially in
Buchanan and about the Heads of Monteith, and coming upon
them unawares, disarmed them.

Afterwards, upon Michaelmass Day [September 29], having
made themselves masters of the boats on the water of Enrick
and Loch-Lomond, about seventy men of 'em possess'd themselves of Inchmurrin, a large isle in the said loch, whence, about
midnight, they came a shore on the parish of Bonhill, three
miles above Dumbarton. But the country taking the alarm by
the ringing of the bells of the several parish churches about, and
being frighted by the discharge of two great guns from the castle
of Dumbarton to warn the country, they thought fit to scamper
off in great haste to their boats, and return'd to the isle, where,
not contenting themselves with beef, which they might have
had, ther being several cows on the isle, they made havock of a
great many deer belonging to His Grace the Duke of Montrose,
whose property the isle is, and row'd off with them towards the
head of the loch, taking along with them all the boats they cou'd
find, and drew them up upon the land at Innersnaat, about
eighteen miles up from the mouth of the loch, and, in a little time
after, went off in a body with their fellows towards Mar's Camp.
Upon what consideration it is not yet commonly known, but so
it is, that, in the end of the last week, they returned to their
former habitations on Craigroyston and the parts adjacent on
the north-east side of the abovemention'd Loch-Lomond, and
upon Monday last, being October 10th, they mustered their
forces.

This their return and rendezvouzing brought the country
about under some frightfull apprehensions. The Jacobits were
at a great deal of pains to perswade people that there was no
harm to be feared from them; that, supposing they shou'd come
doun upon the Lowlands, yet they wou'd spoil them of nothing
but their arms; that it wou'd be their wisdom peaceably to part

with these, because if they shou'd make any resistance, and shed
the blood of so much as one Mc Gregiour, they wou'd set no
bounds to their fury, but burn and slay without mercy. But the
people considered that this was false reasoning; that the quitting
of their arms wou'd be just as wise conduct as when the sheep
in the fable, at the desire of the wolves, parted with their dogs;
wherefore they resolved to do their best to defend themselves
against those miscreants who neither fear God nor regard
man.

For this purpose, and in order to bridle these rebels in their
excursions, a strong guard of one hundred and twenty volunteers
from Paslay, having been sometime before posted at Dumbarton,
and about four hundred voluntiers, partly of the Right Honourable the E. of Kilmarnock's men, partly of the people of Air,
Kilwining, Stevenson, etc., having garrison'd the houses of
Drumakill, Cardross, and Gartartan, it was resolved to retake, if
possible, the boats from them, by which they kept the countrey
round in a terrour....

For effecting this, on Teusday, October 11th, about six a'clock
at night, there came to the Key of Dumbarton, from the men of
war that are lying in the Firth of Clyde, four pinnaces and three
long boats, with four pateraroes, and about one hunder seamen,
well hearted and well armed, under the command of Captain
Charlton, Captain Field, and Captain Parker, with four lieutenants and two gunners. About two or three hours after, there
came up to them a large boat from Newport-Glasgow, with two
large screw guns, under the command of Captain Clark. All
these being join'd by three large boats of Dumbarton, upon the
morrow about nine in the morning they all put off from the
Key, and by the strength of horses were drawn the space of three
miles up the river Levin, which next to Spey is reckon'd the
most rapid river in Scotland.

When they were got to the mouth of the loch, the Paslay
men, and as many more as the boats cou'd conveniently stow,
went on board; and, at the same time, the Dumbarton men, the
men of Easter and Wester Kilpatrick, of Rosneith, Rew, and
Cardross, marched up on foot along the north-west side of the
loch, and after them, on horse back, the Honourable Master

John Campble of Mammore, unckle to His Grace the Duke of Argyle, attended by a fine train of the gentlemen of the shire, viz. Archbald Mc aulay of Ardncaple, Aulay Mc aulay, his eldest son, George Naper of Kilmahew, Walter Graham of Kilmardinny, John Colquhoun of Craigtoun, John Stirling of Law, James Hamilton of Barns, with many others, all richly mounted and well armed.

When the pinnaces and boats, being once got in within the mouth of the loch, had spread their sails, and the men on the shore had rang'd themselves in order, marching along the side of the loch for scouring the coast, they made all together so very fine an appearance as had never been seen in that place before, and might have gratified even a curious person. The men on the shore marched with the greatest ardour and alacrity. The pinnaces on the water discharging their Pateraroes, and the men their small arms, made so very dreadful a noise thro' the multiply'd rebounding echoes of the vast mountains on both sides the loch, that perhaps there was never a more lively resemblance of thunder.

Against evening they got to Luss, where they came ashore, and were met and join'd by Sir Humphrey Colquhoun of Luss, Baronet, and chief of the name, and James Grant of Pluscarden, his son in law and brother german to Brigadier [Alexander] Grant [of Grant], follow'd by fourty or fifty stately fellows in their short hose and belted plaids, arm'd each of 'em with a well fix'd gun on his shoulder, a strong handsome target, with a sharp pointed steel, of above half an ell in length, screw'd into the navel of it, on his left arm, a sturdy claymore by his side, and a pistol or two with a durk and knife on his belt. Here the whole company rested all night. In the mean time, many reports were brought to them, contrived or at least magnified by the Jacobites in order to discourage them from the attempt; such as, that Mc Donald of Glengarry, who was indeed lying with his men about Strafillan, sixteen miles from the head of the loch, had reinforced the Mc gregiours, so that they amounted at least to fifteen hundred men, whereas ther were not full four hundred on the expedition against them; That the loch being narrow at Innersnaat, where the rebels were lying, they might pepper the boats with their shot from the shore without any danger to themselves, being shaded by the rocks and woods. In a word, that it was a desperate project, and would be a throwing away of their lives.

But all this could not dishearten these brave men. They knew that the Mc gregiours and the Devil are to be dealt with after the same manner, and that if they be resisted they will flee. Wherefore on the morrow morning, being Thursday the 13th, they went on in their expedition, and about noon came to Innersnaat, the place of danger. In order to rouse those thieves from their dens, Captain Clark loos'd one of his great guns, and drove a ball thro' the roof of a house on the face of the mountain, whereupon an old wife or two came crawling out and scrambled up the hill, but otherwise ther was no appearance of any body of men on the mountains, only some few, standing out of reach on the craggy rocks looking at them.

Whereupon, the Paslay men under the command of Captain Finlason, assisted by Captain [Francis] Scot, a half pay officer, of late a Lieutenant in Collonell Kerr's Regiment of Dragoons, who is indeed an officer wise, stout, and honest; the Dumbarton men, under the command of David Colquhoun and James Duncanson of Garshaik, Magistrates of the Burgh, with severals of the other Companies, to the number of an hundred men in all, with the greatest intrepidity leapt on shore, got up to the top of the mountain, and drew up in order, and stood about an hour, their drums beating all the while, but no enemie appearing, they thereupon went in quest of the boats which the rebels had seiz'd, and having causually lighted on some ropes, anchors, and oars, hid among the shrubs, at length they found the boats drawn up a good way on the land, which they hurled doun to the loch; such of 'em as were not dammaged they carried off with them, and such as were they sunk or hew'd in pieces. And that same night they return'd to Luss, and thence, next day, without the loss or hurt of so much as one man, to Dumbarton, whence they had first set out altogether, bringing along with them the whole boats they found in their way on either side the loch and in the creeks of the isles, and moor'd them under the cannon of the castle. And thus in a short time, and with little expense, the

Mc greigours were cow'd, and a way pointed how the government may easily keep them in awe.

There are two or three things may be remarked on this expedition.

First, that tho' the Mc greigours deserved extremities, and our men were in a sufficient capacity to have destroy'd and burnt their whole goods and housing, yet they did not take from them to the value of a shoe latchet, save one fork which might have been used as a weapon.

Secondly, The Providence of God was very observable, in that tho' for three days before it had blown a prodigious storm, yet in the morning, when our men were to go on board from Dumbarton, it calm'd, and they got a fair wind in their poop the whole way up the loch. When they had done their business it kindly veer'd about and brought them safely and speedily down the loch, immediately after which, on the Friday's evening, it began to blow boisterously as before.

Thirdly, The cheerfulness of the men who went on this expedition deserves to be notic'd and applauded. They were not forced to it, as the clans are by their masters and chiefs, who hack and butcher such as refuse to go along with them: witness Duncan Mc farland in Rowardennin. But they offer'd themselves voluntarily to it. No wonder, for men begin now[1] to be convinced that all is at stake.

[As the result of this expedition,][2] the M'gregiours were cow'd and frighted away to the rest of the Rebels, who were encamp'd at Strathphillen about 16 Miles from the Head of the Loch, where, being all join'd, as above, they continued till the 18th of October: about which Time they were also joined by Stuart of Appin with 250 Men, Sir John M'Lean with 400, [John] M'Dougal of Lorn with about 50, and a Part of Broadalbine's Men, in all making up, by the modestest Computation, 2400 Men.

On the 17th they began their March towards Inverary, and came before it on the 19th. From the Time of my Lord Ilay's Arrival till now, all possible Means were used to bring in the

[1] This account was written on October 15, upon the return of the expedition to Dumbarton.   [2] *R. 288.*

Duke's Men; but the Clans coming before the Place so very soon, tho' Sir Duncan Campbel's Men, with those of Sir James Campbel of Auchinbreck, the Men of Isla, and several others were on their March to assist the King's Affairs, yet their joining the People within the Town was rendered impracticable: So that they had not above 1000 Men within it when the Clans appeared before it, and these were constantly employed in making the necessary Precautions for their own Defence, from the Time when they heard of the Clans being on their March until they appeared within Sight of the Town, in which Sir John Shaw of Greenock was very useful. The Clans having viewed them, and finding them prepared to give them a warm Reception contrary to their Expectation, thought fit to delay attacking the Town for that Night, but encamped within Half a Mile of that Place.

That same Night, two Servants of Sir Duncan Campbel, mistaking them for the Loyal Party, fell into their Hands, who, after detaining them Prisoners for some Hours, gave one of them his Liberty, upon promising to deliver a Letter to Sir Duncan; which he did, and Sir Duncan deliver'd it to my Lord Ilay. The Letter contain'd a Desire to speak with Sir Duncan next Morning without the Town, and any other two of four or five they condescended on, they having Matters of Importance to communicate to them. The Letter was sign'd by some of the chief Leaders of the Clans. The Earl of Ilay, judging that it was necessary to protract time with them as much as possible, in order to divert their joining the Rebels at Perth till the Troops from Ireland should join the King's Army at Stirling, allow'd Sir Duncan and Colonel Campbel to notify to them, that they would come out and meet with Clanronnald and Glengary next morning, and gave them Instructions to amuse and detain them as much as they could.

Accordingly, next Morning [October 20] they met with these Gentlemen on a rising Ground twixt the Town and their Camp, and acquainted them, that at their Desire they were come out to meet them in order to know their Business: After which, these Rebel Gentlemen told them, They had Orders from the Earl of Mar to oblige them to return home to their

Houses; which if they agreed to, they were ready to give them Assurances that the Shire should remain in quiet. To which Colonel Campbel and Sir Duncan returned, That they received no Orders from the Earl of Mar, and would stay together or go home as they thought fit; That it was their Opinion, That it was more their Interest to return home than theirs. The Rebel Gentlemen told them, That in Case of their Refusal, they had Orders to attack Inverary, and that some of their Number were very forward to begin the Attack. To which they answered, That they would Divert them in the best Manner they could, and wished the forward Gentlemen amongst them might attack them in the Front. The Conversation continued in this joking Manner above an Hour: And the only thing they seem'd to be serious in, and which appear'd to be a Proposal made to them in earnest, was, to concert with his Majesty's Friends in that Place, That neither Party should plunder nor force any Persons to join them. Colonel Campbel told them, That no Person should have the Honour to carry Arms for the King along with them but these who willingly offer'd their Service, and that they had no Power to treat or conclude, having only Liberty from my Lord Ilay to hear what they would propose, and that they would communicate the same to his Lordship. And finally, they promis'd to acquaint them next Day with what his Lordship thought of it.

Next Night [October 21] in the Evening, these Gentlemen sent them Notice by a Letter, That they had communicated what had pass'd to my Lord Ilay, who approved thereof: but the Rebel Gentlemen did not think this Letter (as indeed it was not design'd to be) plain enough; wherefore, the Day following [October 22], they sent another Letter to the Colonel and Sir Duncan, acquainting them therein, That their Letter to them was not express enough, mentioning the two Particulars above-mention'd, and desiring a plain Answer from my Lord Ilay to these two Heads. The Day following [October 23] they return'd them an Answer, signifying in Substance, That his Lordship, as he had no Power, either from the King or from his Brother, to that Purpose, could neither conclude nor so much as treat with any Person in Arms against the Government.

The Day after they received this Letter[1], they march'd off from before the Town of Inverary towards Strathphillen[2]. And immediatly upon their Retreat the Earl of Ilay ordered the above Colonel Campbel, with 800 chosen Men, to follow the Rebels at a convenient Distance, and as near their Rear as possibly he could adventure, in order to disturb their March and to over-awe the Countries through which they were to pass, lest they should join them; which indeed had the desired Success. Upon the first Day's March the Colonel got Notice, That there were 400 of the Earl of Broadalbin's Men left in the Country of Lorn; and having marched all Night, came up with them next Morning, desiring to speak with their Leaders, which accordingly was granted: And the Event of their Communing was, That he obliged them to return home to their own Houses, under positive Engagements not to disturb the Peace of his Majesty's Affairs; which they accordingly performed, and never joined the Rebels.

In the mean time, the Earl of Ilay remain'd at Inverary with 200 Men, and being joined the same Day the Clans went off, or next Morning, by 400 more, waited there till he had got a competent Body of 800 Men together, given the proper Orders to the Deputy Lieutenants for the Security of the Place and Country adjacent, and appointed them not to disband till they had farther Orders. These things took up his Lordship's Time 'till the 11th of November; and then, being advised from Stirling of the Rebels March from Perth in order to cross the River of Forth near Sterling, came with all Expedition to his Majesty's Army a little above Dumblain, accompanied by Sir John Shaw, upon Sunday the 13th about Twelve of the Clock, as they march'd up the Hill to meet the Enemy....

But before we come to a particular Account of that Battel, we shall first look back, reassume the Thread of the History where we left it, and enquire a little into the previous Conduct of the Duke of Argyle...as also of the Rebel General Mar, who continu'd with his Army at Perth, after their Return respectively

[1] October 25.

[2] They joined Mar at Auchterarder, about a week later. See *infra*, p. 112, note 4.

from Leith and Dumblain, With what else may be proper to be
noticed antecedently to that great Action.

We[1] were not long returned to Pearth from Dumblain[2] when
another expedition to Fife was set on foot...to levie the cess[3] of
Dumfermling, a Whiggish toun; and neither that toun, or the
countrie about, which was nearer the ennemie, would pay, being
supported by the ennemie....

Thomas Grahame, who had acquired the title of Major, in
the hills under my Lord Dundee, in the same manner as most
of our commissions were given of late for want of officers, was
named to command fourscore horse and three hundred Highland
foot[4]; they were order'd to march to Dumfermling, which is
fourteen miles from Pearth, but not to goe the direct road; for
they were to marche by Dinnen, to pass under the nose of the
Duke of Argyle's guarnisone at Castell Campbell, six short
miles from Stireling, where he had put some countrie militia,
and after makeing so great a detour to insult them by marcheing
in their sight, Major Graham was with his command to return
to Dumfermling, where he was to raise the cess, and from that
to detache nine horse to Culros and some such number to Saline
towards Stirling....[John] Gordon of Glenbucket[5], who commanded the three hundred foot, tho' a Collonell, was to be under
Major Grahame's command, and James Malcome, without
whome nothing was to be done, was sent alonge to mannage
the whole, haveing been a warriour at Gillicrankie.

They no sooner came to Dumfermling [on Sunday, October
23,][6] then all the gentlemen of the horse seperated into alehouses
and taverns, and after[wards] most went to bed. Glenbucket
put the foot into the Abbey, a place stronglie situated, and took
up his oun quarters in the toun, and placed a sentrie at his door.
Major Grahame placed one sentrie at a bridge, a little without
that end of the toun which leads to Stirling; for, as we had
supposed when at Dumblain, the ennemie would come no other

---

[1] *S. M.* 166.   [2] *Supra*, p. 88.
[3] On October 21, Mar published an order for an assessment upon
the shires of Fife, Clackmannan, Kinross, and Perth.—*R.* 295.
[4] Rae gives them as one hundred horse and two hundred foot.—
Ibid. 294.   [5] The Duke of Gordon's factor.   [6] *R.* 294.

way but the streight road. Major Grahame and James Malcome
set themselves doun to take a heartie bottle: when it was turning
late, [George] Gordon of Buckie, a kinsman of Huntley's,
[? John] Seaton of Lathrie [Lathrisk], and Beatsone of Killrie,
who had more thought and judgment than the others, went and
found out Major Grahame, and told, by all they had heard or
could judge, it would be proper to put out more sentries and
take some other precautions. He ansuer'd them, Mr Malcome
and his nephew Robert, who were present, knew the countrie
better than either they or he did, and had assured him there was
no danger; he drunk on, and they returned.

All this while, Collonell [Charles] Cathcart[1] was lying without the toun with tuo hundred dragoons, and had his spies
goeing out and in, giveing him exact information of everie thing,
and finding all to his wish, dismounted some dragoons, and sent
them [about five o'clock on the morning of the 24th[2]] into the
toun one way, and a captain with [blank in ms.] on horseback
another way. They killed the poor solitarie horse sentrie on the
bridge after dischargeing his pistolls, and, in a word, were in the
middle of the toun before anie bodie knew of them, killed
Forbes, a captain of the Highland foot, who fired both his side-
pistolls and drew his suord amongst the middle of them, did the
same by Glenbucket's sentrie, who did his dutie and fired. They
took eighteen gentlemen prisoners of those who were most alerte
and run out to the streets[3], and very luckie their loss was not
greater. The foot in the Abbey were surprised at the alarme and
keept within, not doubting that the number of the ennemie was
greater in toun than they reallie were, and expected to be attackt
themselves....

No wonder if, after this ruffle, everie one run a different way;
some left their horses sticking in dunghills, in the streets, and
others, when their horses fell in anie narrow lane with justling
or makeing too great hast to get away, left them on the spot,

---

[1] The Duke of Argyll had sent him with a party of dragoons so soon
as he learnt that Graham's force had passed Castle Campbell towards
Dunfermline.—R. 294.   [2] *Ibid.*

[3] Rae mentions seventeen prisoners, and gives the names of the chief
of them.—R. 294.

and came to Pearth on countrie horses, and said they had their horses shot under them; others run to Bruntisland, some to different places of the countrie, some got under beds, others up to garrets, and most of this when the ennemie was gone, who, knowing of the Highlandmen's being in the Abbey, did not stay to dalley in toun, and beat their retreat very quicklie after their comeing in, for they seised nobodie in houses. The foot had longer no patience there, and went off in order next day to Bruntisland[1].

After[2] the conquest of Argylshire[3] we made ourselves...in such a condition that we durst not look at him [Argyll] in front, flank, or rear, and therefor must order the Clans to joyn us, which so soon as they did, we 'd make his Grace of Argyle retire to Berwick and obey the Prince's orders. The Clans blood-thirstie curiositie was soon satisfied in Argyleshire, by seeing folks in armes there readie to receave them and nothing to be got in that countrie, for it 's ill takeing breeches from a High-landman, according to the proverb, most willinglie obey'd, and in their marche towards us, were joyned by Lochiell with the Clan Cameron, and Steuart of Apin with his follouing. Mar order'd them to cantoon at Auchterarduch[4]....They were prittie modest and did not brag much of their success, onlie it was believed the Campbells[5] might at last be brought to marche doun the other side Forth and favour our passage now, the Clans

    [1] Another attempt was made later, and with success, by Lord George Murray and a party of Highlanders to levy the cess at Dunfermline.—
S. M. 192. At St Andrews, where the levying of the cess was resisted, the women of the place behaved with considerable energy against a detachment sent from Perth.—R. 295.

    [2] S. M. 187.

    [3] As has been told (*supra*, p. 109), the Clans in Argyllshire failed in their main purpose—the capture of Inveraray and the opening of a western path of invasion into England.

    [4] It was upon October 25 that the western Clans had withdrawn from before Inveraray (*supra*, p. 109). They reached Auchterarder about November 1 (S. M. 188) and joined Mar on November 11, on his march to Sheriffmuir (R. 301).

    [5] The Campbells were much divided during the whole affair.—Sir Walter Scott's note.

being to marche with us. Linlithgow was commanded out to
Auchterarduch, with the standard squadron and [Lord] Rollo's,
to joyn the Clans....We had been told they were to be nere to
five thousand when Lochiell and Apin joyned, but they were
not more than tuo thousand five hundred[1], being weakned by
desertion in that fatigueing marche [from Inveraray] nere as
much as those tuo Clans strengthen'd them....

The Clans being now with us, we forgot to marche to pass
the Forth, and reprived the Duke of Argyle till my Lord
Seaforth[2], Sir Donald Macdonald, and Frazer[3] joynd us, who
we were expecting every day, as we had done six weeks, or
rather tuo months before, and no greater appearance of his
comeing nou than was then....

[At length, however,] Seaforth being in full marche towards
us, and, after his comeing, our Generall prudentlie foreseeing
there would be no further excuse for staying longer at Pearth,
and that there would be a necessitie of marcheing or makeing a
feint in ten days or a fortnight at farthest, begun to think it was
nou the proper time to fortifie Pearth, I mean make lines about
it....[General] Hamiltone seem'd to look after it for a day or
tuo, but soon wearied of it, and to our eternall shame left the
direction of the whole to a French fellow, who had been a
footman of Beaufort's, and had takne up the trade of being a
danceing and fenceing master in the North, who made the
strangest line that ever was made, which served for no other use
but the jeast of the ennemie's armie; nor had the fellow sense

[1] Rae gives their numbers as one hundred horse and three thousand
foot.—*R.* 301.

[2] Seaforth was meanwhile engaged in the north against the Earl of
Sutherland. The military operations in that district are treated con-
secutively, *infra*, p. 171.

[3] Alexander Mackenzie, Younger of Prestonhall, assumed the name
of Fraser of Fraserdale, on his marriage with Anne, eldest daughter of
Hugh, Lord Lovat. He brought out the Clan Fraser into the Rebellion,
but the celebrated Simon Fraser [of Beaufort], afterwards Lord Lovat,
taking the side of the Government, the Clan came over to him, as the
heir-male and proper Chief, and deserted Fraserdale.—Sir Walter
Scott's note.

enough to face it up, such as it was, so that a man could lay his breast to it, [n]or did he know to make a foot-bank, as I have been told by severall Suisse officers since; tho' it came all to the same, for the frost and want of time would [have] hinder'd the perfiteing of it, being so late of beginning....

About this time we fell to work to make carriages for our cannon, which we had pickt up in severall places, to the number of eleven field-pieces, six of which were brass, and five iron; and all these, tho' we had neither pouder nor ball, were to goe alonge with us when we marched, which time drew near, for Seaforth and Sir Donald MacDonald being in a feu days' marche of us, there was no pretence to shift or delay it longer. Their numbers, till the day we saw them, continued to be near four thousand foot and some hundreds of horse, besides Frazerdale's with his Clan of Frazers, which were augmented proportionallie, and were onlie, in all, seven hundred Macdonalds, about the same number of Mackenzies, and four hundred Frazers, and fortie scrub horse of servants, and others from about Inverness who came alonge with Seaforth; and the great [Lord] Duffus[1] came in his train, on a Galloway of thirtie shillings, as poor as he went North, no bodie haveing takne the least notice of him of all those thousands he proposed to bring out....

Now all hands were set to work about bringing in meale to serve us in our marche; but hou that meale was to be carried, or where we were to marche, we did not know. To pass at Stirveling was impossible; the Foords of Forth was the common storie, but I never heard of anie man of our armie who knew any thing of those foords except Rob Roy[2], who, they themselves said, they

[1] He had undertaken to raise Sutherland against the Earl of Sutherland.—S. M. 69.

[2] The celebrated Rob Roy Macgregor, a freebooter, about whom so much has been said and sung; his attachment to the Jacobite cause was rather overbalanced by his dependence on the Duke of Argyle, who maintained and sheltered him to vex and harass the Duke of Montrose. In a letter to Marshal Wade, after the war was over, honest Rob owns that his inclination induced him to join the King's troops, but that, afraid of imprisonment, he had been compelled to join the rebels; a false step, for which he endeavoured to atone by rendering to the Duke

could not trust....Nor was it to be expected that the Duke of Argyle, who had surveyed these foords and passages narroulie, and spoilt the foords by digging and putting great beams in them with iron pikes, would let us pass them undisturb'd without disputeing the matter, haveing it always in his pouer to be there before us after we had gone higher then Stirveling, where he had nothing to fear if he left tuo hundred men to defend the bridge: Besides it was said he had made lines on all the fords[1], which is not to be doubted he did, if he found them practicable, for we gave him time enough to take all his precautions....Another obvious difficultie arose, the enemie haveing cut the bridge of Doun not far from Stirveling, our onlie way to the Foords of Forth; nor could we pretend to pass that river which is called the Teith, and rather worse to pass then the Forth, as all who knew it said[2]. At other times we talkt of goeing by the Heads of Forth, but still that river of Teith was in our way, nor could we [have] passed it had we tents to ly out so many days marche in that season of the year, in a wild barren countrie, where there was no manner of cover or provisions, which we had not industrie enough to provide or lay up before hand in Pearth, much less to carrie alonge with us....

Seaforth came at last, with Sir Donald MacDonald and Frazerdale[3]. We marched a day or tuo after[4], a la bonne aventure,

of Argyle, from time to time, during the Insurrection, information of the strength and motions of the rebels (see Jamieson's [fifth] Edition [Lond. 1818] of Burt's Letters from the North of Scotland, vol. ii. Appendix).—Sir Walter Scott's note.

[1] It is singular that with so many men in the army from Monteith and the Lennox, they seemed to have been unable to ascertain the real state of these Fords.—Sir Walter Scott's note.

[2] Prince Charles, under more favourable circumstances, since the only considerable force in Scotland was then in his rear, crossed the Teith at Doune on September 12, 1745, and the Forth at the Fords of Frew on the following day.

[3] The force, whose number Rae gives sceptically as eight hundred horse and three thousand foot, included also 'M'Invans, M'Craws, Chisholms of Strath-Glass, and others.'—R. 298.

[4] On November 10.—Ibid. 301.

the blind leading the blind, not knowing whither we were goeing or what we were to doe.

And[1] now, being join'd by all the Troops he had to expect, [the Earl of Mar]...resolved to decamp from Perth and attempt to pass over the Forth into the South Parts of Scotland, in order to march into England to join their Friends in Lancashire[2]. To this End he summoned his Forces together, leaving not above 3000 Men dispers'd in Garrisons at Dundee, Brunt-Island, and other Places along the Coast of Fife: And

Upon the 9th of November he called a great Council of War at Perth[3], where the Rebels agreed to put themselves in Readiness for a March over Forth with the utmost Celerity. And finding themselves Masters of 12,000 effective Men to carry on this Expedition...they determined to march straightway to Dumblain, and from thence to detach 3000 Men to amuse the King's Army at Stirling, which they knew made not full 3000, by making three Sham-Attacks at so many different Places at one and the same Time, as follows: With 1000 they were to attack the End of the long Causeway which leads directly to Stirling-Bridge, and to lodge themselves safe from the Cannon of the Castle in and about the adjacent Houses and Barn-Yards, as if they design'd to force the Bridge: With another Thousand they resolved to make another Sham-Attack at the Abbey-Ford[4], a Mile below Stirling-Bridge; while the third Thousand was to make such another Attack at the Drip-Coble, a Mile and an half above it....While the King's Troops were to be amused with these three Sham-Attacks, the main Body, consisting of about 9000 Men[5], were to attempt to cross the River

[1] R. 298
[2] Forster and Mackintosh surrendered at Preston on November 13, three days after Mar advanced from Perth.
[3] Sinclair does not mention this Council, and affects complete ignorance of the tactics which Mar proposed to adopt. Rae's account would appear to be based on official sources, since he speaks of it as being 'told from Mar's own Cabinet Council.'
[4] Near Cambuskenneth Abbey.
[5] About eight thousand, according to Sinclair, was Mar's total

a little farther up undiscovered, and follow Brigadier M'Intosh into England: And the 3000 Men, [who] were to be employed in these Attacks, had Orders to draw off and follow them with their first Conveniency. The Project was further design'd, that if the Duke of Argyle should abandon Stirling and attempt to encounter that Body of the Rebels after their crossing the River, the 3000 Men above-mentioned were to force themselves into the Town, or press him in the Rear.

Next Morning[1], the Duke of Argyle having Intelligence hereof by his Spies from Perth, and being certify'd of all the Particulars concerted as above, his Grace, to prevent their reaching the Banks of Forth, resolved to possess himself of the rising Ground above Dumblain, keeping the Road from Perth upon his Left, thro' which Road the Rebels must of Necessity come in Order to take Possession of either of the three Places abovemention'd, and there to fight them if he had Opportunity: And accordingly gave Orders to his little Army, which made scarce 3000 effective Regular Troops, made up of Eight small Battallions of Foot, and Five Regiments of Dragoons (as in the Plan below), to be in the utmost Readiness to march next After-noon [November 11]; for the which End he had sent for the Troops that were quarter'd at Glasgow, Kelsyth, and Falkirk[2], and for General Wightman from Edinburgh, to join him at Stirling with all possible Speed. The Names of the General Officers of the several Regiments and the Order of Battle was as follows[3]:

strength.—*S. M.* 208. Keith numbers the army at fourteen battalions of infantry and eight squadrons of cavalry, or about six thousand eight hundred in all.—*K. M.* 16.

[1] Thursday, November 10, 1715.

[2] Late in October, the regiments of Egerton, Clayton, and Morrison [Moryson], and two troops of Evans's dragoons arrived in Scotland from Ireland, and were ordered to wait at Glasgow for further orders from the Duke of Argyll. At about the same time, the Duke ordered forty dragoons and a battalion of foot to Kilsyth, and two hundred dragoons to Falkirk.—*R.* 297.

[3] Actually Argyll's force was drawn up in two lines. *Infra,* p. 129.

His Grace the Duke of Argyle, General.

Lieut. General Whetham.	Major General Wightman.	Lieut. General Evans.
Brigadier Grant.	Brigadier Clayton.	Brigadier Ld Forfar.

Carpenter's Dragoons [3rd Dragoons]	Col. Kerr's Dragoons [7th Dragoons]	Half E. Stair's Drag. [6th Dragoons]	Edgerton's [36th]	Orrery's [R.S.F.]	Clayton's [14th]	Montague's [11th]	Morison's [8th]	Ld Shannon's [25th]	Whitman's [17th]	Ld Forfar's [3rd]	Half E. Stair's Drag. [6th Dragoons]	Evans's Dragoons [4th Hussars]	Portmore's Dragoons [2nd Dragoons]
180	180	90	250	320	240	240	240	340	250	320	90	180	180

And being thus in a Readiness upon the 11th at Night, his Grace, having left the Right Honourable the Earl of Buchan, Lord Lieutenant of the County of Stirling, with the Militia of that Shire, and the Glasgow Regiment, consisting of 500 Men under the Command of John Aird, their Provost, to guard the Town of Stirling[1], Did upon Saturday the 12th in the Morning begin his March towards the Town of Dumblain; and accordingly encamped that Evening upon a rising Ground to the East of Dumblain, betwixt that and the Mountain called Sheriff-Moor.

But before we proceed any further in this Part, we return to

[1] The Glasgow Regiment were order'd to hold themselves in Readiness to march with the Army to give the Enemy Battle; and accordingly were forward to have marched: But, by Reason they wanted Tents, and were not so well acquainted with lying in the Fields as the Regular Troops; and that, if the Glasgow People had marched, as many Regular Troops were to have been left behind in their Room, they were therefore stoped from marching to the Field of Battle; and were left to guard the Town, Castle and Bridge of Stirling, with the Foords upon the River Forth, in conjunction with the foresaid Militia, &c., which they did with great Care and Exactness.—Rae's note.

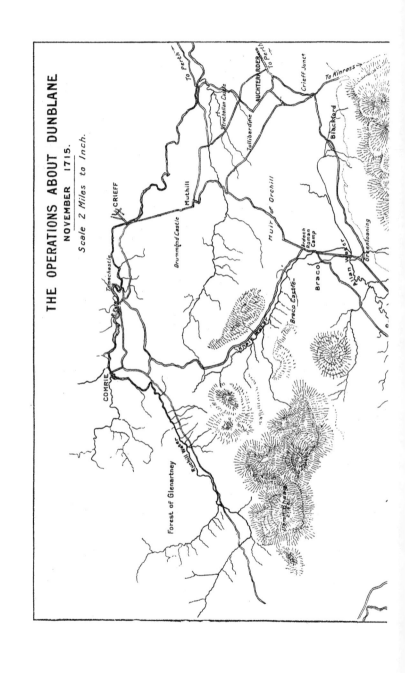

THE OPERATIONS ABOUT DUNBLANE

NOVEMBER 1715.

Scale 2 Miles to Inch.

To Perth

Strathallan Castle

AUCHTERARDER

To Perth

Crieff Junct.

To Kinross

Blackford

Tullibardine

CRIEFF

Muthill

Muir of Orchill

Drummond Castle

Ardoch Roman Camp

Braco

Braco Castle

Greenloaning

Allan Water

Tomachastle

Earn

Moor Moss

COMRIE

Ruchill Water

Forest of Glenartney

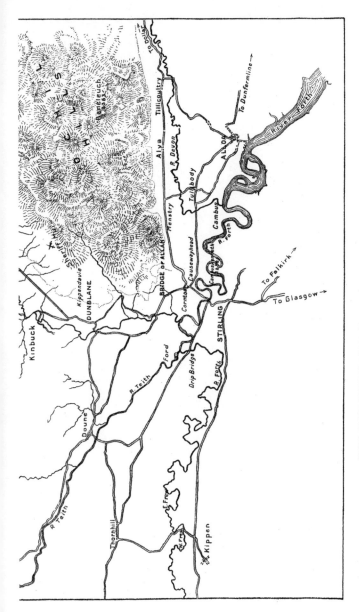

THE OPERATIONS ABOUT DUNBLANE, NOVEMBER 1715

the Earl of Mar, and bring him also to the Field with his Rebel
Army.

The[1] first day's marche [of Mar's army from Perth], we of
the horse cantooned about Dinnen, and the foot in and about
Auchterarduch[2]. That night [November 10] all the Frazers
deserted us, hearing of Beaufort's being arrived in the North,
their other Chief, whome they owned preferable to Frazerdale,
whose title to them was by marrieing ane heiress[3]. Tuo hundred
of my Lord Huntlie's best men who were under the command
of Glenbucket deserted us, as his Lordship said, because they
had been designedlie more oppressed with dutie than any other.
That first night of our cantoonment, orders were sent to us to
be by break of day next morning in the moor of Auchterarduch,
where Mar revieued us, and all our armie drew up in tuo lines,
and afterwards returned to our quarters. In this revieu there
were squabbles about the posts of our squadrons, and [we] were
never so constant in any thing as our being disorderlie....We
halted there all next day [November 11], nor did I stir from my
command. In the evening we receav'd orders to parade in
Auchterarduch moor before day, which we did. So soon as I
came to the parade, my Lord Mar sent for me and told me,
That I and the Fife squadron were the occasion of the armie's
not marcheing the day before[4]. I said, He surprised me, nor
could I conceive how that could be, for I and that squadron...
had keept at our quarters all that day. Then he told me, That
my Lord Huntlie and the Clans, who were to marche before in
a separate body, had refused to marche except he 'd order me
and the Fife squadron alonge with them[5]. I told him, I knew
nothing of the matter, and that it was the same to me, as well

[1] *S. M.* 203.
[2] Mar left John Balfour of Ferny behind in command of Perth.—
R. 301. He had with him three battalions for the defence of the town.
—*K. M.* 16.   [3] *Supra*, p. 113.
[4] Mar's official account attributed the delay to 'some Interruptions.'
—*P. H.* 54.
[5] This had already been urged by the Clans some days before Mar
began his advance, and Sinclair, who expresses himself as being at that
time 'wearied of Huntley's horse,' undertook to accompany them 'if

as to the [Fife] gentlemen, where or with whome we were to marche. He said, It was now resolved I should goe alonge with them to please them, and likewise said, He believed I had ane influence on Huntlie, and spoke pressinglie to me to encourage him. I ansuer'd, I was not well acquainted with my Lord Huntlie, but that I would doe all that depended on me; nor had I then the honour of his Lordship's intimacie[1].

I joyn'd the Clans, who by this time were beginning their marche. They consisted of Sir Donald MacDonald's, Captain of Clan Ronald's, Glengarie's, Glencoe's follouings, all Mac-Donalds, Bredalbins, the MacCleans, the Camerons, Steuart of Apins, and the few that were left of Huntlie's Strathdoun and Glenlivet men who had not deserted, for the greatest part of them had gone home. All were under the command of Generall Gordon[2], as I was likwise with the three squadrons which I commanded, Huntlie's tuo, and the Fife squadrons. I marched on the front with the horse, haveing detached tuo avant guards, and the foot folloued. The gross of our armie, under the command of Mar and Generall Hamiltone, were to follow us soon after[3], to cantoon that night at Arduch, and we were to take post at Dumblaine, eight miles further. It was then the tuelft day of November. We continued in full marche till three of the afternoon; about which time our Quarter-Masters, who had left us a little before, came back with a lame boy, who had run

ever they marched seperatlie on any expedition, and wanted horse.'—*S. M.* 189.

[1] 'With more talent than Huntly, and at the same time with less power and influence, the MASTER [of Sinclair] obtained the credit of being his adviser, and chief of the Mutineers, or, as they were called, of the Grumbling Club. He was very sensible of all this, and wrote *recentibus odiis*, which may [be] an apology for the savage ferocity with which he attacks not only Mar but Marischal and others.'—Sir Walter Scott's Preface to *S. M.* xix.

[2] Brigadier Ogilvy was with Gordon.—*R.* 301.

[3] Mar's main body paraded, early on the morning of the 12th, on the Moor of Tullibardine, and then marched after the Clans under General Hamilton's command. Mar proceeded to Drummond Castle to meet Lord Breadalbane.—*P. H.* 54.

as hard as he could to tell us that the Duke of Argyle was marcheing through Dumblaine with his whole armie towards us[1], and said the Ladie Kippendavie had sent him, whose husband[2] was in the armie with us....Upon this, the Generall [Gordon[3]] sent ane express to Mar, and I detached half a dozen of the horse to goe as nere to Dumblaine as possible to reconnoitre the enemie, and Gordon order'd me to halt and draw up the horse, and ordered the foot to doe the same, the boy still affirming he had seen the enemie, and saying he was satisfied to be hanged if we did not find it so[4].

[1] Argyll's official account, sent to the King by Colonel Charles Harrison, was to the effect, that the Duke, learning on the 12th that Mar's army had reached Auchterarder, 'was obliged either to engage them on the Grounds near Dumblain, or to decamp and wait their coming to the Head of Forth. He chose the first on many Accounts, and amongst others, that the Grounds near Dumblain were much more advantageous for his Horse than those at the Head of the River; and besides this, by the Frost then beginning, the Forth might become passable in several Places, which the small Number of his Troops did not enable him to guard sufficiently. He likewise received Advice, that the 12th, at Night, the Rebels designed to encamp at Dumblain; upon which, judging it of Importance to prevent them by possessing that Place, he marched the 12th in the Forenoon, and encamped with his Left at Dumblain, and his Right towards the Sheriff-Moor.'—P. H. 36.

[2] Stirling of Kippendavie, whose house is not distant from the field of battle.—Sir Walter Scott's note.

[3] Gordon's force was at that time about two miles to the west of Ardoch. Hamilton, upon receiving Gordon's message, 'drew up the Army so as the Ground at the Roman Camp near Ardoch would allow. A very little after, the Earl of Mar came up to the Army [from Drummond Castle], and not hearing any more from Lieutenant General Gordon, who was marched on, judg'd it to be only some small Party of the Enemy to disturb our March, ordered the Guards to be posted, and the Army to their Quarters, with Orders to assemble upon the Parade, any time of the Night or Day, upon the firing of three Cannon.'— P. H. 54.

[4] Argyll's advance to Dunblane was wholly unforeseen by Mar, who expected to occupy that place unopposed, and concluded that Argyll would fight 'at the passage of the river' Forth.—K. M. 16. The Duke's motives for not doing so are set forth in note 1, *supra*.

We had no sooner halted then [Quartermaster-General]
Peter Smith[1]...order'd us to marche on, and the foot folloued.
As we were thus in motion, we met severall of the countrie
people, who said the generall report was that the Duke of
Argyle was of this side Dumblain; and now it was beginning to
be dark, and we had marched a mile from the place we halted,
when I told Generall Gordon, who rid alonge with me all the
while, That it would be of very bad consequence at any time to
stumble in our marche in the dark on the Duke of Argyle's
whole armie, which must be alreadie posted in some stronge
ground, otherwise we must [have] heard more of them, but of
the worst of consequences at present, when the great bodie of
our armie was at such a distance from us....

Upon this, we drew up again on a riseing ground in the
moor, and those we had sent to reconnoitre returned, telling
that they had heard of the enemie, but it turning dark, they did
not care to venture for fear of being kidnapt....Next thing to be
thought of was to take up some stronge ground, where we were
to be under armes all that night, or till we heard from my Lord
Mar; for now it was to be supposed that the enemie were posted
of this side of Dumblaine, and could not be above tuo miles from
us. We were also to think of our horses, which could not be fit
for anie bussieness next day if we were not near to some farm-
house whence fourage could be got. I proposed to Generall
Gordon to pass the river of Allen, which was within tuo hundred
yards of our right as we were then drawn up, and told him,
That I had observed some very good barn-yards on the other
side before it grew duskish; for it was not yet dark....He ansuer'd,
He 'd goe and see what was to be done; and rid off, with tuo-
three more with him, and at last found a little hollow, hard by
on the river side[2], where there were tuo little farme-houses and
corn-yards. He came back and led us thither. He gave me a
guide to lead the horse into the ground allotted for them, who

    [1] 'Formerlie a surgeon in the armie, and made ensigne in Douglas
regiment after the peace.'—*S. M.* 205.
    [2] The place where the Clans halted, and where Mar and the main
body joined them later, was Kinbuck, which lies close to the left bank
of the Water of Allan.—*P. H.* 55.

carried us doun a hollow way which leads to the houses, and told me it was the Generall's orders to put our horses into those caile-yards which he sheu'd us, to which we could find no entrie but through the houses; so I lighted, and with my oun hands broke doun the walls, the louer part made with drie stone, and above with turf or faile. The first yard not being able to containe us, we broke doun the next wall, and did so with another, till the three squadrons got place. These yards made the bottom of the hollow; all the ground about had a sudden rise from the houses and yards for tuo hundred paces, except toward the north, where we were hard upon the river, which was behind us; for it can't be properlie said we had front or rear, more than it can be said of a barrell of herrings. In this uneven ground, with a hollow way in it, to better the matter, were we packt in, and all the foot round us, almost as much straitned as we. What the Generall did that lookt at all like a sojer was, to call for a horse-guarde, to send patrouiles a good way round us.

I, with the gentlemen of the horse, took up one of those houses, and the Marquise of Huntlie, Generall Gordon, and the Heads of Clans took up the other. We were not longe got in when Southesque came with the Angus squadron, and told me of Mar with the whole armie's following us; and Mar came soon after him, which was then about nine of the clock, for we had takne a longe time to settle all in that confusion in the dark[1]....So soon as he lighted he came into that house which I had takne up...and askt, What intelligence we had got? Which I told him. He treated it with ane air of neglect, as if he had a mind to accuse us of fear, and said he 'd lay anie monie that it was not true. Afterwards he called for Generall Gordon, who

[1] 'A little after the Army was dismiss'd [cf. note 3, p. 121], the Earl of Mar had an Account from Lieutenant-General Gordon, that he had certain Intelligence of the Duke of Argyle's being at Dumblain with his whole Army. Upon which [Gordon] was ordered to halt till the Earl should come up to him, and ordered the three Guns to be fired; upon which, the Army form'd immediately, and marched up to Lieutenant-General Gordon at Kinbuck, where the whole Army lay under Arms, with Guards advanc'd from each Squadron and Battalion, till break of Day.'—*P. H.* 54.

came alonge with Huntlie. And when the Generall told him
the same he said, He knew the contrarie; and to this there was
no answer to be made....My Lord Huntlie...took me alonge
with him, and I left my quarters to Mar....After that I laid me
doun in the straw betuixt Captain of Clan Ronald and Sir John
MacClean, and sleept till day.

All that night did our armie ly in that small circumference;
and I believe eight thousand men, for we were about that
number, were never packt up so close together since the inven-
tion of pouder....Houever, that night we had the good luck not
to be discover'd by the enemie, as I have been since told, any
more than if we had been all buried....

Next morning [November 13], by six of the clock we drew
out of that ground and formed in tuo lines in the plaine[1], above
that place where we had lyen that night. At sun-riseing we
discover'd a command of horse[2] on the high ground to the south
of us, at a good mile's distance[3], which appear'd to us a stronge
squadron; even then we pretended to pass the river of Teith in
order to try the Heads of Forth or the Foords, tho' it was
believed the Foords were render'd impassible by the enemie, and
agreed to by all that neither the Teith nor the Forth were to be
passed at that season of the year, the rivers being so high; nor,
without these obstacles, had we anie more provisions left to
serve us one day's marche in a countrie where nothing was to
be got for ourselves or horses; so all that was possible for us to
have done was to marche three-four miles further to the Teith,
and return starved back to Pearth. So soon as that command of
the enemie's horse appear'd, reconnoitrers were sent out; they

[1] The army formed 'on the Moor, to the Left of the Road that leads
to Dumblain, fronting to Dumblain.'—*P. H.* 55.

[2] 'Next Morning [November 13] his Grace being informed by his
advanced Guard that the Rebels were forming, he rode to a Rising-
Ground, where he viewed the Enemy distinctly, and found, as they
pointed their March, they designed streight upon our [right] Flank [on
Sheriffmuir].'—Colonel Harrison's account, in *P. H.* 37.

[3] 'When the Army was forming, we [of Mar's army] discover'd
some small Number of the Enemy on the Height of the West End on
the Sheriffmuir, which looks into Dumblain.'—*P. H.* 55.

came back and told us the enemie were all about the inclosures of Kippendavie. After this we lost a great dale of time. I believe his Lordship of Mar, who did not expect the enemie, not knowing what hand to turn himself to, and being then conscious of his want of abilitie for such ane undertakeing, was stunned[1]....

Now it was past eleven of the clock before it seems our Generall took his resolution, and I, as well as everie bodie at this moment, admire what he could be thinking of all that time, for it was not his part to make the disposition, which was done soon; but there he was out of his element. Had he been scribling in his chamber at Pearth, his resolution had been soon takne, and orders sent to the commanding officer to attack, right or wronge, without further consideration.

At last, all Lords, Commanders of Corps, and Heads of Clans were called for to a little round spot of riseing ground betuixt[2] our lines, where Mar stood. Being all met, his Lordship, to doe him justice, which I think I am oblidged in consciens to doe, it being the onlie good action of his life, made us a very fine speech...and concluded it was his opinion we should attack the enemie, who were so near us, and inlarged on the whole in very stronge and moveing terms....My Lord Huntlie was the onlie man who spoke in our Council of War[3], and, I think, haveing own'd the truth of what my Lord Mar said, askt, If the gaineing a battle would recover our liberties and give the decisive stroke to our affair as we were then circumstanced, and w[h]ither we

[1] Apart from Mar's competency, the project of attacking Argyll had an objection, real or assumed, which was urged by Huntly—namely, that if the army crossed the Forth, the Chevalier, who was expected daily, would be cut off from it. Sinclair, who frankly despaired of success, suggested to Huntly and others that they should fight only after learning from Argyll whether he had power to negotiate full and satisfactory terms with them. Failing that assurance, however, he was resolute to fight.—*S. M.* 209.

[2] 'In the Front of the Horse on the Left.'—*P. H.* 56.

[3] According to Keith, Huntly 'made some insinuations that it wou'd not be fit to remain in unaction till the King's arrival.'—*K. M.* 17. This is directly contrary to Sinclair's statement already noticed, *supra*.

could pretend after that to resist the force of England and its allies without forraigne aide?...Mar took no notice of what my Lord Huntlie said, and desir'd the vote to be stated, Fight or Not; and all unanimouslie, to doe them justice, with ane unexpressible alacritie called out, Fight. And the moment most went to their posts....

We were no sooner got to our posts when a huzza begun, with tossing up of hats and bonnets, and run through our whole armie on the hearing we had resolved to fight; and no man, who had a drope of Scots blood in him, but must [have] been elevated to see the cheerfullness of his countriemen on that occasion; and, for my oun part, in spite of my reason, I made no manner of doubt of gaineing the victorie, and by that unaffected livelieness that appear'd in everie man's looks I begun to think that Highlandmen were Highlandmen[1].

I have alreadie said we had been formed all that morning in tuo lines: Marishall's, Linlithgow's [Stirling squadron] and Huntlie's tuo squadrons were on the right of the front line, and Southesque's [Angus squadron], Rollo's [Perthshire squadron], and mine [the Fifeshire squadrons] were on the left of the rear line, by orders. From our meeting at our Councill of War we did not loose half-ane-hour, when [General] Hamiltone broke our lines each in tuo colloms, and order'd the four squadrons of horse on the right, with tuo thousand Highlandmen who compos'd the collom of the right of the first line, to marche and take possession of that high ground where the ennemie's horse appear'd. My Lord Drummond...put himself on the head of those four squadrons; so he and Marishall commanded them, and Generall Gordon commanded the foot....The second colume on the left of the first line marched likwise by the right, and folloued the other at a great distance; then the first colume of the second line marched by the right, as did the second [i.e. left] colume of the second line, so that the three [Fifeshire] squadrons fell into the rear of that colume which marched last off the

---

[1] Sinclair held a very low opinion of the Highlanders' fighting qualities. He admits that their conduct at Sheriffmuir corrected his judgment.—
S. M. 211.

ground, and had orders to follow that colume, which, it was
saide, would carrie us to the left. Rollo was next the foot, and
Southesque next him, and I last[1]....

By the time we begun to move off our ground, the four
squadrons of horse with Drummond and Marishall, and the first
colume of the foot, with them who had made so great haste to
the top [of the hill on which Argyll's cavalry had appeared],
were nere the ennemie, and beginning to form; but Drummond
and Marishall, instead of formeing on the right of that colume
with their four squadrons, formed on the left, which made the
center of the foot[2], it seems not knowing their left hand from
their right, thought themselves well there. We observing them
form so quicklie, and all the other three colums, who were
marcheing most irregularlie at some distance, the one before the
other, mended all of us our pace, and folloued as fast as we could
run, the three squadrons continueing, according to order, to

---

[1] Cf. *P. H.* 55.

[2] Of this march in column Mar's official account states, that 'by the
breaking of their Lines in marching off, they fell in some Confusion in
the forming, and some of the second Line jumbled into the first, on or
near the Left, and some of the Horse form'd near the Center, which
seems to have been the Occasion that the Enemy's few Squadrons on
the Right were not routed as the rest.'—*P. H.* 56. Marischal's mistake
was even more serious than Mar's official narrative declares. As Sir
Walter Scott comments, 'This mistake, by which the left of the Earl of
Mar's army was left unsupported by cavalry, occasioned the loss they
sustained, the Duke of Argyle being thus at liberty to outflank their
infantry, and charge them with his dragoons, which he could not have
done had they been protected [on their left] by cavalry of their own.'
The mistake would have been avoided, as Sinclair (*S. M.* 229)
remarks, if Hamilton, instead of advancing the army in order of column,
had marched with a straight front towards the enemy, as the ground
allowed him to do. Hamilton's reason, no doubt, was that drawn up as
the army was before it advanced, it was necessary to extend the line
towards Dunblane in order to contain Argyll's left. Keith ascribes the
mistake not to Marischal but to the foot: 'one columne of foot enclining
to the right, and another to the left of the Earl Marischal's squadron of
horse, that regiment, which shou'd have been on the right, found itself
in the center.'—*K. M.* 18.

follow the last colume of the foot, who keept us at a gallop, inclineing towards the ground our left designed to take up. When we had advanced prittie well that way with the haste we made, ane Aide-de-Camp of Kilseyth's came to Rollo, who, being nixt the foot, was on the front of the three squadrons of horse, and order'd the three squadrons to the right of the whole armie with all possible expedition[1], as did with the same breath some one from Mar, and one Lewis Innes from my Lord Huntlie, by Mar's order. Rollo's squadron obey'd at once and went off at full speed, and gave the order back to Southesque's, who did the same to me onlie with a cry, and went after Rollo....

It was more than our necks were worth not to follow our first orders[2], except we had seen ane Aide-de-Camp, and [I was for] goeing to the left alone, but dreading misconstruction, thought it best to follow the others, haveing takne witness that I foresaw the consequence, and gallopt as hard as I could after them, who I could not overtake till they were posted on the right of the whole foot, Major Balfour calling always to me that I would ruine the squadron, we rid so hard that our horses were sunk by that time. I cant tell who posted the tuo squadrons[3], but whoever did it, did well[4]; they with the line of foot made ane obtuse angle; for haveing a little hill nere our flank, we did not know whence the ennemie's horse of the left wing would come; if they came with their foot on the south side of the hill to our front, it was easie for us to make half a wheel that way; or if they came on the north side of the hill, we had no greater wheele to make, and could not be attackt in the rear; all I can

[1] Unfortunately for Mar, though his right, which he was strengthening at the expense of his left, was hidden from the enemy's view, his weakened left was clearly seen from the Duke's position, enabling Argyll to 'stretch to the Right,' distributing his cavalry equally between his right and left wings.—*P. H.* 37.

[2] *i.e.* to take position on the left.   [3] Rollo's and Southesk's.

[4] Writing from Stirling on the day after the battle, General Wightman confirms Sinclair's commendation: 'I must do the Enemy that Justice to say, I never saw Regular Troops more exactly drawn up in Line of Battle, and that in a Moment; and their Officers behaved with all the Gallantry imaginable.'—*P. H.* 49.

say [is], that it was the onlie thing I saw done there with judge-
ment, and took my post as they were draun up, upon their right.

[Meanwhile,][1] on the 13th in the Morning...the Duke of
Argyle [had] advanced to a rising Ground to take a View of the
rebel Army, which he could easily discern in full March towards
him. But another Hill on his Left intercepted his Grace's View
of the whole Extent of their Left Wing[2], by which Reason it
was impossible for him to guess at the true Extent of their Line,
or how far they outflank'd him.

His Grace's Army amounting to 3500 men, of which 1200
were Dragoons, was drawn up upon the Hights above Dumblain
to the North-East of that Place, which lay about a Mile and a
half from his Left, and a wet boggy Mire or Morass call'd
Sheriff-Muir on his Right.

The Order of the royal Army was thus[3]; the First Line was
composed of six Battallions of Foot in the Center, with three
Squadrons of Dragoons upon the Right and Left; the Second
Line was composed of two Battallions of Foot, and two Squadrons
of Dragoons on each Wing[4]. His Grace commanded on the
Right at the Head of Stair and Evan's; General Witham com-
manded the Left; and Major-General Wightman the main
Battle or Center....

The Duke of Argyle, who till now supposed that the Morrass

---

[1] *C. A.* 189.

[2] This does not tally with other accounts. General Wightman states
distinctly: 'The Right of their Line, which vastly outwing'd us, lay in
a hollow Way, which was not perceiv'd by us, nor possible for us to
know it, the Enemy having Possession of the Brow of the Hill; but the
Left of their Army was very plain to our View.'—*P. H.* 46. Sinclair's
account makes it equally clear that the left and not the right of Mar's
army was exposed to Argyll's observation.

[3] It was about eleven o'clock in the morning when the Duke left the
hill from which he had been observing Mar's movements, and put his
army into position to resist the impending attack.—*R.* 303.

[4] 'The second Line was compos'd of two Battalions [of foot] in the
Center, one Squadron [of horse] on the Right, and another on their Left,
and one Squadron of Dragoons behind each Wing of Horse in the first
Line.'—Colonel Harrison's account, in *P. H.* 37.

of Sheriff Muir was unpassable, saw that the two or three Nights
Frost had made it capable of bearing; and the Rebels coming
down the Moor with an Intent to flank him, having their Right
much extended beyond the Point of his Left, hearing their
Bagpipes at a great Distance, found himself obliged to alter the
Disposition of his Front to prevent his being surrounded, which,
on Account of the Scarcity of General Officers, was not done
so expeditiously as to be all form'd again before the Rebels begun
the Attack[1].

The Left Wing of the Duke's small Army fell in with the
Centre of theirs, which consisted, especially the first Line, of
the Flower of the rebel Army[2]; the Clans [were] animated by
the Presence of their respective Chiefs, who led them on to the
Attack with uncommon Bravery.

They began the Action[3] by a general Discharge of their Fire

---

[1] 'Yet notwithstanding of [the drums] beating a great while, the strict
Orders not to stir from their Arms the Night before, and the Officers
doing their utmost to get them together, it was about Twelve before
they were ready to March: But that not being a fit Time to punish for
Breach of Order, the Duke was forced to pocket up the Matter till a
more convenient Season.'—*R.* 304. He had already caused thirty rounds
of ammunition to be served out to each man.—*Ibid.* 302.

[2] 'The Earl of Mar plac'd himself at the Head of the Clans, and
finding the Enemy only forming their Line, thought fit to attack them
in that Posture; he sent Colonel William Clepham, Adjutant-General,
to the Marquis of Drummond, Lieutenant-General of the Horse on the
Right, and to Lieutenant-General Gordon on the Right of the Right of
the Foot, and Major David Erskine, one of his Aids-de-Camp, to the
Left, with Orders to march up and attack immediately: And upon their
Return, pulling off his Hat, wav'd it with a Huzza, and advanc'd to the
Front of the Enemy's form'd Battalions; upon which, all the Line to the
Right, being of the Clans, led on by Sir Donald MacDonald's Brothers,
Glengary, Captain of Clan-Ranald, Sir John Maclean, [Alexander
Macdonald of] Glenco, Campbell of Glenlyon, Colonel of Broadalbin's,
and Brigadier Ogilvy of Boyne, with Colonel Gordon of Glenback at
the Head of Huntley's Battalions, made a most furious Attack, so that in
seven or eight Minutes we could neither perceive the Form of a Squadron
or Battalion of the Enemy before us.'—Mar's account, in *P. H.* 57.

[3] The Duke's left was not formed when the Highlanders at-

Arms, and received the first Fire of the royal Troops without shrinking[1], which is a sure Signal that these kind of Militia will stand to the last; but at the first Fire, the Capt. of Clanronald, who led them on in Chief, was kill'd[2], which had like to have struck a Damp upon the Rebels, as they had a Respect for that Gentleman that fell little short of Adoration. But Glengary, who succeeded him, starting from the Lines, waved his Bonnet, and cried three or four times, Revenge[3]; which so animated the Men, that they followed him like Furies close up to the Muzells of the Muskets, push'd by the Bayonets with their Targets, and with their broad Swords spread nothing but Death and Terror where-ever they came.

The three Battallions of Foot on the left of the Duke's Centre[4] behaved gallantly, and made all the Resistance they could make, but being unacquainted with this Savage Way of Fighting, against which all the Rules of War had made no

tacked. Indeed, General Gordon was adjured by 'Captain Livinston of Dumbarton's regiment, with great oaths, To attack the enemie before they were formed.'—*S. M.* 217. Rae explains that Argyll's left was still forming when 'they found a Body of the Enemy's Foot which had lain conceal'd...to be just on their Front'; while Mar's cavalry, 'being still to their Left,' were 'in Condition to take them in Flank.'—*R.* 305.

[1] 'The order to attack being given, the two thousand Highlandmen ...run towards the ennemie in a disorderlie manner, always fireing some dropeing shots, which drew upon them a generall salvo from the ennemie, which begun at their left, opposite to us, and run to their right. No sooner that begun, the Highlandmen threw themselves flat on their bellies; and when it slacked, they started to their feet. Most threw away their fuzies, and drawing their suords, pierced them everie where with ane incredible vigour and rapiditie, in four minutes' time from their receaving the order to attack.'—*S. M.* 217.

[2] Sinclair describes him as 'the onlie [one] who attackt with the foot on horseback; who, it was said, dyed, leaving his curse on his follouers if ever they deserted the countrie's cause: He was, without dispute, one of the best men we had.'—*S. M.* 227.

[3] Or, more fully, 'Revenge! revenge! to-day for revenge, and to-morrow for mourning!'

[4] They represented 'just the half of our Foot.'—Wightman's account, in *P. H.* 47.

Provision, they were forced to give way, fell in among the Horse, and help'd the Enemy to put them in Confusion; so a total Rout of that Wing of the royal Army ensued[1]. General Whitham, with some of the Horse[2], riding full Gallop to Sterling, gave out there with certainty that all was lost; but the General was mistaken in that, as well as in the Opinion he form'd of the Men he run from that Morning before the Engagement.

Upon the Right Wing of the royal Army the Duke of Argyle commanded in Person, and charged at the Head of Stair's and Evans's Dragoons[3], attack'd the Enemy's Left, consisting chiefly

---

[1] 'We drove the main Body and Left of the Enemy in this manner for about half a Mile, killing and taking Prisoners all that we could overtake.'—Mar's account, in *P. H.* 57. The squadrons of Marischal and Drummond, breaking from the position which they had wrongly taken on the centre, wheeled to the right, 'all broke and scattred, everie man for his own hand, rideing as hard as his horse could carrie him' in pursuit of Argyll's broken left. Sinclair had great difficulty in preventing his squadrons on the right wing from following also, and Sir Walter Scott condemns him for his inaction. But if, as Sinclair asserts, he had already heard of the rout of Mar's left, he was probably justified in holding his unbroken cavalry in reserve. Cf. *S. M.* 218, 226.

[2] Rae explains their rout as follows: 'The Left of the King's Army, commanded by General Whetham, observing a great Cloud of the Highlanders break thro' the Center close by them, and gathering apace, could make no guess of their Number, they standing so thick and confused, and intercepting their View, so as they could neither hear nor see what was acted upon the Right, which the circular Ground on which the Army stood would of it self have impeded without any other Obstruction, and all Communication or Intelligence by Aid de Camp or otherwise being intercepted, made them firmly believe that the Duke and the Right of the Army were either entirely beat, or at least surrounded by the Rebels; nor did they find themselves in Condition to resent it or rescue them, in case it had been so.'—*R.* 306. According to Mahon, the rout of Argyll's left continued as far as Cornton.—*History of England*, vol. i, 262.

[3] The Duke engaged Mar's left with five battalions of foot, five squadrons of dragoons, and one squadron of volunteers.—*P. H.* 38. The volunteers, about sixty strong, were commanded by the Earl of Rothes, and were placed behind Evans's dragoons on the right.—*R.* 300.

of Horse, with such Intrepidity, that notwithstanding the Rebels shew'd they wanted neither Courage nor Inclination to stand, yet were obliged to give way, and were put into Confusion. The Duke pursued them towards the River Allen, which he was obliged to do, in regard that tho' the Distance is not above two Miles, yet in that Space they attempted to rally again near a dozen of Times, and wherever the Ground would afford them any Advantage, endeavoured to make a full Stop; so that the Duke, having to do with Troops of that Disposition, who likewise out-number'd him, was obliged to follow his Blow, least he should have lost the Advantage he gain'd, and have all his Work to do over again[1]; nor was it in his Power to succour his Left, the Rout of that Wing happening so suddenly; and the Officer that commanded that Wing leaving the Field almost at the first Fire of the Rebels, there was no Opportunity to rally the broken Troops a second Time.

[1] This account of the rout of Mar's left does not mention the fact that they were not fully formed when Argyll attacked, nor that the Duke had pushed out a body of cavalry under Cathcart across the morass on his right to outflank Mar's left flank.—*R.* 304, 305. Sinclair's account brings out both points: 'In what manner our three colums [*i.e.* left wing] run away, none of those amongst them could tell, nor where the flight begun, everie corps putting it off themselves on each other, as is usuall. Most agreed that few of them had ever formed, and those who did, begun to fire at a great distance; that the three colums fell in with one another in that running up the hill, and when they came within sight of the Duke of Argyle's right wing, which was alreadie formed, they were in disorder; and the last confusion, when his [*i.e.* Cathcart's] dragoons made a mine [an attempt] to attack them through the morass, which happned to be betuixt them....I have often wonder'd to see so few killed on all that ground over which he [the Duke] pursued with the dragoons. The onlie reason I can conceave was, his being oblidged to goe about the morass, which gave our people a great advantage in the flight doun hill, and that the frost was stronge enough to bear them on foot, when the dragoons' horses sunk deep in the moor, our's in the mean time getting over the river of Allen.'—*S. M.* 225. Some currency was given to the explanation, that Hamilton's A.D.C., Lawrence Drummond, 'Laurie the Traitor,' told him treacherously the right had already given way.—*P. H.* 61. Cf. *S. M.* 240.

Brigad. Gen. Wightman followed close after the Duke with three Battallions of Foot[1], and ran a very great Risk of faring in the same Manner with the rest, if the Rebels had but common Prudence, for no sooner their Right understood the Disaster of their Left than they form'd again, and returned back to the Field, following close on the Rear of Wightman's Battallions, to the Number of 5000[2]; some say that Body was led on by

[1] Wightman says 'with a little above three Regiments of Foot.'— P. H. 47. They were those on the right centre.

[2] The position of the field at this point was as follows: The left of both armies was in full flight, Mar's towards the Water of Allan, Argyll's towards Dunblane. Argyll's left centre was broken and in retreat, and Mar's centre was in pursuit of it. Argyll's right centre, under Wightman, was following to support the Duke's pursuit of Mar's left. The only force, therefore, which remained intact in its original position was Mar's right wing, where Sinclair had kept his squadrons in hand. They, with such of the foot and horse as had rallied and returned from the pursuit of Argyll's centre and left, left Mar with a force which still was greater than Argyll's whole army, and was in possession of the original field of battle. The horse took up their position on the Hill of Kippendavie, slightly in the rear of Argyll's original line, whence they could see the whole extent of the field (R. 304, 306). Here, joined by some of the foot, they faced north and awaited Argyll and Wightman (P. H. 50). These movements are described in the following accounts: 'The Right of the Rebels, which had been all this while unactive, seeing now, by the Retreat of our [Argyll's] Left, that that Part of the Field was empty; and being encouraged to join that other Party of theirs who had broke through our Center, join'd them: And crossing the Field of Battle, in Number then about 4000 Men, marched up to the Top of that Part of the Hill called The Stoney Hill of Kippendavie, where they stood without attempting any Thing, with their Swords drawn, for near four Hours Space.'—R. 306. Sinclair gives the following account, whence it appears that an attack was expected from the direction of Dunblane before Argyll returned from his pursuit of Mar's left to Allan Water: 'We were no sooner on the top of that little hill [Kippendavie] then we perceaved their [Argyll's] left wing of dragoons forming, as they return'd from the flight, above Dumblaine, but could see nothing of all the enemie's foot and our oun horse and foot, betuixt them and us the ground was so hollow and waved, except a few scattred here and there at great distances. At first comeing up to that little hill, our three squadrons were carried

General Gordon, others by General Hamilton, others by them both, and others, and indeed with more Probability, said they were headed by Glengary, and that he, upon being ordered to attack these Battallions, returned for Answer, that the Clans had done enough, and that he would not hazard them to do other People's Work (meaning the Horse), and remain'd upon a Hill where he seem'd to form his Men as if for some new Action[1].

The Duke having by this Time entirely broke their Left, and push'd them over the River Allen, return'd to the Field; and Wightman, facing again to the Right, took Possession of some Enclosures and mud Walls, which would serve for a Breast-Work in Case they were attack'd[2], as they judged by the

in to a small pound fold, I don't know how or by whose order, where, instead of makeing a large front to intimidate those above Dumblain, we made no greater than that of one squadron, so that no man could stir, far less wheel in squadron. I represented to them the risque they run if attackt from any hand, for then all knew the ennemie [*i.e.* Argyll and Wightman] was in our rear as well as our front [at Dunblane]. We defiled out of it at tuo openings, one by one; and haveing extended our front, to keep them in awe that were now formed above Dumblaine, we were told the Duke of Argyle was comeing up in our rear from the pursuite of our left wing.'—*S. M.* 220.

  [1] This story, which appears to lack confirmation, bears some resemblance to the following one of Rob Roy: 'There was another Thing very observable in that Days Service, viz. That one Robert Roy Mac-Grigor, alias Campbell, a noted Gentleman in former Times for Bravery, Resolution, and Courage, was with his Men and Followers within a very little Distance from the Earl of Mar's Army, and when he was desired by a Gentleman of his own to go and assist his Friends, he answer'd, If they could not do it without me, they should not do it with me: That is, If they could not conquer their Enemies without him, he should not assist them in the doing of it.'—*P. H.* 62.

  [2] 'The inactivity of the rebel army was so great, that they neglected all the advantages of a most excellent position on the summit of a rising ground, round which Argyle was obliged to march, and when, if they had but thrown down stones, they might have disordered him. It was on this occasion that Glenbucket exclaimed, "Oh for an hour of Dundee!"'—Sir Walter Scott's note, in *S. M.* 223. The following accounts illuminate this concluding episode in the battle:—

  'As I had kept that part of our Foot which first engag'd in very good

Countenance and Numbers of the Enemy they should; in this
Posture both Parties stood looking at one another, but neither

Order,' writes Wightman, 'his Grace join'd me with five Squadrons of
Dragoons, and we put the best Face on the Matter to the Right about
[the enemy being now in his rear], and so march'd to the Enemy, who
had defeated all the Left of our Army. If they had had either Courage
or Conduct they might have entirely destroy'd my Body of Foot; but
it pleased God to the contrary....We march'd in a Line of Battle till we
came within half a Mile of the Enemy, and found them ranged at the
Top of a Hill on very Advantageous Ground, and above Four Thousand
in Number. We posted our selves at the bottom of the Hill, having the
Advantage of Ground, where their Horse could not well attack us; for
we had the Convenience of some Earth-Walls or Ditches about Breast
high; and as Evening grew on, we inclined with our Right towards the
Town of Dumblain in all the Order that was possible.'—*P. H.* 48.

Rae supplements Wightman with the information, that Argyll, having
re-formed his army, advanced to the hill with the Scots Greys on his
right, Evan's and Stair's dragoons on his left, and the foot in the centre;
that the foot lined the turf-wall or 'fold-dyke'; and that a single cannon
was placed in position in front of both wings, which, in case the enemy
attacked, were to deliver two discharges before the Duke's cavalry were
to charge.—*R.* 308.

Mar, in his short letter to Colonel Balfour, writes, that after his
pursuit of Argyll's left centre and left wing 'to a little Hill on the South
of Dumblain,' he re-formed 'most of our Horse and a pretty good Number of our Foot, and brought them again into some Order. We knew
not then what was become of our Left, so we return'd to the Field of
Battle. We discern'd a Body of the Enemy on the North of us, consisting
mostly of the Grey Dragoons, and some of the Black. We also discover'd
a Body of their Foot [Wightman's] farther North upon the Field where
we were in the Morning; and East of that a Body, as we thought, of
our own Foot, and I still believe it was so. I form'd the Horse and Foot
with me in a Line on the North Side of the Hill where we had engaged,
and kept our Front towards the Enemy to the North of us, who seem'd
at first as if they intended to march towards us; but upon our forming
and marching towards them, they halted, and march'd back to Dumblain.'—*P. H.* 50.

Sinclair, continuing his account (*supra*, p. 134), writes: 'After lookeing at one another for some time, our foot begun to assemble and draw
nere [from their pursuit towards Dunblane], at least some hundred, I

caring to engage; when towards Evening the Duke drew off towards Dumblain, and the Enemy towards Ardoch[1], without molesting one another[2].

believe three or four; and some few of the horse, who came back, drew up in the rear of my squadron, as if they design'd making a fourth rank. On seeing the foot, I order'd to advance to the enemy, and they [the enemy] wheel'd and went off, for the little time they were in our sight, at great leasure, but after they got upon the descent made great haste back to the Duke of Argyle, who we observed comeing to meet them with a bodie of horse and foot from pursueing our left wing, a large mile from us, and nearer Pearth then where we were draun up in the morning....Our foot and horse being almost all return'd from pursueing [Argyll's infantry and left wing], we formed into tolerable order, the one half of our horse being draun up on the right of the foot, and the other on the left, and marched to that bodie which was joyned by the Gray Dragoons and marcheing to us in order of battle, and were then scarce persuaded it was the ennemie [Some imagined Argyll's returning right to be Lord George Murray and Stewart of Invernitie, who had received orders to march from Burntisland with five hundred men, 'and had joyn'd the Mac-gregors and MackFiersons'].....The ennemie made the first halt, and we, in complaisance to them, did as much, and stood lookeing at one another about four hundred yards distance, for half ane hour; our horse upon the wings advanced before the foot a hundred yards....We halted in expectation that the tuo thousand foot would advance and take up that voide betuixt us, which would [have] formed our whole line, haveing gone so far to encourage them, but lookt longe in vaine over our shoulders, for they stood like stakes....The night comeing on, the Duke of Argyle seem'd first to make a feint as if he was moveing towards us, and inclined after to Dumblain, and it being almost dark, we soon lost sight of them.'—*S. M.* 221.

[1] Mar's official account says: 'The Earl of Mar remain'd possess'd of the Field of Battle and our own Artillery, and stood upon the Ground till Sun-set; and then, considering that the Army had no Cover or Victuals the Night before, and none to be had nearer than Braco, Ardoch, and Adjacents, whereby his Lordship expected the Left to rally, and the Battalions of the Lord George Murray, Innernyhe [Stewart of Invernitie], M'Pherson, and Mac-Gregor to join him, resolved to draw off the Artillery, and march the Army to that Place.... But these Battalions [Murray's, etc.] did not join us till the next Day Afternoon, before which the Enemy was return'd to Stirling.'—*P. H.* 58.

[2] From Argyll's official returns, his losses appear as follows—Killed:

Monday[1] [November] 14. The Earl of Mar drew out the Army early on the Morning, on the same Field at Ardoch they were on the Day before. About Eleven a-Clock we perceived some Squadrons of the Enemy on the Top of the Hill near the Field of Battle, which march'd over the Top of the Hill, and a little after, we had an Account of their marching to Sterling[2]. Upon which, the Earl of Mar march'd back with his Army, who continued about Auchterarder.

Tuesday 15. Rested[3].

Wednesday 16. The Earl of Mar left General Hamilton with fourteen officers and two hundred and seventy-six men; Wounded: eleven officers and one hundred and seventy-six men; Prisoners: ten officers and one hundred and twenty-three men; Total losses: six hundred and ten, or about one-fifth of his army.—*R.* 310. Mar estimated his losses at 'not above sixty private Men killed, but several of our Officers are taken.'—*P. H.* 53. Eighty-two of his officers and gentlemen were lodged as prisoners in Stirling Castle.—*Ibid.* 42. Clanranald and Strathmore were killed.

The cause of Mar's small losses was due in part to the nature of the ground over which the left was pursued. It was due also to the fact that the Duke's artillery never came into action. He brought six 3-pounders and eighteen gunners on to the field, designing to form three batteries before the centre of his army. But the battery on the right had not unlimbered when Argyll's right joined with Mar's left, and the guns of that battery, presumably, formed the two which Argyll brought to bear upon the Hill of Kippendavie after his return from the pursuit to Allan Water. The other two batteries were involved in the rout of Argyll's left before they had fired a shot.—*R.* 308. Mar had eleven cannon (*S. M.* 200), all of which he claimed to have brought off the field, except two, whose carriages broke down.—*P. H.* 59. But according to *R.* 308, six of Mar's guns were captured and brought into Stirling upon the day following the battle. Keith (*K. M.* 20) states that five guns fell into Argyll's hands, owing to the gunners running away with the horses when the left broke.

[1] Mar's official narrative in *P. H.* 60.

[2] They were a body of dragoons whom Argyll sent to bring off the wounded.

[3] Keith explains that it was impossible to undertake any further movement against Argyll, because the Highlanders had lost their clothes, having cast them off as they advanced to battle on the 13th.—*K. M.* 21.

the Horse to canton about Duplin, and Lieutenant-General Gordon, with the Clans and the rest of the Foot, about Forgan and Adjacents, and went into Perth himself to order Provisions for the Army, the want of which was the Reason of his returning to Perth.

Thursday 17. The Earl of Mar order'd General Hamilton to march with the Horse and some of the Foot to Perth, and Lieutenant-General Gordon, with the Clans, to Canton about that Place.

News[1] was brought us [at Perth] that the same day we fought the Duke of Argyle's army our troops in England had surrendred to the Generals Carpenter and Wills, who had penned them up in the toun of Preston....I shall only touch this as it influenced our affairs in Scotland, where it had several bad effects: first, it gave the enemy oportunity to draw down forces from England against us, and to employ all the Dutch troops which they had brought over (consisting of 6000 men) against Scotland[2]. A second bad effect was the disuniting us amongst ourselves; for several of our party, seing that the English, which we always looked on as our principal strength, were quelled, and indeed had never made any appearance equal to their promises, having never been above eight hundred men, began to think of making terms for themselves; and accordingly the Marquess of Huntly formed a party in our army, who proposed to send to the Duke of Argile to know what terms we might expect if we submitted. The Duke answer'd, he had no orders to treat with us in general, but that every one who in particular wou'd adress himself to the King's clemency might expect pardon. This opened a door to all particular treaties, and many suspected that even our General, the Duke of Marr, from that time forward held a correspondence with the enemy, more for his own particular interest than for the general advantage of his party.

[1] *K.M.* 22.

[2] The regiments of Newton and Stanhope set out from Preston about November 27 and reached Glasgow on December 19. At about the same time 6000 Dutch auxiliaries arrived in England. They came in accordance with an article in the Treaty guaranteeing the Protestant Succession in Great Britain.—*R.* 327. The two English regiments were disbanded in 1718.

After[1] our returne to Pearth...the Duke of Athole's vassals would no more obey the Marquise of Tullibardine or his brother Lord George, his Grace haveing takne care to shew them where all was goeing; and the loss of their friends at Prestone[2], who they lookt on as alreadie hang'd by follouing the orders of Tullibardine, stun'd them....The Laird of Weems' vassals, who had joyned Struan, were nou more against than for us, and Struan's, betuixt the Duke of Athole and Weems, durst not move tho' they 'd had a mind. [Stewart of] Garntullie's vassalls were in the same apprehensions of the Duke of Athole.

Not to goe further into that detaile, betuixt exemple, fear, and the inclination the whole had to stay at home, the tide turned upon us, oueing in a great measure to the influence the Duke of Athole had on his nighbourhood; for of those who Mar called his oun vassalls, and run away before we came out of Pearth, of that hundred men, for that was all, not one ever came back to us. Nobodie ever pretended Drummond's would, for Lord Strathallen and Logie, who had given him the name of their folks, were now prisonners, and neither his Lordship of Drummond's oun or their's would stir at this time, not being Highlandmen, and only forced out in the beginning by Tullibardine, and had not stay'd longe with us....Bredalbine's three hundred men were on the same foot with the rest, they were gone home; and his Lordship [being] too cunning not to see through the whole affair, we could never promise much on his friendship....

While in this state, [Coll Macdonell of] Keppoch[3], a Highland Chief and vassall, or rather tennant, of Huntlie's, came to Pearth with tuo hundred and fourtie men. He had never been with us before; but hearing of a battle, and that there was plunder, got his men together and robbed the other Highland-

[1] *S. M.* 258.

[2] Lord Nairn, Lord Charles Murray, and their followers.

[3] The MacDonalds of Keppoch were always a very independent and untameable Clan....Like their neighbours the Camerons, they were considered as particularly addicted to depredation on their neighbours, and claimed as an honour the character which others, and Lowlanders especially, imputed to them as a reproach.—Sir Walter Scott's note.

men who were goeing home stragling with the pillage of our baggage and what they had takne out of the Low Countrie, and haveing secured it, he and his folks took ane itching to see that countrie where so many good things were got, being so often invited, and being told before he left home that we were in a very good condition, haveing banged the ennemie....Colin Simpson, who had the delivering of the bread, told me Mar had ordered him to give him [Keppoch] bread for five hundred if he called for it, and by no means to stand with him, and please him at any rate. The leader stay'd and receaved a good pay, but the men went home, the greatest part of them, in a few days after, and not longe ere all were gone, [and] took what they liked best on the road that they might not return emptie handed.

The reports of the Duke of Argyle's paying us a visit terriefied from time to time[1]; but when these went over, we knew to make some pleasant lye succeed to them, which again elevated our spirits. To make all readie for our retreat, we had sent the horse to cantoon over the Tay in the Carse of Gourie....The French dancing master was still at work [on the fortifications of Perth], but never advanced, and did not compleat one part of his lignes, which, if he had, would have been to no purpose as they were contrived....

While we were languishing and falling out of one fainting fit into another...Huntley communicated to me and told me he had seen the forme of ane Association that Mar designed to steale in upon us that evening....Without any further advertice-ment, it was given out in orders at three of the clock that all Lords, Commanding Officers of everie Corps, Chiefs of Clans, with one of the most considerable gentlemen of everie countie, should be at Mar's quarters before five of the clock that night....

No sooner we were met then Mar threw doun tuo draughts of ane Association on the table, telling us that it was thought

[1] Argyll, like Mar, lay inactive during the weeks which followed Sheriffmuir. However, he bombarded the Jacobite garrison at Burnt-island, and took possession of the place on December 19. Its evacuation was followed by that of other Jacobite positions on the Fifeshire coast. Shortly after, the Duke sent Colonel Cathcart to occupy Dunfermline. —R. 338. Cf. S. M. 331.

fit by those who knew our present circumstances, that we should enter into new tyes and bonds oblidgeing us never to desert one another, and that the verie shew and appearance of unanimitie and firmitie, as things stood, would be of no small consequence to us, and for that reason [he] had called us to signe either of these tuo draughts of ane Association, which he order'd to be read, and begged of them not to shew the least mark of disunion, since the ennemie must certainlie know all that passed there[1]....

We[2] agreed that nixt day, Major Balfour, Sir James Kinloch, and Mr Ogilvie, should aske leave to speak to Mar in the name of a great many gentlemen of distinction; which Mar granted. To be short...they proposed a capitulation in the name of the whole: And his Lordship ansuering, You can't get it; it was said, It will be no small satisfaction to be sure of that, and then we 'll know what to expect, and nothing can sement us so stronglie as a refusall [from the Duke of Argyll] of that kind.... Mar askt, What should become of the King? They ansuer'd, His Lordship could solve that question better than they, for they knew nothing about him, nor what had or what would become of him; they hoped he was well and would continue so, but that neither they nor his Lordship, they believed, expected him.... And Mar, being hard pressed by them, and heated and in confusion, own'd to them he wisht the King would not come, and that he had sent to stop him....

Our three Deputees returned to Mar in the morning, and

---

[1] Sinclair's long account amounts to this: Mar wished to counteract the influence of that party among his followers which regarded further remaining in arms a hopeless enterprise. Of that party, Sinclair and Huntly were the leaders. Huntly was suspected, probably on good grounds, of a desire to make a separate peace in order to save his northern estates from the Earl of Sutherland, though Sinclair, to whom the Earl Marischal communicated that as Mar's reason in proposing the Association, denied the truth of it. Cf. *S. M.* 274 *et seq.*

[2] Sinclair and the 'mutineers.' Though Sinclair does not mention the fact, he and Lord Rollo had before December 27 made private overtures to the Duke of Argyll. Cf. Lord Townshend's letter to the Duke, in Mahon, *History of England*, vol. i, App. p. xlix.

his Lordship proposed Collonell Laurence[1] as the fittest man to
be sent to the Duke of Argyle, and said, It would be the gaining
of time to send him, because if they imployed any other they
must first send a trumpet to get a safe conduct. Mr Ogilvie,
Major Balfour, and [Smith of] Methvin[2]...came and told us of
the proposale. It was a surprise to hear that Mar, who had been
so much against the thing before, appear'd all of a suddain to
shew us the most expeditious way of doeing what we were so
fond of; it put us on doubting and diveing into the advantages
Mar could reap from such a choice....The result was, that...
Laurence was dispatched with offers of a submission, provided
the Duke of Argyle had pouer to give us such a capitulation as
could secure our lives and fortunes. He returned next day late
and went to Mar, to whome he made the report....His Grace
of Argyle bid him tell us, He 'd imploy his influence at Court to
get a capitulation, and was to send one to London for that purpose,
who, Laurence said, was my Lord Roxbourough; and Argyle
further promised, When he got a return, he'd let them know.

[Very[3] shortly after these events,] Huntlie was to leave Pearth
...being everie day more and more urged to goe North by letters
from thence, to put a stop to Southerland's progress[4], who had
been at Elgine, within six miles of his house, with fifteen
hundred men, and was to be supposed would not be longe of
guarnisoneing his houses and disarming his tennants and vassalls,
who could not be got together without his oun presence; which
if he did not give a check to in time, there was nothing to hinder
Southerland to cut off our communication from all the sea-coast
touns, and attack ourselves at Pearth with ane armie four or five
times greater than ours; for his numbers must have suelled on
the road, where there were enough disaffected to us in that
longe tract which might readilie joyn the gaineing side....

[1] Lieutenant-Colonel Herbert Lawrence, of Montague's regiment,
had been made prisoner at Sheriffmuir.—*P. H.* 52.

[2] He had taken Sir James Kinloch's place, Mar having refused to
meet the latter.—*S. M.* 286, 292.

[3] *S. M.* 316.

[4] Seaforth also had been called to the North to meet the crisis, after
being with Mar only about a week.—*S. M.* 243.

Huntlie went North a day or tuo after his appointed time[1], and I...follow[ed] him, haveing given so much umbrage that I could be of no further use to the cause, which now was not onlie desperate but sunk.

This[2] was the Situation of the Rebel Army when the Chevalier landed in Scotland, and by his Presence convinc'd his Party that the Mountains of Promises they had so long fed themselves with from France were all meer Illusions: For instead of bringing with him eight or ten thousand men, with which the Earl of Mar flatter'd those he had embark'd into this Undertaking, he took Shipping at Dunkirk, on Board a small Ship that had formerly been a Privateer, of eight Guns, and landed at Peterhead in the North of Scotland on the 22d of December, with only six Gentlemen in his Retinue, among whom was the Marquis of Tinmouth[3], Son to the Duke of Berwick.

We[4] had long been impatient for his coming into Scotland, and when many had given him over, and some were gone Northward in Discontent occasioned by Delay, on a sudden we were told he had appear'd at Sea in the Offing about the Height of Montrose, and had made the Signals[5] and passed by. This News was brought by Express from Montrose, and filled all his Friends with incredible Joy; the Soldiers, who had been told of great Forces that were to come with him, were particularly en-

[1] He had arrived at Castle Gordon by December 25.—*S. M.* 324.

[2] *C. A.* 231.

[3] James Francis Stewart FitzJames, son of James Duke of Berwick, born 1696, died 1738.   [4] *P. P.*

[5] On October 7, anticipating the Chevalier's arrival upon the western coast, Mar had issued the following order from Perth:—

'*Signals upon the West Coast.*

A White Flag on any of the Topmast-heads, pulled up and down for several Times; and the Answer from the Shore, a white Cloath shown on the nearest Eminence.

Upon the Signal, a Boat to be sent off, and the Word from the Boat, Lochaber.

The Answer from the Ship, Lochyeal.

The People who make the Signal to know of Horses and Carriages

If any Ship be seen chased, Boats to be immediately sent off.'—*R.* 434

courag'd with the News, and promised themselves great Things, not doubting but there was a great Fleet with him, little thinking that this great Monarch, as we thought him, and all his Foreign Troops were embark'd in one small Ship of less than 200 Tun Burthen....He was now arriv'd on the Coast, and when he came to the Height of Montrose, as above, thought to have Landed there; but a Ship appearing as Cruising near the Coast, it was taken for an English Man of War, which caused them to stand off to Sea, steering Northward till Evening, when making Land again, they resolved to run right in for the Shore, be it what part it would. This took up most of the Night, and before Day they found themselves opposite to Aberdeen, a calm Night and a clear Sea, that is to say, clear of Enemies; and finding that they had the Command of the Shore, so that if they had spied a Sail they might Land any where before an Enemy could have come up, Upon this Assurance they kept on till they came fair with Peterhead, a Promontory near to Aberdeen, and standing in, they Mann'd out their Boats and landed the Ch[evalier].

There[1] remains yet to answer one question which you may naturally ask, as most people do, on this subject, and that is, Why the Chevalier delay'd his comeing so long?

To answer this Question to your Satisfaction I must tell you That I have what I shall here relate from Persons of unquestionable Veracity, who were then upon the Place, Eye and Ear Witnesses of what past, and so you may safely rely upon it.

You have certainly heard what was generally said of the Chevalier's Sister's [Queen Anne] Inclinations towards him whilst She was in Possession of his Throne: But whatever there was of truth in that, what I am well assured of is, that he was at last so little satisfied with what was said to him from thence, that he was fully resolved whilst She was yet alive to have gone into Scotland, and, in order to that, had already prepared a Declaration or Manifesto to have been there published upon his Arrival.

How he was hinder'd from putting this Design into Execution by some real Friends that were themselves imposed upon, and by other pretended Friends who were at the Bottom real Enemies, is a Mystery which Time may discover.

[1] *M. J.*

Upon the first News of his Sister's Death he immediatly took Post, resolved to endeavour at any Rate to get into some Part of his Dominions, but was stop'd by those who had Power to do it effectually. Being then forced back to Lorain, he made and published his Protestation, which it's likely you have seen, and which I can assure you was drawn entirely by himself.

From that Time, as before, he had nothing in his Thoughts but how and when he could assert his own Right and deliver his People. He saw little Ground to hope for Succour from any Foreign Prince, and had only the Affections of his People and the Advice of his Friends on this Side the Water to rely upon: Their interest seemed now more than ever linked to his, and they being upon the Place, and consequently best able to judge of the fittest time for his Coming to them, it must be allow'd that it had been no ways prudent nor advisable to him to act contrary to their Opinion. And yet it is most certain that it was only by following their Advice, contrary to his own Judgment and Inclination, that so much time was lost. Some of them in England insisted on having a certain Number of regular Troops to make Head at first, without which they said nothing was to be attempted[1]; and though he sent them Word over and over, That after all the Endeavours he could use he found it absolutely impossible to obtain any Troops, yet they persisted for several Months in the Opinion, and by that Means the most favourable Time he ever had was lost. Other Friends there pretended that the Dispositions of the People would still grow more favourable towards him, and that there was no Danger but Advantage by delaying.

Thus, though he had several Times fixed a Day for his Departure, he was still forc'd to delay that he might not act contrary to the Advice of his Friends, and at another Time because he found that his Enemies had Discover'd his Design and taken infallible Measures to intercept him. But as soon as his Friends began to see and own the Mistakes they had been in, he, without any regard to the many Dangers he had to go through,

---

[1] Cf. Bolingbroke's letter to Mar on this matter, dated September 20, 1715, in Mahon, *History of England*, App. p. xix.

set out from Commercy the 28th of October, and went incognito through a great part of France to the Coast of Brittany;
and to avoid falling into the Hands of many that were laid upon
the common Roads to intercept him, he was obliged to cross the
Country through By-ways with onely three People with him.
His Design was to go to England if Things appeared favourable
there, or, if they did not, to go to Scotland.

When he arrived at St Malo's, he found the Duke of
Ormond returned from the Coast of England, to which he had
gone some Days before in Hopes to have found Friends ready to
join him; but that having failed by some Accidents of Dis-
coveries, he was forced to return[1]. Upon this he was resolved
to go into Scotland, and it not being thought safe for him to
go thro' the British Channel, he had been advis'd to go round
Ireland, and by a Message from his Friends in Scotland it was
propos'd to him to land at Dunstaffnage, which was at that
Time in their Possession; but soon after, the Enemy came to be
Masters of it, by the Clans not performing what they were
charg'd with in Argileshire, as is afore mentioned. His Friends
immediatly informed him of this Change by a second Message.
And this confirm'd him in the Resolution he had himself before
taken, of changing all his Measures, and in place of taking that
long tedious Way, which was indeed the safest, to take a much
shorter, though a more dangerous Way for being intercepted
by the Enemies Ships. He sent therefore immediately to prepare
a small Ship privately for him at Dunkirk, which was accordingly
done, tho' not without Difficulty.

He was now a second Time obliged to traverse a great Part of
France, and that on Horse-back, in the very coldest Time of this
hard and severe Winter, exposed to greater Danger than in the
Forth, from the greater number of those who lay in Wait for him
on all the great Roads, which obliged him to travel by unfre-
quented Routs, where there was bad enough Accommodation;
and yet all this Time in that terrible Cold he never had the least
Ailment or Indisposition.

It was about the middle of December (our Style) before he

[1] Cf. Mahon, *ibid.* App. p. xxxi.

could reach Dunkirk[1]. He was there informed that there was a Man of War then lying in that very Road, and that there were a great many more cruizing on the Coast of France, England, and Scotland, all of them in Wait for him. But he, without any regard to these Dangers, went immediately on Board this small Ship[2] with only three Servants, and conducted by good Providence, arriv'd safe at Peter-Head, where he landed the 22 of December (old Style)[3].

[The[4] Chevalier] being come on Shore, with a Retinue of Six Gentlemen only, the Ship immediately returned for France with the News of his safe Arrival, and Lieutenant [Allan] Cameron [who had come from France with him] was sent Express to Perth, where he arriv'd on the 26th [of December], with the acceptable Tidings to the Earl of Mar, who presently mounted with the Earl Marischal, General Hamilton, and 20 or 30 Persons of Quality on Horseback, and set out from thence with a Guard of Horse to go and attend him. The Pretender and his five Companions having lodged one Night in the Habite of Sea-Officers at Peterhead, and another at Newburgh, a House of the Earl of Marischal, on the 24th they passed incognito thro' Aberdeen with two Baggage Horses, and at Night came to Fetteresso, the principal Seat of the Earl of Marischal, where he stay'd till the 27th, when the Earl of Mar, Marischal, and Hamilton came up to wait on him. Having dress'd and discovered himself, they all kiss'd his Hand and own'd him as King; thereafter they caus'd Him to be Proclaim'd at the Gates of the House; then General Hamilton was sent over to France to sollicit Supplies for his Service.

He design'd to pursue his Journey next Day towards Perth;

[1] 'Having lurked some Days [before] in several Ports on the Coasts of Britany, in the Habit of a Mariner.'—*R.* 351.

[2] 'A French Ship, formerly a Privateer, of 8 Guns, well mann'd and arm'd.'—*Ibid.* 351.

[3] The ship sailed first towards Norway, and then altering her course, steered towards Scotland, and arrived at Peterhead after a seven days' voyage.'—*Ibid.* 351. Three letters of the Chevalier to Bolingbroke written after his arrival, which express his hopes and fears, are in Mahon, *History*, App. pp. xxxiv–xxxix.   [4] *R.* 351.

but he was seized with an aguish Distemper, which detain'd him for some Days at Fetteresso: During which Time, his Declaration[1] dated at Commercy [on October 25] was dispersed and published in several places under his Influence, and Copies of it were dropt in the Night Time in the Streets of some loyal Cities and Towns, where His Friends and Adherents durst not publish it otherwise[2]....

The Pretender being recovered of his aguish Distemper, which had detain'd him at Fetteresso, went from thence to Brechin on Monday the 2d of January [1716]; he staid there till Wednesday, when he came to Kinnaird; on Thursday to Glames; and on Friday, about Eleven o'Clock in the Morning, he made his publick Entry on Horseback into Dundee, with a Retinue of about 300 Men on Horseback, having the Earl of Mar on his Right, and the Earl of Marischal on his Left. His Friends desiring it, he continued about an Hour on Horseback in the Market-Place, the People kissing his Hand all the while, and then he went and dined at Stuart of Garntully's, where he also lodged that Night. On Saturday he went from Dundee to Castle-Lion, a Seat of the Earl of Strathmore's, where he dined; and after, to Sir David Triplin's[3], where he lodged; and on Sunday the 8th of January he arrived at Scoon, about two Miles from Perth. Upon Monday the 9th he made his publick Entry into Perth, where he viewed some of the Soldiers quartered in the Town who were drawn out for that Purpose, and returned the same Night to Scoon.

At[4] the first News [of the Chevalier's arrival] it is impossible to express the Joy and Vigour of our Men [at Perth]: Now we hop'd the Day was come when we should live more like Soldiers, and should be led on to Face our Enemies, and not lie mouldring away into nothing, attending the idle Determinations of a disconcerted Council; but our Joy was very much abated when

[1] It is printed in *R.* 456.

[2] On December 29, at Fetteresso, the Chevalier received Addresses from the Episcopal clergy and Magistrates of Aberdeen.—*R.* 352, 354. The authorities of Marischal College, Aberdeen, also presented an Address.

[3] Threipland, of Fingask, Perthshire.   [4] *P. P.*

we came to hear that there was no Troops arriv'd, only about Eighty Officers, which in Truth there was not by above half the Number.

We were indeed Buoy'd up with the Account spread Abroad, that the Troops were shipping off, and might be expected in a very few Days, that the Ch—— being willing to encourage his Friends with his Presence, and eager to be at the Head of his Armies, could not be easie in staying any longer for the Shipping the Troops, but resolv'd, tho' with the extreme hazard of his Person, to venture alone, and came away before. This Tale took pretty well, and we being willing to hope for the best, acquiesc'd, tho' we profess'd our selves to be very much disappointed....

The Ch—— was Lodg'd at Schone, about two Miles from Perth, and they talk'd of Preparations for a Coronation, but I never found that he was in haste for the Ceremony; and I believe most firmly that he was not forward because he, I mean his Friends that he brought over with him, found from the beginning that it would not do, that the Foundation was ill laid and could not support him, and that he would be obliged to quit the Enterprize with Dishonour. However, the Coronation was much spoken of[1], the Place also seeming to concur happily with the Proposal, being the very Spot where all the antient Kings of Scotland were Enthron'd and Crown'd.

I had thought here to have set down my Observations at large of the Person who was then call'd King, and in whose Quarrel we were now in Arms; but I will not take that Freedom here as was intended, because I know not whether it may turn to Good or Ill, according as into whose Hands these Memoirs may happen to fall. However, in brief, his Person is tall and thin, seeming to encline to be lean rather than to fill as he grows in Years. His Countenance is pale, and perhaps he look'd more pale by Reason he had three Fits of an Ague, which took him two Days after his coming on Shore; yet he seems to be Sanguine in his Constitution, and has something of a Vivacity in his Eye that perhaps would have been more visible if he had not been

[1] A proclamation was issued from Scone, appointing January 23 as the date of the Chevalier's coronation.—R. 360.

under dejected Circumstances and surrounded with Discourage-
ment, which it must be acknowledg'd were sufficient to alter the
Complexion even of his Soul as well as of his Body; and I was
told, that as soon as he was on Board the Ship which carried
him away he spoke with a different Spirit, and discover'd such
a Satisfaction as might well signify that he look'd upon himself
before as a meer State VICTIM, appointed for a Sacrifice to
expiate the Sins of other Men, and that he was escaped as from
certain Destruction. His Speech was Grave, and not very clearly
expressing his Thoughts, nor overmuch to the Purpose; but his
Words were few; his Behaviour and Temper seem'd always
composed; what he was in his Diversions we knew nothing of,
for here was no room for those Things, it was no Time for
Mirth, neither can I say that I ever saw him Smile: Those who
speak so positively of his being like King James VII must excuse
me for saying that it seems to tell me they either never saw this,
or never saw King James VII; and yet I must not conceal that
when we saw the Person who we called our King, we found
our selves not at all animated by his Presence, and if he was
disappointed in us, we were tenfold more so in him; we saw
nothing in him that look'd like Spirit; he never appear'd with
Chearfulness and Vigour to animate us: Our Men began to
despise him; some ask'd if he could Speak; his Countenance
look'd extremely heavy; he car'd not to come Abroad among us
Soldiers, or to see us handle our Arms or do our Exercise; some
said the Circumstances he found us in dejected him. I am sure
the Figure he made dejected us, and had he sent us but 5000
Men of good Troops and never come among us, we had done
other Things than we have now done.

The[1] Duke of Argyle [meanwhile] being assured that the
last of the Dutch Troops were come past the Borders in order
to join him, and that the great Train of Artillery, which was
ship'd off at London for this Expedition, was Wind-bound in the
Mouth of the Thames, and seeing that the Season of the Year
promised rather a continued Storm than any Hopes of a Change
of Weather, and that the Circumstances of His Majesty's Affairs

[1] R. 361.

required all possible Dispatch, His Grace...upon Wednesday the 3d of January sent Brigadier [Lewis] Petit, a notable Engineer, and the Commissary of the Scots Field Train to Edinburgh, with express Orders to make up a Train of twelve battering Guns of eighteen, twelve, and nine Pounders, and six small Field-Pieces of six and four Pounders from Edinburgh Castle and Berwick, to be added to the six three Pounders formerly at the Camp at Stirling, with four Mortars and two Haubitzers, making in all twenty-four Pieces of Cannon, four Mortars, and two Haubitzers; And to hire out of the Dutch and British Troops such Men as had Skill in Gunnery, to the Number of fifty, for Gunners and Matrosses, to be added to the old Scots Corps of Gunners then at Stirling, consisting of twenty, with Power to appoint proper Officers. They were likewise ordered to get what Ammunition and other warlike Stores would be necessary for the said Train, and 9000 Men[1], either for Siege or Battle, in Readiness with the utmost Expedition, together with Pontoons for crossing Rivers, &c.; which accordingly was fallen about on the 4th with all possible Diligence....

On the 21st of January, Colonel [Joshua] Ghest with two hundred Dragoons was detached from Stirling to reconnoitre the Roads leading to Perth, which were covered with a very deep Snow, and to discover, if possible, the Posture of the Enemy. ...His advancing so far as he did alarmed the Enemy to that Degree as to put all the Town of Perth in a Hurry....Nor was their Fright over till a Party of Horse, being sent to Tullibardine, and from thence every Way to view the Roads, sent Word that all Things were quiet, and that no Enemy appeared. However, from this Time till the Rebels left Perth, there was nothing to be seen but planting of Guns, marking out Breast-Works and Trenches, digging up Stones in the Streets and laying them with Sand to prevent the Effects of a Bombardment, and in a Word, all possible Preparations were made as if they had really intended to defend the Place (tho' some think their Leaders had no such Design), insomuch that all our publick Accounts at that Time

[1] Argyll's army, which was now about three times its strength at Sheriffmuir, included fourteen squadrons of horse and twenty battalions of foot, besides artillery.—*R.* 363.

assur'd us, That the Pretender and his People resolved to Fight His Majesty's Army.

Soon after, the Duke of Argyle sent out General [William] Cadogan[1] with a strong Detachment of Horse and Foot to take Post at Dumblain, and to send a Party to Down...and on the 24th his Grace marched out to Dumblain with two hundred Horse, and taking from thence General Cadogan with as many more, went to view the Roads as far as Auchterarder, and returned at Night to their respective Quarters. This March put the Rebels into so great a Consternation that some of their smaller Garrisons abandoned their Posts, and retired behind the River Ern: And many others of the Rebels repaired to the Banks of that River, where, they gave out, they were resolved to make a Stand and fight the King's Army commanded by the Duke of Argyle. And having Intelligence that His Grace had posted 3000 Men as his Advance-Guard at Dumblain and Down, they sent 3000 Highlanders of the Garrisons of Braco, Tullibardine, and other neighbouring Garrisons, who, pursuant to the Pretender's Orders[2]...burnt the Towns and Villages of Auchterarder, Crieff, Blackfoord, Dunning, and Muthel, with what Corns and Forrage they could not carry off: Whereby the poor Inhabitants were exposed to the open Air in that stormy Season, and it is said, some poor decripted People and Children, who could not get fast enough out, were smothered in the Flames.

Upon[3] Tuesday the 24th of January 1715–16 a Detachment of the Clans of betwixt five and six hundred men did...march

[1] He had been sent to Scotland owing to the Government's dissatisfaction at Argyll's dilatory movements, and succeeded him in the command.

[2] This order was signed on January 17.—*R.* 360. The author of the *Proceedings at Perth* remarks: 'Nor was this Severity to be blamed in us if our Resolution to defend our selves had held; for as it was, it put the National Army to very great Extremities, some of the Troops [when they advanced upon Perth] having no Lodging but upon the Snow for two or three Nights, nor any covering but, as the French say, *Sou les Belles Estoielles,* under the most glorious Stars.'

[3] *B. A.*

from Perth about nine a Clock at night. This Detachment consisted of Sᴿ Donald M'Donald's, Clan Ranald's, Glengarie's, Lochyells, Appin's, M'cleans, and Cappoch's men, under the respective Officers of theire own Clans, but commanded in chiefe by Clan Ranald, Brother and Successor to him who was kill'd at the Battle of Sherrifmoor....

Clanranald, coming to Octerarder upon Wednesday the 25th of January about 4 in the morning, found every body fast asleep. Sentries were placed, and all precautions taken by him that no intelligence might be carry'd to the King's Forces, of whom they falsely supposed a party to be within two miles.

Then Partyes were ordered to every House in the Town to let none stirr out of doors, which they broke open without allowing any body time to put on theire Cloaths....

Betwixt nine and tenn, a party of about two or three hundred of the Rebells Foot, with some few Horsemen (not of the Clans), march'd by Clanranald's order for Blackfoord, a Country Town two miles to the westward of Octerarder on the road to Stirling....

This being done, he [Clanranald] gave publick orders in these words, Go and Burn all the Houses in the Town, Spare none except the Church and Mrs Paterson's.

This Mrs Paterson's was the house where the Jacobites kept theire Conventicles during the time of the late Ministry and before the Rebellion....

Such as heard these orders run to theire houses to throw out theire goods, but theire houses being almost all at the same time invested and set on fire, it was little they cou'd get thrown to the doors, and what was, was immediately snatch'd upp and plunder'd by the Rebells, being it was with great difficulty they cou'd save theire children and infants....

Clanranald now, seeing every house on fire and many of the best fall'n down, rode along the streets, conveen'd his men and march'd. All the way he pray'd the people whom he saw weeping to Forgive him, but was answer'd with silence, and so departed to do the like in other places. His men, before they went, seized all the horses they cou'd find to carry off theire plunder....

When [the party sent to Blackford] came to James Maitland's house, they halted, fed their horses, and then they sent out parties to all the houses of this town or village...and burnt down houses, corns, and every thing to the ground....

It would be endless to give account of all the hardships and acts of barbarous cruelty done: It may be easily imagined, considering the season of the year, the vast load of snow that lay then on the ground, the poor people, man, wife, and child, without the shelter of a house, without cloaths, meat, drink, or any thing to support them, and little or no hopes of relief....

Upon Saturday the 28th January 1715–16, about five a clock att night, Lord George Murray with the Regiment of Rebells under his command, consisting of about 300 men, came to the village called Dunning, lying about six miles Southwest of Perth in the Lord Rollo's interest....The Souldiers having spent about the space of four hours in prepareing the meall and refreshing themselves therewith and [with] all they could find in the town, about nine the drums began to beat, and according to orders formerly given them, they all appeared in arms in the midst of the town, where their Collonell intimat to them the order he had for burning the village, and commanded them immediatly to begin the execution thereof, and so a mellancholy and dismall Tragedy commenced; they in a moment were scattered in files through the whole town, and began to kindle the houses, lofts, and corn yards....

The number of families that had their houses burnt that night within this little and small village and the confines thereof were thirty three, besides barns, byres, and stables....

On Sunday the 29th by three in the morning, the Captains Stewart and [Lord George] Murray with a detachement...came to Dalreoch, a barrony belonging to M[r] Haldane of Gleneagles. ...The first thing the party did was to carry a great quantity of the threshed straw, and laying it round the stacks and houses, putt fire to all att the same time, so that with much adoe the servants and those that were in the houses escap'd; horses and cattle he had none, being taken away by the Rebells long before that time....

Upon Saturday the 28th day of [January] 1715–16, a party of the Clans, about fifty men, consisting of the M[c]Donalds, M[c]Cleans, and Camerons, under the command of the Captain of Clanranald, came from Drummond Castle (where they were quartered) to the town of Muthill under silence of the night, betwixt eight and nine of the clock, and without any advertisement given or time allowed the people to carry out their household furniture, sett the town on fire, and burnt down houses, household furniture, and corn stacks to ashes....The loss sustained by the inhabitants of this town...amounts to the summ of six thousand and ninety six pounds seventeen shillings and ten pennies Scotts money, which is about five hundred pounds Sterling....

Upon the [28]th of January 1715–16 came to Crieff about three hundred and fifty of the Clans, mostly McDonalds and Camerons....They began the Tragedy att one Thomas Caw his house in the west end of the town, thus: the said Thomas and his unkind guest Captain Cameron discourseing together on matters of indifferency, Cameron all of a sudden goes to the door, immediately returns, sayes to his men lodged in the same house with him, Up! To your arms! Fire the house! and that moment Cameron with his own hands kendled the house. Thus they surprizeingly fired all the houses in town; only some particular houses where they expected goods of any value they delayed till the best things were taken out, which they immediatly carried off....

Sir, from thir few instances of the many severities we mett with, it 's easie for you to conjecture what must have been the sad and fatall consequences of such inhumane, barbarous, popish-like, and hellish cruelty....The poor women (*horresco referens*) exposed to the open fields with their sucking infants, and scarce a ragg left to cover them from ane extremity of cold: Likewayes severall vigorous men and women (I might name) were struck with such terror that they survived the burning but a very few dayes. These are a few of the many unavoidable consequents of such barbarities. Many have dyed since, and no doubt their deaths occasioned by cold contracted in barns, stables, and old hutts where they were oblidged to lodge, and that in a very rigorous season as has been of many years, having no cloaths save what honest, charitable neighbours were pleased of their goodness to bestow. To say no more (this being too mellancholly

a subject to insist further upon), I presume, were there a particular
account geven (by some sufficient hand) of the bad usage the
people of this Stewartry of Strathearn mett with from the Rebells,
it could not miss to produce ane utter abhorrence of a popish
Pretender in the heart of any thinking man, who countenanced,
yea even ordered the execution of such cruelties[1].

[On[2] January 24] the Duke went to view the Roads [from
Dunblane towards Perth]: it thawed suddenly, and the Thaw
was followed with a great Fall of Snow, which was every where
two or three Foot deep, and suddenly froze again, which rendered
the Roads extreamly difficult, especially for the Foot; insomuch
that some of the Officers were of Opinion, that they ought not
to march till the Season was a little more settled: But his Grace
having received positive Orders from Court to march forthwith
against the Rebels, he resolved to surmount all Difficulties, and
to march as soon as the Artillery and some of the Dutch Forces
at Edinburgh, and the Regiments of Newton and Stanhope, who
were quartered at Glasgow, could come up to join him, which
they did two or three Days after.

The Train of Artillery from Berwick[3] and some of that from
Edinburgh arriv'd at Stirling upon the 26th; But the making...
such other Instruments of War as the Magazines here could not
furnish took up till the 28th before the last of our Convoy was
got clear [from] Stirling: On which very day, Colonel [Albert]
Borgard with the English Train, which had been so long
detained by the Stormy Weather, arrived in the Road of Leith[4]
...[and] marched up to Stirling with all possible Speed, where he

---

[1] On January 26, the Chevalier issued a declaration authorising
relief to be given to those of Auchterarder and Blackford who had
suffered by the destruction of their homes. Shortly before he sailed from
Montrose, on February 4, he wrote to the Duke of Argyll regarding a
sum of money which he proposed to distribute among the sufferers. The
declaration and letter are printed in the Maitland Club's *Miscellany*,
vol. iii, 446–49.   [2] *R.* 365.

[3] It consisted of ten cannon and two mortars.

[4] The personnel of the Artillery Train is in Charles Dalton's *George
the First's Army*, i, 283. The warrant for its despatch was dated November 14, 1715.

arrived on the 29th in the Morning, and was just in Time enough to go along with the Army....

And now the Roads being in some Measure repaired, and all Things in Readiness, the Duke began his March on Sunday the 29th of January...and marched to Dumblain, leaving the Government of the Town and Castle of Stirling to the Garrison of the Castle. That Morning a Detachment of 200 Dragoons and 400 Foot with two Pieces of Cannon approaching the Castle of Braco, eight Miles from Stirling, the Rebels in Garrison there abandoned the same, and the Troops, when they came up, found it deserted. The next Morning the same Detachment marched towards Tullibardine to dislodge the Rebels from thence, and to cover the Country People, who, to the Number of about 2000 Men, were employed in clearing the Roads of Snow, and making them otherwise practicable for the more commodious March of the Army, which that Day [January 30] advanced to Auchterarder, where, the Rebels having burnt all the Houses, as above, the poor Soldiers had no Lodging but the cold Snow, nor any other Covering than the fine Canopy of Heaven.

We[1] [at Perth] were now...arriv'd to the Crisis of our Affair; for on the 28th of January an Express came in from Sterling, where we had our Spies, assuring us, That Argyle would March the next Day, That all was in readiness, the Carriages provided, and the Horses for the Baggage come in, and that General Cadogan was already advanc'd with the first Line of the Army to Dumblane, 2000 Men being employed to remove the Snow, which indeed we thought impassable.

In this Situation, it may be said the Council sat continually to deliberate what was to be done; nor did their first Measures and Resolutions seem to concern the Grand Question, whether we should defend our selves or no? But as if that had been no Question, the Consultations generally turn'd upon the Question, in case of a resolv'd Engagement.

Never Men appear'd better disposed for Action than ours of the Clans; the Gentlemen embrac'd one another upon the News, drank to the good Day, and prepar'd as Men that resolved with Chearfulness to behave themselves as Scots Gentlemen

[1] *P. P.*

used to do; the common Soldiers, the Followers and Dependants of the Chiefs, were as Gay and Chearful as if an extraordinary Solemnity had been upon their Hands; nothing dejected or unpleasing was to be seen among us; our Pipers play'd incessantly, and we shook Hands with one another like Men invited to a Feast rather than call'd to a Battle. In pursuance of these Resolutions, as we thought them, for Fighting, Measures were taken to bring our Troops together, and Post our selves in such a manner and to such Advantage as it might be easy to subsist and yet easy to draw together upon a Signal....

In the Council held that Evening [January 28], it seems that every Man was order'd with Freedom to speak their Minds of the Method of Resisting, and whether the Army should post it self in the City [Perth] and defend it, or March out and Fight in the open Fields? The first who gave his opinion was, as I remember, a French Officer, to whom they shewed great Respect, and who, they said, was also a good Engineer. He told them, That...as the Case now stood, that neither was the National Army strong enough to Besiege a Town whose Garrison would be superior to their whole Army, neither was the Season such as would permit the Army to lie in the Field, no, not those few Days requisite; nor if they could lie Abroad could they make any work of their Siege, not being able to break the Ground, to dig Trenches, or raise Batteries in order to carry it on; and therefore, since the Town could not be carried by Scalade, he thought they would do well to suffer themselves to be Attack'd in the Town, when he did not question they should give a very good Account of themselves.

He then proposed the posting the Horse behind the River, which being then frozen over, and passable both for Horses or Carriages, might either receive those who might be push'd by the Enemy or advance to share of the Advantage which might be made; he gave them Notice of a little Spot of Ground without the Town, which formerly had held a Windmill, and on which there was a House, all which was compassed in by a large old dry Mote, and that if a good Body of Foot was posted on that Piece of Ground with four Pieces of Cannon, the Town could not be Stormed till they were dislodged....

But the next Day [January 29] all these happy Measures came to nothing, and the Confusion and Hurry without Doors was equal to the want of Concert within; for we could find that they agreed in nothing, that they not only differ'd in their Opinion of general Things, but also of every thing; and in a Word, here they broke in upon all they had done before, as shall appear presently.

The great Men were up all Night, and nothing was seen but posting to and fro between Schone and Perth. The Case, as we afterwards learned, was this, viz. That all the Military Men were positive in their Resolutions for Fighting; the Earl of Mar, two or three Clergymen who kept with him, and some others, who for the Sake of the Times I do not name, were resolv'd not to put it to the Hazard; their Pretence was the Safety of the Ch——'s Person: Whether that were the true and only Reason I shall say more of by and by; but nothing is more true than that we who were Soldiers and Voluntiers did not believe them. We told them we had as much Concern for the Safety of the Ch——'s Person as they had, and if we were for putting it to hazard, it was not without the hazard of our Lives; and to shew the Sincerity of our Resolutions we were willing the Ch—— should Retreat to some Place of Security, and let all that had a Value for his Cause Fight for it like Men, and not bring Things this Length, to turn our Backs like Scoundrels and Poltrons, and not strike a Stroke for him when he was come so far to put Himself and His Fortunes upon our Services and Fidelity. We carried this so high that some of our Number ruffled the great Men in the open Streets, call'd them Cowards, and told them they betray'd the Ch—— instead of advising him. One of them, an Intimate of the Earl of Mar, stop'd and talk'd some time with our People, who indeed began to threaten them if they offer'd to decline fighting: 'Why, what would you have us do?' said he. 'Do,' says the Highland-Man, 'What did you call us to take Arms for? Was it to run away? What did the Ch—— come hither for? Was it to see his People butcher'd by Hangmen and not strike a Stroke for their Lives? Let us Die like Men and not like Dogs. What can we do, says the other? Let us have a Council of War, says the Soldier, and let all the

General Officers speak their Minds freely, the Ch—— being present, and if it be agreed there not to Fight, we must submit.

This was not the only Ruffle; they met with a bold Norlander of Aberdeenshire who threaten'd them in so many Words, That the Loyal Clans should take the Ch—— from them, and that if he was willing to Die like a Prince, he should find there were Ten Thousand Gentlemen in Scotland that were not afraid to Die with him.

Things began that Night to be very disorderly and tumultuous, and I know not what it might have ended in if some more discreet than the rest had not interposed, who satisfied the Soldiery by telling them there would be a great Council in the Evening; That the Ch—— desir'd all that were his Friends would acquiesce in such Measures as should be resolv'd on there; That if it was adviseable to put it to the Hazard, the Ch—— would take his Fate with his faithful Friends; if it was otherwise advised, he would do as they should direct, or to this purpose: And accordingly a great Council was held in the Evening of the 29th, and the most weighty and ultimate Debates taking up so much Time that it could not be concluded that Night, it was renewed the 30th, when the fatal Resolutions of giving up their Cause were taken, on the same unhappy Day that the Grandfather of the Ch—— was Beheaded at the Gate of his Pallace by the English Usurper, a Day unlucky to the Family, and which, as it Dethron'd them before for almost Twelve Years, so it seems to have extirpated the very Name of Stuart at last, and left the Race to God's Mercy and a state of Pilgrimage without hope of Recovery....

When the Council was set [January 30], the Ch—— spoke a few Words, and they were but few indeed, to let them know that they were met to consider of the present Situation of their Affairs, and to give their Opinions in what was to be done; that their Enemies were preparing to Attack them, and that it was necessary to consider of the properest Measures to defend themselves; and that he had order'd every Thing to be laid before them, and desir'd that every Man would freely speak their Opinion, that what ever was resolv'd on, it might be with their general

Agreement and Consent and might be Executed immediately, for that no Time was to be lost.

The Ch——— having spoken, the Earl of M[ar] took the Word, as was appointed, and open'd the Case in a long Speech to the Purpose following:

He told them, That ever since the Battel of Dumblane, I think he said the Victory of Dumblane, he had endeavoured to keep the Army together, and to put them in as good a posture for Service as possible, having two Expectations on which they all knew their whole Affair depended upon, (viz.) the coming of the Ch———, and the rising or Landing of the D[uke] of O[rmon]d in England, as had been concerted and agreed between him and the said D——— of O———d, as well before his going from England as since; that the first of these had answer'd their Expectation, and the Ch——— was happily arriv'd, having also caused to be brought to them powerful Supplies of Money, Arms, Amunition, and other Necessaries, as well before as since his Arrival, all which had come safe to their Hands, not one Vessel having fallen into the Enemies Hands[1]; but that their Friends in England had met with many Disappointments, and their Designs having been betray'd, the chief Gentlemen on whom the D——— of O———d relied for Assistance had been taken up, so that their Measures had been entirely broken; and that when the D———, not satisfied with the Advices he receiv'd, had Sail'd even to the very Coast of England, and had actually gone on Shore there, yet he found their Friends so dispers'd and discouraged that it was impossible to bring them together without a sufficient Force to be landed from Abroad, to make a stand and give time for those who were well-affected in England to come together in Safety; That upon this Disappointment, his Grace was gone back to France, where Preparations was making for his Descent upon England with such a Power as should protect their Friends, and give them Opportunity to show themselves in a proper Manner and Place.

[1] Several vessels with supplies followed the Chevalier to Scotland. One stranded near St Andrews, and another was lost near Arbroath.— R. 351.

That these Things however have brought the Weight of the War upon them in Scotland, and not only so, but had caused those Succours which they expected from Abroad to be stopp'd and reserv'd for the said Expedition of the D—— of O——d, which was now in a great Forwardness in the Western Parts of France. But...it was to be now consider'd of, whether they were in a Condition to maintain themselves in their present Situation or not....

These Things being thus laid before them, the Debates began; a Lowland Gentleman speaking first told them, as we were inform'd, That...he made no doubt but they might defend the Town of Perth till the Enemies Foot should perish in the lying before it....On the other Hand, as he said, supposing they thought it advisable to Retreat, they might do it with all the leisure imaginable, leaving about 2000 Men in the Town, and before those Men could be oblig'd to Surrender, the Army might be posted in what Advantageous part of the Kingdom they thought fit.

A Highland Officer stood up next. 'I am ashamed,' says he, 'to repeat what I hear in the Streets and what the Town is full of, (viz.) That we are met here to resolve to run away like Cowards from an Enemy who we have once already seen in the Field like Men. I hope none here will doubt wheather we dare see them there again or no. I am perswaded there is not a Man in the Troops I have the Honour to be at Head of but had rather Fight and be Kill'd than turn their Backs and Escape... [and] for my share, I do not see the least Reason for Retreating.'

Upon this Speech it was said the Ch—— appear'd a little terrified...[and] as soon as the Officer had done speaking, the Ch—— look'd at a French Officer, who was also an Engineer, and who had formerly advis'd the fortifying the Town of Perth with a compleat Rampart....

This Gentleman told them, however, That it would be needful that they should come to a speedy Resolution in this Case; for that if he had order to prepare for a Defence, he must desire as much Leisure as possible, and must have as many Workmen press'd in from the Country as could be had....

In a Word, all the Generals or other Officers who came over

with the Ch——, and all those who belong'd to the Clans of
Highland Men, were unanimously for Fighting.

The Arguments for Fighting were the Subject of many
Hours Debate, for many more spoke their Opinions than those
above-mention'd; it came then to the turn of those who were in
the Secret to act the part they had agreed on....

So the Grand Council was adjourn'd to next Morning
[January 31]; but notice being given to a certain Number
selected for the Purpose to meet in an Hour or two after, they
had a private Meeting accordingly, and here the Lord Mar
open'd to them the whole Mystery, telling them in a few Words,
That...there were many Reasons which made it inconvenient
to make publick all the Circumstances of their Affairs, and those
especially which made it necessary to Retreat; but that it was
evident they were come now to a Crisis, in which it was advisable not to Retreat only, but to put an end to the Design in
general for a time....

But this was not all: there was it seems at this Secret Committee, or Cabinet of their Chiefs, a Piece of Secret News
communicated to them....This News was, that the Ch——
had two Days before receiv'd a certain Account that some of the
Chief of those who had appear'd in Arms in favour of this
Undertaking had wickedly entred into a Conspiracy...to make
their Peace at the expence of their Friends, and to seize upon
the Person of the Ch——, and deliver him up to the Duke of
Argyle.

This seem'd to fill the Assembly with Horror, and...united
them in the Resolution of Retreating.

The Council having determin'd [to retreat from Perth], it
was immediately made publick, tho' all imaginable Care was
taken to prevent sending the News of it to the Duke of Argyle:
No Body went to Bed that Night but those who had nothing to
remove but themselves, and the Ch—— came from Schone very
early, some said it was but little after Midnight[1]; and in the

---

[1] 'The Pretender, finding that Time was not to be lost, retired that
Evening from Scoon to Perth, where, having supp'd at Provost Hay's,
he rested some Hours.'—R. 367.

Morning[1], Things having been all ready, the Troops began to
File off, and by Afternoon most of the Forces were o'er the
River Tay, which at that Time was so hard Frozen, tho' a deep
and swift River, as to bear both Horse and Man.

We were not long leaving the Town, nor were the National
Troops long behind us in taking Possession; for expresses having
carried the News of our Flight, a Body of Dragoons enter'd the
next Day [February 1][2]; however, they could not all come
together under two or three Days, and having Notice that we
retir'd in a Body and were not to be insulted by a small Party,
they did not immediately follow: By this Means we had leisure
to proceed with the less Confusion, and to make such Provision
for subsisting the Troops as prevented the usual Disorders in a
flying Army; for we had four or five Days March of them.

Leaving[3] Perth [on January 31] and retiring Northwards...
[we] came in two days to Montross and Brechen. Neither of
these Places are tenable, tho' we had been provided, as we were
not, with a sufficient Number of Men, Ammunition, and Provisions: but Montross being a good Harbour, where we expected
our Succours from Abroad, we were unwilling to quit it so long as
we could remain safe in it. We thought, indeed, that the Enemy
would have made a Halt at Perth, and not have marched so
quickly after us, as we soon found they did, they being within a
few Miles of us before we had certain Intelligence of it, tho'
great Pains had been taken to be informed of their Motions[4].
The Earl of Panmure, not being recovered of the severe Wounds

[1] About ten o'clock. The Chevalier followed about noon 'with Tears
in his Eyes, complaining that instead of bringing him to a Crown, they
had brought him to his Grave.'—*R.* 367.

[2] Argyll and Cadogan, with four hundred horse, entered Perth about
one in the morning of February 1. They were followed by the rest of
the army before night fall.—*Ibid.* 367.

[3] *M. J.*

[4] The Duke followed in pursuit very rapidly. On February 2 a
detachment of his force occupied Dundee shortly after the Chevalier
had left the town. On the 4th his vanguard was at Arbroath. By the 6th
he designed to arrive at Stonehaven, by which time the Chevalier and
Mar had abandoned their army.—*R.* 368, 369.

he had received at the battle of Sheriffsmoor, was not in a Condition to march along with the Army, which otherwise he would have done; upon which the Chevalier advis'd him, as he pass'd Dundee, to endeavour to get off in the first Ship he could find, and by accident finding a little Bark at Arbroth, went off in it for France.

Before this time several People had very seriously represented to the Chevalier the deplorable Circumstances in which his Affairs now were on all Sides; that being over-power'd in Scotland, no Appearance of any rising in England, nor any News of the Succours he expected from Abroad, he had no Course at present to take that was consistent with what he owed to his People in general, to those who had taken Arms for him in particular, and to himself upon their Account, but by retiring beyond Sea, to preserve himself for a better Occasion of asserting his own Right and restoring them to their ancient Liberties.

It was indeed hard to bring him to think of this, but those about him found it now high time to press the Matter more than ever, the Enemy being within three Miles upon their March towards us. They therefore again represented to him the impossibility of making a Stand any where 'till they should come to the most inaccessible Places of the Mountains, where in that Season of the Year, there being so much Snow on the Ground, there could be no Subsistance for any Body of Men together, and where no Succour could come to them; That when his small Army was divided into lesser Bodies, they could not avoid being cut off by the Enemies Troops, who would then be master of all the Low Countries, and especially by the Garrisons they had in Inverlochy and Inverness, which they would reinforce; That as long as they knew he was in the Kingdom they would pursue him, even with the Hazard of their whole Army, his Person being the chief Object of their Pursuit, as his Destruction was the only thing that could secure their Usurpation; whereas, if he were gone off, they would not pursue with that Eagerness, nor would they find their Account in harrassing their Army in the Snow and excessive Cold of the Mountains to pursue the scatter'd Remains of the Loyal Party, who might sculk in the Hills till Providence should open a Way for their

Relief, or that they could obtain Terms from the Government; That his Person being with them would defeat even these faint Hopes, and that, in short, whilst he was in the Kingdom they could never expect any Terms or Capitulation but by abandoning him or giving him up, which rather than ever consent to they would be all, to the last Man, cut in Pieces.

Tho' the Chevalier was still extremely unwilling to leave his Loyal People, who had sacrificed their All with so much Zeal and Alacrity for his Service, yet when he considered that as Things then stood, his Presence, far from being a Help and Support to them, would rather be an Occasion of hastening their Ruin, he was sensibly touch'd to find himself for their Sakes under a Necessity of leaving them. There was no answering their Reasons, nor any time to be lost, the Danger encreasing every Moment. He therefore at last told them that he was sorry to find himself obliged to consent to what they desired of him. And I daresay no Consent he ever gave was so uneasy to him as this was.

In the mean time, fresh Alarms coming of the Enemy's approaching, Orders were given for the Army's marching on [from Montrose] towards Aberdeen[1], and the Resolution was taken for his going off in the Evening [February 4]. It happened very Providentially that there was just ready in the Harbour a small Ship[2] that had been designed to cary a Gentleman he was then to have sent to a Foreign Court. This Ship was now pitched upon to transport him; she was but a small one and could carry but few Passengers, and therefore, to avoid Confusion, he himself thought fit to name those who should attend him. The Earl of Mar, who was the first nam'd, made Difficulty and begg'd he might be left behind; but the Chevalier being positive for his going, and telling him that in a great Measure there were the same Reasons for his going as for his own, that his Friends would more easily get Terms without him than with him, and that, as Things now stood, he could be no longer of any Use to them in that Country, he submitted.

The Chevalier likewise ordered the Marquis of Drummond to go along with him; this Lord was then lame by a Fall from his

[1] 'To be ready to march about eight at Night.'—R. 369.
[2] The *Maria Teresa* of St Malo, of about ninety tons.—R. 369.

Horse, and not in a Condition to follow the Army, and was one of the four—with the Earl of Mar, Lord Tullibardien, and Lord Lithgow—against whom there was then a Bill of Attainder passing. The Chevalier would have willingly carried with him the other two Lords, but it happened that they were both then at a distance, Lord Tullibardien at Brichin with a part of the Foot, and Lord Lithgow at Bervie with the Horse. Lord Marischal, Gentleman of his Bedchamber, was also order'd to go, tho' he seem'd very desirous to stay and share in the Fate of his Country-men[1]. Lieut. General [Dominick] Sheldon, Vice-Chamberlain, had the same Orders, as had also Coll. [William] Clephan, who had left the Enemy. Lord Edward Drummond[2], who was also Gentleman of his Bed-chamber, happen'd to be with Lord Tinmouth[3] at five Miles distance, and so could not go with the Chevalier as he intended they both should, but he wrote to them to follow in a small Ship that was then in the Harbour; but the Master of this Ship was frighten'd and went away without carrying any Body.

The Chevalier then order'd a Commission to be drawn for Lieut. General Gordon to command in Chief, with all necessary Powers inserted, and particularly one, to treat and capitulate with the Enemy. He left also with the said General the Reasons of his leaving this Kingdom, and all the Money that was in the Pay-master's Hands or that he had himself (save a small sum for defraying his own and Company's Charges), and left orders for a sum of Money (if there should be any left after paying the Army) to be given to the poor People who suffer'd by the burning of A[u]chterarder and some villages about it, which had been thought necessary to be done to prevent the Enemy's March, tho' very much against his inclination, which made him delay it from time to time until the Enemy was actually on

[1] Cf. *K. M.* 28. He states that Marischal was not only convinced that the situation was not desperate, but that he brought Mar to the same conclusion, and that Mar undertook to represent Marischal's views to the Chevalier.

[2] Sixth titular Duke of Perth, d. 1760.

[3] Son of the Duke of Berwick. He had arrived in Scotland with the Chevalier.—*R.* 351.

their March: and the Chevalier left a Letter with General
Gordon for my Lord Argyle[1], to be delivered when the said
Money should be given, desiring that it should be distributed
accordingly.

About 9 a clock the Chevalier went on board the Ship, which
was about a Mile at Sea. Lord Marischal and Colonel Clephan
came some time after to the Shore, but by an Accident found no
Boat, and so could not go off, tho', as the Boat-men who carried
the Chevalier assure us, he stay'd for them till near Eleven a
Clock, but could stay no longer because of the nine Men of War
that were cruising thereabouts; and it was great good Luck that
the Ship, having stayed so long, got out of their Reach before it
was Day-light.

As soon as the Chevalier parted [at Montrose] we marched, and
...advanc'd towards the Highlands; for there was no Stand could
be made at Aberdeen[2], nor could we think of going to Inverness,
that being still in the Enemies Hands. Some went to Peterhead
and thought to have got off in a Ship they found there, but...
were soon forc'd back by a Man of War....

Thus I have given you true Matter of Fact and a sincere
Account of our unfortunate Condition. Whatever may now be
our Fate, we have still one solid Ground of Comfort, that the
Chevalier hath (as we hope) got safe out of the Reach of
his Enemies; for in the Safety of his Person lies all our Hopes
of Relief, and we look on him as the Instrument reserv'd by God
(and he now seems the only one[3] in the ordinary Course of
Providence) to rescue these Nations in due Time from their
present Oppression and the lawless Dominion of Foreigners[4].

[1] Dated February 4. It is in the Maitland Club's *Miscellany*, vol. iii,
447.

[2] Gordon evacuated Aberdeen on February 7. The Duke and a
small body entered the town next day.—*R.* 370.

[3] The Chevalier as yet was unmarried. His only surviving sister had
died in 1712.

[4] The Chevalier landed at Gravelines seven days after his departure
from Montrose, and proceeded to St Germain. He was coldly received
by the French Regent and, shortly after, curtly dismissed Bolingbroke
from his service.—Mahon, *History of England*, vol. i, 285.

The[1] Duke of Argyle, being arrived at Aberdeen on [February] the eighth, as was said, sent Major General [Joseph] Sabine with a Party of Foot to Peterhead, and Colonel [William] Ker with a Detachment of Dragoons to support them, and Major General [William] Evans with 200 Dragoons, and Colonel Campbell of Finah with 400 of his Men (who marched as an advanced Guard to the Royal Army), to endeavour to intercept the Horse of the Rebels, if, finding they could not get off at Peterhead, they should make towards Frazerburgh. Some of them embarked near Peterhead and got safe to France; but others were obliged to return and follow their flying Army to the Hills, and were got to Frazerburgh a March before General Evans. When he came to Frazerburgh he found the Pretender's Physician, who surrendered to him; but the rest of the Party being gone to Bamff, he detached after them Colonel Campbel with 40 Dragoons and 400 Foot, and soon returned. The Duke having sent several of the Forces in Pursuit of the Rebels as far as Murray, Brigadier [Alexander] Grant came to Inverness, and my Lord Lovat and he planted Garrisons of their own Men in Seaforth's House at Brahan, Chisholm's House at Erchles, and Borlum's House at Borlum, and Colonel [William] Grant, who commanded an Independent Company, with a Party, took Possession of Castle-Gordon....These Garrisons continued till they were relieved by the regular Troops, but the Rebels thought not fit to give them any Trouble.

For their main Body marched straight West thro' Strath-Spey and Strath-Don to the Hills of Badenoch, where they separated. The Foot dispersed into the Mountains on this side of Lochy, and the Horse went to Lochquhaber; agreeing, however, to meet again upon Notice from the Pretender. And here, being advised that two French Frigats were come for their Relief and would lay in Pentland Firth till they should hear from them, the Lord Duffus, Sir George Sinclair, General [Thomas] Eckline [Echlyn] and others, about 160 Gentlemen in all, well mounted on Horseback, made a Sally from the Hills, and crossing the Shire of Murray, came to the Sea-side near Burgh, where they got several large Barks, which carried them

[1] R. 370.

to the Orkneys, Arskerry, and other of the Islands, from whence most of them found Means to get into the Frigats, which carried them safe to France. Other Ships coming afterwards carried the rest to Gottenburg in the Sweedish Dominions....Amongst those was Lord Duffus....There were yet with the Rebels in Scotland many of their Chiefs, as the Marquis of Tullibardine, the Earls Marischal, Southesk, Linlithgow, and Seaforth, who, having broke his Submission, joined them again in their Flight to the Northward, the Lord Tinmouth, Sir Donald M'Donald, and several others of the Heads of the Clans, who sheltered themselves for some Time in the Mountains from his Majesty's Troops who pursued them through the North, and from thence some made their Escape to the Isle of Sky, the Lewis, and other of the North-western Islands, till Ships came for their Relief to carry them abroad....

But to return to the Duke of Argyle, whom we left at Aberdeen; the Passage being left clear between that and Inverness, his Grace ordered four Battalions of Foot and a Regiment of Dragoons, designed to be quartered in that Part of the Country, to march to Inverness on the fifteenth of February: And...having thus gloriously finished the most laborious and hard Campaign that ever was known, he left the Command of his Majesty's Troops to Lieutenant General [William] Cadogan, and returned to Edinburgh the 27th of February. And in a Day or two after, set out for London, where he arrived on the 6th of March[1].

We[2] shall now proceed to speak of the Affairs in the North of Scotland, which have hitherto been almost untouch'd.

No sooner did the Pretender's Design of invading Britain with a Power from Abroad, and Mar's Endeavours to raise a

[1] Cadogan, towards the end of February, sent a detachment which pacified the Lewis, though the Earl of Seaforth succeeded in escaping to France. Another detachment was sent to Skye in quest of Sir Donald MacDonald, who also escaped to France. Glengarry submitted; Lochiel, Keppoch, and Clanranald consented to disarm, and Cadogan was enabled to leave Aberdeen for Edinburgh about April 27, leaving General Sabine in command.—R. 373.

[2] R. 328.

Rebellion at Home, appear to the World, than the Friends of
the Government, on this Side and beyond Inverness, began to
rendezvouze and inlist their Men who had Arms, and endeavoured
to provide those that wanted, as well as they could: But when
they had done [so], there was still a great Want of Arms,
Ammunition and Money, with which, if the Government had
only supplied them, they might easily [have] found double the
Number of the Men they had in Arms for his Majesty's Service,
and prevented the Rebellion in those Parts from arising to the
Height which it afterwards came to.

On[1] the 15th[2] of September [upon the news of Mar's raising
the standard at Braemar on September 6] the Laird of M'Intosh[3]
conveened his Men at Farr, as was given out, to review them;
but in the Evening he marched streight to Inverness, where he
came by Sun-rising with Colours displayed, and after he had
made himself Master of what Arms and Ammunition he could
find, and some little Money that belonged to the Publick, proceeded to proclaim the Pretender King, under the Name of
James the VIIIth of Scotland, and IIId of England. At this time
Jean Gordon, Lady Culloden, found it absolutely necessary for
the Safety of a great many of the King's Friends and their
Goods to shut up the House of Culloden, where she had taken
in great Store of Provision. Her Husband [John Forbes], then
Member of Parliament, tho' at London, had some very good
Arms in his House, and ordered One Hundred Men to be taken
in, knowing that the Rebels could not omit to Garison it, being
a very strong House, and so near Inverness that it hinder'd any
to go or come from it on that side of the Water of Ness; which
M'Intosh finding, sent a Message to the Lady to give up the
House, but she refusing it, he went himself and spoke to the Lady
over a Window, but to no purpose. She understood that there
was no Means but the Rebels would use to have that House,
which might be so troublesome to Inverness, that now there

---

[1] *P. H.* 142. Patten prints this narrative as 'The Lord Lovatt's
Account of the taking of Inverness; with other Advantages obtain'd over
the Rebels in the North of Scotland.'

[2] The 13th, according to *R.* 329.

[3] 'By the Instigation of his Friend, M'Intosh of Borlam.'—*Ibid.* 329.

was a Garrison of Four Hundred Men settled, of the name of M'Kenzie of Coull[1].

Upon the 20th of September, M'Intosh march'd with six Hundred Men, the first of all the Clans, towards the Earl of Mar, who then had set up the publick Standard of Rebellion. The want of Cannon was the only Thing that grieved the Lady Culloden; but being informed that there was a Merchant Ship lying in the Harbour of Inverness, which had six Guns on Board and a number of Ball for them, she detached a Party of Fifty Men under Silence of the Night by Boats, who had the six Pieces of Cannon before it was Day mounted upon the House, to the great Surprize of the Jacobites in the Town, who look'd upon that Cannon as their Security.

While this Loyal Lady was Fortifying her House, she had the good Luck of being assisted by the Arrival of Mr Duncan Forbes[2], her Brother-in-Law, who from that time distinguished himself both by his Wit and Resolution, that if Things were acted by the Rebels according to the Hardness expected from them, it might be improper to have such a Governor and Governess in one House, and some other Places not so well served.

The Earl of Seaforth, who was nominated Lieutenant-General and Commander in Chief of the Northern Counties to his Majesty K. James the VIIIth (for so was the Designation then), was not Idle, gather'd his Men from the Lewes and all his Inland Country to the Place of Brahan, where Sir Donald M'Donald of Slate with Six Hundred Men and the Laird of M'Kinnon with One Hundred and Fifty join'd him. Alexander M'kenzie of Frazerdale, who assumed a Command of the Name of Frazer by his Lady, had forced together Four Hundred of that Name, which, with the Hundred Men that [Roderick Chisholm of] Chisolme (who is Vassal to that Family) had, made up Five Hundred under Frazerdale's Command, which

[1] The Mackenzies garrisoned Inverness after Mackintosh had marched off to join Mar.—*R.* 330.

[2] He had come from Leith in the ship which brought the Earl of Sutherland to the North. The Earl reached Dunrobin Castle on September 28.—*Ibid.* 330.

lay at and about Castledouny, five Miles from Brahan and six from Inverness: But the Frazers of Struy, Foyer[1], Culduthell[2], &c., kept the rest of that Name on Foot for the Government, having Assurance that the Lord Lovat, their Natural Chief, was at London, firm for the Protestant Succession, and daily expected. This procured them not only the Ridicule but the Objects of the Rebels Threats. Frazerdale, finding his Party few to what he expected, resolved, if it was possible, to bring those Gentlemen into their Party, and so wrote to Struy and Foyer that he wanted much to meet with them in order to satisfy them with the Justice and Reasonableness of what they were to Rise for, and that he hoped either he should satisfy them or that they would him.

The Gentlemen, upon his Letter, resolved to Trust him and show him freely that they would continue firm to the Protestant Succession as by Law established: And having come with One Hundred and Fifty Men near his House of Castledouny, they were told he was at Brahan with my Lord Seaforth, from whom they immediately received a Message by one Donald M'Urchison, Factor to the Lord Seaforth, That he understood they had got in Arms, and that answerable to his Power as Lieutenant-General and Commander in Chief of those Counties, he demanded them to join him and have themselves Listed to serve his Majesty K. James the VIIIth. To which they return'd answer, That they were Protestants of the Low-Church, and that they would let his Lordship know so much whenever he pleased. But in the mean time that his Message was delivered them, he detached Six Hundred Men commanded by M'kenzie of Frazerdale, Aplecross, and Fairburn, with an Order to take them Dead or Alive; but by good Luck it was one of the most boisterous Nights that could be, and when they came to the Place, they found that they had been appriz'd of their coming and had got themselves in a Posture of Defence, which obliged them to return half-starved with Cold and Hunger....

The Earl of Sutherland, who was sent down from Court to

[1] Hugh Fraser.

[2] Alexander Fraser, Lieutenant of one of the three Independent Companies.—Dalton, i, 237.

Command in the North of Scotland[1], had got of the Mackays, Rosses, Monroes, and his own Men, One Thousand Eight Hundred together at a Place in Ross called Alnes, and thought proper to divert Seaforth from joining Mar; that the King's other Friends in the North, who were in readiness to join him if they could come together, they would have been able to give the Earl of Seaforth, or Huntley, or both, Battle: But Seaforth, finding himself Four Thousand strong, and Sutherland but One Thousand Eight Hundred, thought it was fit to take the Advantage, and so marched[2] directly towards Alnes where Sutherland lay; who found that by retiring to Sutherland, Seaforth would be for some time diverted, and he would save his Men from fighting so unequally[3]. Seaforth coming to Alnes[4], which is the Monroes Country, allowed his Men to commit all the Barbarity that could be expected from Turks, destroyed all the Corn and Cattle in the Country, took of every thing that was useful within as well as without Doors, lodged their Men in the Churches, where they kill'd Cattle and did every thing disrespectful to Places of Worship, and treated the Ministers, of all the People, the worst, took some Gentlemen Prisoners, and now believed that since Sutherland retired all the Cause was gain'd there.

Next Care was to come to Inverness and settle a stronger Garrison in it, reduce the pitiful Whig-house Garrisons, as they called Culloden and Killravock Houses, and Force all the silly People who stood out along with them.

Being come to Inverness, General Seaforth called a Council of War, where were present the Lord Duffus, Sir Donald M'Donald, Frazerdale, M'Kinnon, the Chisolme, and several other Officers, besides Sir John M'Kenzie of Coul, the Governor,

---

[1] His commission as Lieutenant-General of Horse and Foot is dated November 16, 1715.—Dalton, i, 235.

[2] On October 9.—R. 331.

[3] He retreated towards Sutherlandshire, though he was opposed in that step by the Monros and Mackays, who refused to follow him.—Ibid. 331.

[4] On the day after Sutherland withdrew. Seaforth remained there till October 15.—Ibid. 331.

where it was resolved that Culloden House must be reduced at any Rate, and so commanded Mr George M'Kenzie of Grumziord [? Greinord] to go with a Trumpet along with him and Summon the House formally to Surrender. Coming to the Place, Grumziord ordered the Trumpet to Sound, and called to Mr Duncan who kept the House. Mr Forbes not only told him but shewed him that the House was not in their Reverence, and so Defiance was returned for Answer. But in a second Council of War, the Lord Duffus was sent in order to reduce Mr Forbes by Reason, or otherwise to assure him of the hardest Treatment if the House was taken. But my Lord returned without Success, and so a Disposition was made for the Siege, and the Party for the Attack order'd; but finding that the House was strong, and the Governor and Garison Obstinate and Brave, after twelve Days Deliberation marched forward toward their Grand Camp at Perth. From Inverness they marched[1] to Strath-Spey, the Laird of Grant's Country, where they found the Grants all in Arms in order to secure their Country from harm; they only asked some Baggage Horses to the next Country, and Quarter'd their Men civilly, and returned the Horses home next Day; and so they joined the Earl of Mar at Perth, where they continued till the decisive Stroke of Dumblain, from whence they returned[2] in a hundred Parties, to the Satisfaction of many who were very careful of Disarming them in their Retreat. But the Four Hundred Frazers that Mr M'Kenzie had brought there four Days before to Dumblain, hearing that the Lord Lovat was come Home, deserted that Cause, and came Home full Armed with their Affection to their Natural Chief; and their Love to the Protestant Interest, for which that Name distinguished themselves since the Reformation, was plainly seen in their Services thereafter till the Rebellion was extinguished.

On the 5th of November the Lord Lovat with Mr Forbes of Culloden arrived at Culloden's House, from whence my Lord wrote to the Gentlemen of his Name that stood for the Government to come and receive him: Ross of Killravock and Forbes of Culloden conducted him with Three Hundred Men

[1] On October 24. Seaforth had received an urgent summons from Mar.—*R.* 332. [2] *Supra*, p. 143.

by Inverness, near the Bounds of his own Country; he was informed that M'Donald of Keppoch[1] was marching with Three Hundred Men to reinforce Sir John M'Kenzie of Coull at Inverness. My Lord had concerted with Captain George Grant, who then Commanded that Name in Absence of his Brother [Alexander] Ross of Killravock, and Forbes of Culloden, that he should go through all his Countries and get all his Men together, and that then they would invest Inverness. But finding now that Kepoch was on his March, resolved to intercept Kepoch in his Road, and so resolved to cross the River Ness; but just as he was ready to cross, he gets an Account, That what were not marched to Perth of the M'Intoshes were in Arms, ready to go into Inverness and strengthen that Garrison. Upon which, having consulted the Gentlemen that were with him, resolved to disperse those M'Intoshes, and so came directly on his Way to the Place where he heard they lay, and on his Way found two or three of their chief Gentlemen, which bound themselves for the peaceable Behaviour of such as were at Home, and that they would give up their Arms, and give in any thing they could afford in Inverness, when they were Masters of it. His Lordship, having on the 7th of November crossed the Water, resolved to throw himself in directly betwixt Kepoch and Sir John, who, hearing of his coming, resolved to Sally out, and that Kepoch on one side and he on the other would Attack him. But Kepoch, finding himself not safe to go forward, returned home by the Country of Urquharts, belonging to the Laird of Grant, where he did several Barbarities, and carried off three or four Gentlemen Prisoners, in hopes they would relieve themselves by a Booty, which they not yielding to, he dismissed in two or three Days. Upon News of Kepoch's suddain retiring, my Lord Lovat marches streight to the Town of Inverness[2], and in his Way found some Cows that belonged to the Garison, kept by a Guard, which he took, and chased in one other Party to the Town. Having settled his Men within a Mile of the Town, ordered a Party to the side of the Firth to stop any Boats

[1] Coll Macdonell, 'Coll of the Cows'; died 1723?

[2] He came before it on November 9, the day on which Mar's Council at Perth decided upon the advance to Sheriffmuir.—*R.* 333.

coming with any Succours of Men or Provisions to the Garrison, and now he began to think that it was not reasonable to be Idle a Minute, and so acquaints Ross of Killravock and Forbes of Culloden, who had the Town Blockaded on the East side Ness, that it was proper to attempt the Town, since the Grants were Eight Hunder'd on their March[1]. Mr Duncan Forbes, a Man that was most active in these Affairs, hardly giving himself rest, was order'd to go and concert some things with my Lord Lovat; and Arthur Ross, Brother to the Laird of Kilravock, a young Gentleman that had been Captive in Turkey for many years before and but just come home, was order'd to Cover Mr Forbe's passing the River with a Party: He, finding the Rebels Guard Relieving their Centinels by the River side, pursued them so close to the heart of the Town, that he entering the Tolbooth Door, where the Governor had Lodged himself with his Main Guard, he was by the Centinel within Shot through the Body, and thereafter he discharged two Pistols he had under his Sash among the Guard, and had they not crushed his Sword-Hand in forcing the Door close, he might have lived some longer time then he did, which was but about Ten Hours.

At the Alarm of this Shooting, the whole Garrison got to Arms, Firing so from all quarters that the six or seven Men that came up with Mr Ross had very good luck to escape. The Death of this Gallant Gentlemen so vex'd my Lord his Brother and all his other Friends, that they swore Revenge of his Blood, and accordingly summoned the Town to send out their Garrison and Governor, or if they did not, they would Burn the Town and put them all to the Sword. The Governor, expecting no great Favour from East or West side, was in a surprise. My Lord ordered all the Men to be ready[2], which the Governor finding, on Saturday the Tenth of November got together all

[1] According to the prearranged plan, Sutherland with the Mackays, Monros, and Rosses was to invest Inverness on the north. They arrived too late, however.—R. 333.

[2] Lovat took post at the west end of the bridge. Captain George Grant was upon the south side, to enter the Castle street, and the Morayshire men, to the number of about three hundred, were to attack the East Port.—R. 334.

the Boats he could find, and with high Water made off with all imaginable Confusion, to the Joy and Grief of the sundry Parties within. Ross of Killravock and Colloden's Men lay at and about Colloden, the Eight Hundred Grants to the Westward of them two Miles, and the Lord Lovat, who had got of his Name Five Hundred together on the North and West side of the Town, Marched all in, having prepared Bullets [Billets] for their Men. They now found it convenient to let the Earl of Sutherland know that they had the Town: And his Lordship, receiving my Lord Lovat's Letter, returned him a very kind Letter, wherein he was glad his Lordship by his Conduct and Diligence was sufficiently intitled to the King's Favour, and that none would more truly represent it than he.

At this time the Earl had got together his Men and the others that were with him in Ross, and was to March forward to join that considerable Body that were then together at Inverness: His Lordship, being Thirty Six Miles from Inverness, Marched his Men, being a considerable Number, to the Western Division of Ross, where they Encamped, and his Lordship, with the Lord Rae, Monro of Fouls, and several other Gentlemen came into Inverness on Tuesday the [15]th of November; which Day we had the joyful News of his Grace the Duke of Argyle's Victory at Dumblaine, which was observ'd with great solemnity of Joy; and two Days thereafter, having left Col. Robert Monro of Fouls[1] Governor of Inverness there with a suitable Party, the Earl of Sutherland with his Men, and the Lord Lovat with a part of his Men, went to the place of Brahan[2], and oblig'd all the responsible Men of the M'Kenzie's that were not with my Lord Seaforth at Perth, to secure their peaceable Behaviour, and return the Arms taken from the Monroes by my Lord Seaforth before, and release the Prisoners, and that they would not assist my Lord Seaforth directly or indirectly, and that they would Answer to his Lordship of Sutherland any Sum of Money he required for the use of the Government upon

[1] Captain of an Independent Company.—Dalton, i, 237.

[2] They marched out of Inverness on November 19, having fortified the Castle with some cannon which they had taken from a ship in the harbour.—R. 334.

a due Advertisement, and that the Lord Seaforth's House of Brahan would be made a Garrison for his Majesty King George.

Things being put in this order in that Country, the Monroes being left at Inverness, the Earl of Sutherland marched with his Men, the Frazer's, the M'Kay's, the Ross's, Killravock's Men, Culloden's, and Sir Archibald Campbell, Tutor of Calder, with a Party of Two Hundred to Murray, to bring that Country's Disaffection to good order, and divert my Lord Huntley from Crossing the River Spey[1], who made the Rocks in that Country resound his Resolutions, having got, as he gave out, new Orders and a Detachment sent with General [Thomas] Eclin to him from Perth: But they were not long in that Country when things were put in that Condition[2] that the Earl of Sutherland came back to Inverness, and left the Lord Lovat, Killravock, Sir Arch. Campbell, &c., behind, to act as he directed them and as Matters required. The Murray Jacks being put in pretty good Order, the King's Authority own'd over all the Country, it was thought proper to send Hugh Frazier of Foyer to Sterling, to let the Duke of Argyle know how matters stood, and receive his Grace's Command. The whole Country betwixt Fort-William and Aberdeen being in the Rebels Hands, except Murray and Strath Spey...he went forward for Dunstafnage, and from thence to...Sterling, where he arrived the 17th of December, and was introduced to his Grace the Duke of Argyle.

This[3] Success in reducing Inverness, and the Activity of the Friends of the Government there, oblig'd [the Earl of Seaforth] to separate again[4] very soon from the Rebels at Perth, and return home for the Safety of his Country; where he arriv'd about the first of December [1715]; and towards the End of that Month drew his Men together, and concerted with the Marquis of Huntley, who was likewise returned with his Men from Perth[5], to attack Inverness on both Sides. The Earl of Sutherland,

[1] This was in December, after Huntly had left the camp at Perth. *Supra*, p. 144.

[2] 'Inverness was again in Hazard of being attacked by the Rebels, who were now gathering together after their Return from Sheriff-Moor.' —*R*. 335.

[3] *R*. 336.   [4] *Supra*, p. 143.   [5] *Supra*, p. 143.

having Intelligence hereof, resolved to reduce the Earl of Seaforth, lest he should be engaged by him and Huntley at once;
and, in order thereunto, march'd out of Inverness 300 of his
own Men, with about as many of the M'Kays, under the Command of Mr Patrick M'Kay of Scourie, 300 Grants, under the
Command of Captain George Grant, 200 of the Rosses, under
the Command of Hugh Ross of Brealangwel, with about 200 of
Colonel Monro's Men, the rest of his Men being left to keep
the Town; with these he marched to the Moor of Gilliechriest,
where they were join'd by 500 of my Lord Lovat's Men.
Seaforth had there rendezvouzed about 1200 Men, being all he
was able to make of them who had fled from Sheriffs-Moor;
but finding my Lord Sutherland and the Gentlemen with him
resolute to force him to an Engagement, he made his Submission
to the Government, which was transmitted to Court....Where-
upon the Earl of Sutherland return'd to Inverness with all his
People, upon the first of January, 1716. And, in a short Time
after, the Marquis of Huntley came also into Terms of Submission, which he observed better than the Earl of Seaforth did
his.

For, but a few Days after his Submission to the Government,
having received Intelligence of the Pretender's Landing, he
drew his People together again, placing Parties upon the several
Passes and Ferries, who robb'd a great many of my Lord Sutherland's, Lord Rae's, and East-Ross Men of their Arms, as they
were going home, upon the Faith of the late Submission. He
likewise sent a Party of 2 or 300 Men to possess the Town of
Chanrie, to interrupt the Communication between Inverness
and Ross. Of which my Lord Sutherland having Intelligence,
he sent Colonel Monro with a Detachment of 200 Men
(whereof 50 were of his own, the rest of the Earl's Men, the
M'Kays and of Rosses each as many) in Boats from Inverness,
to dispossess them of that Place. The Rebels, discovering them
before they got to Chanrie, drew up on the Shore: Whereupon
the Colonel landed his Men a Mile from the Town; but as he
was marching up to attack the Party near Chanrie, Sir John
M'Kenzie of Coul appeared on his Rear with 3 or 400 Men:
Upon which the Colonel judged it more proper to retire to his

Boats than to expose the Handful of Men he had with him, to
the evident Danger of being surrounded by the Enemy; and
accordingly marched back, ordering the Sutherland Men, with
the M'Kays and Rosses, to embark first, and afterwards went
on Board with his own Men; but the last of his Boats sticking
fast on the Ground, by which Time the Enemy was come up to
the Shore, firing on the Boats; which the Colonel with his own
50 return'd, and kept a close Fire upon the Enemy for a considerable Space, the rest of the Boats steering off all the while to
Sea; notwithstanding of all the Signals given to bring them to
the Shore....Whereupon the Colonel, having got off his Boats,
returned to Inverness: Which the Earl of Sutherland, with the
other noble and honourable Gentlemen abovementioned, continued to defend till the End of the Rebellion, that they were
relieved by the regular Troops.

CHAPTER III

PRESTON, 1715

I[1] must...go back into Northumberland, and give some Account of the Rising and Motion of the Rebels on that Side, as also of some of their Measures and Marches, till they came and joined the Highland Foot at Kelso as above[2].

There had been Measures concerted at London by the Pretender's Friends some time before the Insurrection in Northumberland broke out, to which Capt. John Shaftoe, a Half-pay Officer, since executed at Preston, and Capt. John Hunter of North-Tyne in the County of Northumberland, who had a Commission from Queen Anne to raise an independent Company but did not, assisted: Besides these two, there was one Capt. Robert Talbot, an Irishman and Papist, formerly in the French service, who likewise being acquainted with the Design in August, 1715, took Shipping at London and went to Newcastle. By this Gentleman the Resolutions taken at London were first communicated to their Friends in the North of England, and Means us'd to persuade and prepare the Gentlemen they had embark'd with them to be ready to rise upon Warning given....
The principal Men entrusted with these Negotiations were Colonel Oxburgh, Mr Nich. Wogan, Mr Charles Wogan, and Mr James Talbot, all Irish and Papists: A second Class of Agents consisted of Mr Clifton, Brother to Sir Gervase Clifton, and Mr Beaumont, both Gentlemen of Nottinghamshire, and Mr Buxton, a Clergyman of Derbyshire. All these rid like Gentlemen, with Servants and Attendants, and were armed with Swords and Pistols. They kept always moving, and travelled from Place to Place till Things ripened for Action. The first Step towards their appearing in Arms was when, about the latter

---

[1] *P. H.* 20.   [2] *Supra*, p. 98.

end of September, the Lord Derwentwater had notice that there was a Warrant out from the Secretary of State to apprehend him, and that the Messengers were come to Durham that were to take him. This Lord went to the House of one Mr B———n in his Neighbourhood, a Justice of the Peace, who, if zealously affected to His Majesty's Government or that Lord's Interest, might have honourably enough taken him or at least persuaded him to surrender, which, it is presumed, would not have been Matter of great Difficulty to have been done. Here it is supposed he went from thence to the House of one Richard Lambert, thought more private and least suspected. Mr Forster, likewise having Notice of the like Warrant against him, went from Place to Place, 'till at last he came to the House of one Mr Fenwick of Bywell. The Messenger in pursuit of him was got within half a Mile of that Place, but staying or calling for a Constable to his Aid, whether the other had notice thereof or not, yet he found time to out-distance the Messenger, so that he never overtook him 'till they met at Barnet, when the Messenger brought Ropes to pinion him that had led him such a Dance. It has been reported (not without good Reason) that Mr Fenwick had given shrewd Demonstrations, if not plain Evidence, of his good Inclinations to join the Rebels. Upon this News they had a full Meeting of the Parties concern'd in Northumberland, where, consulting all the Circumstances of their Friends and of the Interest they were embark'd in, they boldly resolved, since there was no Safety any longer in shifting from Place to Place, that...they would immediately appear in Arms....

Pursuant to this Resolution, an Appointment was made, and Notice of it sent to all their Friends to meet the next Morning, which was the 6th of October, at a Place called Green-rig, which was done accordingly; for Mr Forster, with several Gentlemen, in Number at first about Twenty, met at the Rendezvous, but made no stay here, thinking the Place inconvenient, but rode immediately to the top of a Hill called the Waterfalls, from whence they might discover any that came either to join them or to oppose them. They had not been long here before they discovered the Earl of Derwentwater, who

came that Morning from his own Seat at Dilston, with some
Friends and all his Servants, mounted some upon his Coach-
Horses, and others upon very good useful Horses, and all very
well arm'd. In coming from Dilston-Hall they all drew their
Swords as they marched along Corbridge and through that Town.
They halted at the Seat of Mr Errington, where there were
several other Gentlemen appointed to meet, who join'd the
Lord Derwentwater, and then they came on all together to the
Places appointed, and where the forenamed Company attended.
They were now near 60 Horse, most Gentlemen and their
Attendants; when, calling a short Council, it was concluded to
march towards the River Coquett, to a Place called Plainfield:
Here they were join'd by others who came straggling in, and
having made some stay here, they resolved to go that Night to
Rothbury, a small Market-Town: Here they stay'd all Night;
and next Morning, being the 7th of October, their Number still
encreasing, they marched to Warkworth, another Market-Town,
upon the Sea-coast and strong by its Situation, famous formerly
for a Castle, the Body of which still remains, and an ancient
Cell cut out of a solid Rock. Here they continued[1] till Monday,
during which time nothing material happened, except that on
Sunday Morning, Mr Forster, who now stiled himself General,
sent Mr Buxton their Chaplain to Mr Ion, the Parson of the
Parish, with Orders for him to Pray for the Pretender as King,
and in the Litany, for Mary Queen-Mother and all the dutiful
Branches of the Royal Family, and to omit the usual Names of
King George, the Prince and Princess; which Mr Ion wisely
declining, the other, viz. Mr Buxton, took Possession of the
Church, read Prayers and Preached. Mean while the Parson
went to Newcastle to consult his own Safety and acquaint the
Government with what happened. The next thing they did was
openly to proclaim the Pretender as King of Great Britain, &c.
It was done by Mr Forster in disguise, and by the sound of
Trumpet and all the Formality that the Circumstances and
Place would admit. It may be observed that this was the first

[1] William, fourth Baron Widdrington (d. 1743) with thirty horse
joined them on the 8th.—*R.* 239.

Place[1] where the Pretender was so avowedly Pray'd for and Proclaimed as King of these Realms....

On Monday the 10th of October they marched to Morpeth, a very considerable Market-Town belonging to the Earl of Carlisle, and gives Title to his Eldest Son. Upon their March to this Town their Number got a considerable Addition; At Felton-Bridge they were joined by 70 Scots Horse, or rather Gentlemen from the Borders, and they had been considerably encreased before in their March from Warkworth, at Alnwick and other Places; so that at their entring this Town [Morpeth] they were 300 strong, all Horse, for they would entertain no Foot, else their Number would have been very large; but as they neither had nor could provide Arms for those they had mounted, they gave the common People good Words, and told them that they would soon be furnished with Arms and Ammunition, and that then they would list Regiments to form an Army. This was upon the Expectation they had of surprising Newcastle, in which case they did not question to have had as many Foot as they pleas'd. Here Mr Forster receiv'd an Account that Mr Lancelot Errington[2] and some others had surprised the Castle in the Holy Island, which is a small Fort guarded by a few Soldiers sent Weekly from the Garrison at Berwick. Errington undiscovered took Boat and went to Sea, and with his Companions landed under the Cover of the Wall, and got into the Fort by Surprise[3], though he kept the Possession but a very little while; for the Governor of Berwick having an immediate Account of the Action, and resolving if possible to recover the Place before Errington could be supply'd with Men and Provisions, detach'd a Party of 30 Men of his Garrison, with about 50 Voluntiers of the Inhabitants, and marching over the Sands

[1] Warkworth was the place, and October 9 the date, at which the Chevalier was first proclaimed in England. The other Jacobite movements in England were comparatively trivial and were easily suppressed. Cf. *The Political State of Great Britain*, vol. x, 343 *et seq*.

[2] 'Master of a Ship at Newcastle.'—*R. 241*.

[3] In another account Errington is said to have been acquainted with the garrison, and to have inveigled its members on board his ship.—*Ibid*

at Low-water-mark, attack'd the Fort and took it Sword in Hand; Errington himself, attempting to make his Escape, was wounded and taken Prisoner with several others; he with his Brother afterwards got out of Berwick in Disguise. The Design of taking this Fort was, to give Signals to any Ships that seem'd to make to the Coast to land Soldiers; for by the Assurances they had from Friends beyond Sea, they expected them to land on that Coast with Supplies of Arms and Officers; but they never came till they were gone for Scotland, and then Two Ships appeared off at Sea, and made their Signal, but having no Answer from the Shore, made sail Northward.

The Rebellion was now formed, and they were all in a Body at Morpeth, promising themselves great things at Newcastle, and several Gentlemen joined them there, and several of the Country People came in and offer'd to List, but they still declined them, and prepared to march to Newcastle. But before they went, Mr Buxton the Clergyman, taking on himself the Office of a Herald as well as of a Churchman, Proclaimed the Pretender. They had a Party that went and seized the Post at Felton-Bridge, and one Thomas Gibson, a Blacksmith of New-castle, whom they apprehended and detained as a Spy, which it is thought he was from Alderman White of Newcastle, a zealous Gentleman for the Government; he afterwards became an Evidence against some of the Rebels at their Trials. Here it was that they receiv'd their first Disappointment, viz. in the Affair of Newcastle, which they expected should open its Gates to them; but finding some Delay in it, they promised themselves to have it in a few Days, and in the mean time they turned a little to the Westward and marched to Hexam, an ancient Town famous for its Privileges and Immunities and its once stately but now ruinous Cathedral, formerly for many Years a Bishop's Seat, of which three were Canoniz'd. This Town is distant from Morpeth 14 long Miles: Here they were join'd by some more Scots Horse. From this Town they all march'd, few or none knowing whither, and went three Miles distant to a Heath or Moor adjoining to Dilston, the Seat of the Lord Derwent-water, and there they made a Halt; this was with Design, as was thought, to go to Newcastle for the Surprize of that Town, which, as above, they hoped to have done sooner. It is certain they had a great many Friends there, and it was reported among them that Sir William Blackett would join them....

The Rebels that had gone out of Hexam to the Moor, as above, returned again to their Quarters, having certain Intelligence from some of their Friends in Newcastle, that even before any Regular Forces entred that Town, the Magistrates and Deputy-Lieutenants having first had some Suspicion, and soon after, positive Intelligence[1] of the Designs of the Rebels to surprise the Town, had effectually prevented it, and had taken all imaginable Precaution for their Security, raising immediately what Men they could, securing and imprisoning all Papists and suspected Persons, arming and encouraging the Inhabitants for their own Defence...so that the Town was full of Horses and Men, both Townsmen and Countrymen unanimously declaring for King GEORGE....

In the middle of this Hurry also, a Battalion of Foot and part of a Regiment of Dragoons being order'd out of Yorkshire for the Security of the Town, having made long Marches, they came to Newcastle, and then all their Fears vanished: But they were all farther eas'd of these Disorders a few Days after; for Lieutenant-General Carpenter having been ordered by the Government to go in Pursuit of the Rebels with Hotham's Regiment of Foot[2], Cobham's [1st], Molesworth's[3], and Churchill's[3] Dragoons, for which purpose he set out from London the 15th of October and arrived at Newcastle the 18th[4], where he began to prepare for attacking the Gentlemen at Hexam, waiting a little for the coming up of the Troops.... But the Rebels...staid there but three Days[5], tho' they were not idle during that time; for first they seized all the Arms and Horses they could lay their Hands on, especially such as belong'd

[1] 'Some say, from my Lord Justice Clerk at Edinburgh.'—R. 242.
[2] Raised July 1715, disbanded 1718.
[3] Disbanded November 1718.
[4] Part of Hotham's regiment reached Newcastle on October 9, and the rest of it with Cobham's dragoons arrived on the 12th, in advance of Carpenter.—R. 243.
[5] They left Hexham on October 19.—R. 256.

to those who were well-affected Subjects to the King. Next, here Mr Buxton went to the Minister of the Town and desired him or his Curate to read Prayers, commanding that in them he should mention the Pretender by Name as King James III. The Minister modestly declined it (for there was no speaking boldly to them), so Mr Buxton officiated and performed as usual.... The Night before they left the Town, they were all drawn round the Cross in the Market-Place, where the Pretender was proclaimed and the Proclamation fixed to the Cross, which remain'd there several Days after the Rebels were gone....

Here [at Hexham] the Rebels had notice of the Viscount Kenmure, Earls of Nithsdale, Carnwarth, and Wintoun, who had taken Arms in Nithsdale, Dumfries-shire, and other Places in the West of Scotland, having entred England to join them, and that they were come to Rothbury.

[For][1] the Viscount of Kenmure having received a Commission from the Earl of Mar to head the Pretender's Friends in the South Parts of Scotland, a Resolution was taken to raise a Rebellion there, about the same Time the Rebels took Arms in Northumberland; and for that End, several of the disaffected Nobility and Gentry in these Parts repaired to the Borders, and ...assembled in Parties at the Houses of some of their Friends, moving secretly from Place to Place, in order to put Matters in a Readiness for the speedy Execution of their traiterous Designs.

But their Motions and Designs were not kept so secret as not to be observ'd by some of their Neighbours: And on Saturday the 8th of October, when the People of Dumfries were conven'd in the Church, it being the Preparation for the Sacrament of the Lord's Supper, Mr Gilchrist, one of the Baillies, received a Letter from an honest Countryman, dated at Lockerbridge Hill, wherein he advis'd him of the Jacobite Design to surprize and take Possession of the Town next Day in time of the Sacrament; which being communicated to the Provost and some others, who supposing...this Alarm was only an Amusement, they made no further Use of it than only to double their Guards, and all things continued peaceable.

On Monday the 10th of October, the Inhabitants of the

[1] R. 246.

Parishes of Torthorrald[1] and Tinwal[2], having further Intelligence of the Enemy's Design, immediately put themselves in Arms and marched to Lockerbridge-hill, from whence they sent an Express to Dúmfries, to acquaint the Magistrates and Mr Robinson, Minister at Tinwal (who was there at the Time), and to offer their Service to the Town that Night if the Magistrates pleased. But the Magistrates, apprehending no Danger, sent an Express to tell them that they might retire to their Houses that Night, and to desire them to be in Readiness to come to their Assistance upon a Call: And accordingly, tho' some was for accepting their Offer, an Express was sent out, and they retired home.

Upon Tuesday the 11th of October early in the Morning, an Express from My Lord Justice Clerk arriv'd at Dumfries.... After this Letter was read, there was no longer Doubt of the Rebels Design to surprize Dumfries....And it being consider'd that there was a Rendezvous that Day of the fensible Men in the Stewartrie of Kircudbright at the Leaths-Moor, it was instantly resolved that four of their Number...should forthwith repair to that Place and desire the Gentlemen there met, with a competent Number of armed Men, to come into the Town that Night. And the Provincial Synod being to meet that Day, it was agreed that this should be kept secret till after Sermon.

Accordingly, these Gentlemen mounted their Horses without any Delay, and in a few Hours came to the Place of Rendezvous, where they met with the Deputy Lieutenants and several other Gentlemen; but many of the People were by that Time dismiss'd: So soon as they had communicated to those Gentlemen the Contents of the Letter, Expresses were sent to all Quarters ...requiring the fensible Men with their best Horses, Arms, and other Accoutrements, to repair to Dumfries next Day....

After Sermon, the People of Dumfries being appriz'd of the Rebels Design to seize that Place, they were instantly put in Arms, and suitable Precautions were taken for Defence of the Town against any sudden Attack. The Ministers of the neigh-

---

[1] James Gordon of Boytath, Captain.
[2] John Johnston in Syde, Captain.

bouring Parishes went out that Afternoon and return'd that
Night with their fensible Parishioners armed. Expresses were
also sent to the Loyal Gentlemen and People in the adjacent
Country, and the Town was provided next Day with a con-
siderable Body of armed Men from the several Parishes in
Nithsdale and Galloway, all Volunteers; and many more were
willing to come had they been provided with Arms. Nay, 'tis
very remarkable, that their Motions were so quick on this
Occasion, that...those who liv'd in the remotest Parts of the
Country, and were latest in getting the Alarm, were all in
Dumfries within two Days after....

Several Gentlemen and others who had good Information
came to the Place of Rendezvous on Wednesday, according to
the publick Intimation that was made for that Effect. And as
Sir William Johnston of Westerhall came there, he order'd his
Servants to follow him with seventeen stand of Arms for the
Use of his own Militia, which he had sent up that Morning, or
some short Time before, to Brado-Chappel, about half a Mile
from Lochmaben, to be lodg'd in the House of Mr John
Henderson of Bradeholm 'till he had Occasion for them. But
some Jacobite Gentlemen with the Lord Viscount Kenmure
and Earl of Carnwath, who were drawn together the Night
before at a Gentleman's House not far from thence, being
advis'd of these Arms, came up that Morning and seiz'd them.
Having thus got the Arms, which they very much wanted, and
being join'd by several of their Friends in these Bounds, they
took their Rout towards Moffat in Order to join the Earl of
Winton, who, with a Party of Lothian Gentlemen and their
Servants, about seventy in all, was then on his March to that
Place, where accordingly they met and quarter'd that Night....

About Eleven at Night, a Bank was beat thro' the Town
[Dumfries], and Intimation was made to all Townsmen and
Strangers who were provided with Horses, to appear in the
Streets with their best Horses and Arms by the next Beat of
the Drum.

Accordingly, next Morning[1] by one of the Clock, an Alarm
was given (which was certainly very surprizing to the most of
[1] Thursday, October 13.

the People, who were at that Time unacquainted with the
Occasion of it), and a considerable Body of Horse and Foot
drew up in the Streets, which were illuminated[1] for that Purpose,
all of 'em shewing their Readiness to march whithersoever there
might be use for their Service. But the Night was so very Dark
that it was judged impracticable for the Foot to march: And
therefore leaving those in the Town, the Horsemen march'd
out a little after three, arriv'd at Lochwood early in the Morning,
and returned again that same Forenoon with My Lord Lieutenant [the Marquess of Annandale]....

It would seem that the Rebels at Moffat were not as yet
appriz'd of the Posture of his Majesty's Friends at Dumfries,
nor so much as knew that they had any Intelligence of their
traiterous Design to surprize them: For, that same Forenoon,
they march'd out of Moffat and took their Rout directly towards
Dumfries, and about two a Clock were advanced within a Mile
and a Half of that Town, not doubting but in a short Time
they should be Masters of it: But here their Eyes were speedily
open'd to see their Disappointment; For James Robson, Servitor
to a Neighbouring Gentleman, whose Son was with them,
advis'd them that the Town was full of People well arm'd, who
were then in Readiness to give them a warm Reception. Upon
this Information the Rebels made a Stand to consult what
Measures were next to be taken, whether to make an Attack,
or to retire till their Number (which was now about 153 Horsemen well mounted) should be increas'd by the Accession of
others of their Party. 'Tis reported the Viscount of Kenmure
told them, that He doubted not but there were as brave Gentlemen there as himself, and therefore he would not go to Dumfries
that Day. Hereupon they retir'd to Lochmaben, where they
lodged that Night with Mr Paterson, one of the Bailies of
Dumfries, Mr Hunter, Chirurgion, and Mr Johnston, Post-
master there, who had been sent out to reconnoitre them. They

[1] From this Time till October 20th, all the Windows that look to
the Streets, &c., were illuminated the whole Nights over, as well as at
any publick Solemnity, for the Conveniency of the People in Arms,
and that they might observe the Motions of Disaffected Persons. The
Strangers had also free Quarters allow'd them.

treated their Prisoners civilly enough, and dismist them next Day, when the Town had set at Liberty three of their Friends who had been incarcerate there as suspected Jacobites.

As soon as the Enemy appear'd within Sight of the Town [Dumfries], My Lord Lieutenant, with Concurrence of the Magistrates and Gentlemen present, caus'd barricade all the Avenues, stop the High-Ways, cast up some Entrenchments for the present Necessity, reinforced all the Guards, and put the Men into a suitable Posture for making a vigorous Resistance in case of an Attack. And when it was known that the Rebels made a Stand, most of the Gentlemen, and the whole Body of Men there assembled in Arms, were animated with such Zeal and Courage that they would have gone out to encounter them in the Fields, and pursue them in their Retreat; Nay, all of them were clear for surprizing them next Morning in their Quarters at Lochmaben: The Lord Lovat[1] made offer of his Service to go at their Head; But my Lord Marquis [of Annandale] would not allow them to go out, judging it not expedient for the Reasons aftermention'd.

The next Day[2], there was a general Rendezvous at the Moat, both of the Horse and Foot, where they were review'd by my Lord Lieutenant....

My Lord Marquis being inform'd of the People's Discontent, because they were not allow'd to pursue the Rebels, on Saturday the 15th his Lordship was pleas'd to call for the Ministers then in Town to come up to his Chamber, where he made a long and pathetick Speech to this Purpose: Shewing, 'That he was very well pleas'd to observe the People's Zeal and Courage against the Enemy; But yet, that it would not [have] been expedient for him to have led them out against them that Day they appeared before the Town, nor even since that Time, In regard all he had got done was to appoint their Officers, who had not as yet had Time to view their Arms, whether they were sufficient

[1] Lord Lovat, 'who had been some Years out of the Kingdom, and was then returning to his own Country, arrived there [Dumfries] with five of his Friends and Servants,' on October 11.—R. 250. Cf. *Major Fraser's Manuscript*, vol. ii, 30.

[2] Friday, October 14.

or not; that they had no Field-Officers to command them, for which Cause he had written to the Duke of Argyle for Officers, Ammunition, and Arms; That a rash attack, before they knew their Officers and had their Arms in good Order, might endanger the whole Cause; That much depends on the first Success....' Moreover his Lordship added, 'That if the People would be patient till Things were in Order, he would go upon their Head and venture his Life and Estate in the Defence of our Religion, our King and Country.' And finally, his Lordship desired the Ministers to use their Endeavours to convince their People of the Reasonableness hereof, and of how much Importance it was to the Government to secure and Defend the Town of Dumfries, and to perswade them to rest satisfied till Things were in better Order.

This wise Speech (as the Event has proved it) was satisfying to many; and in the beginning of the following Week his Lordship review'd the People again at the Moat: And having desired the Ministers then on the Spot to wait upon him, he made a handsome Discourse (to the same Effect) to the several Companies, with which they declared their Satisfaction by several Huzza's.

But...we shall return and give some farther Account of the Rebels. On Thursday [October 13], when they entered into the Town of Lochmaben, they proclaim'd the Pretender there as their King. Upon their Approach, the People of that Place had put their Cattle in a Fold to make Room for their Horses; But the Beasts having broken the Fold, some of them drew home to the Town a little before Day: And a Townsman going to hunt one of them out of his Yard, call'd on his Dog named Help: Hereupon the Centries cry'd, Where? And apprehending it had been a Party from Dumfries to attack them, gave the Alarm to the Rebels, who got up in great Confusion....

On Friday they marched to Ecclefechan[1], where, after they had put up their Horses and secured their Arms (some say in the Prison-House), they instantly met with such another surprizing Alarm: For, Sir Patrick Maxwel of Springkell coming

[1] On their way thither, they formed their force into two squadrons, under the command, respectively, of the Earl of Winton and the Earl of Carnwath. Kenmure commanded in chief.—*P. H.* 35.

up with about fourteen Horsemen, they suppos'd it was a Party to attack them. Hereupon they call'd for their Trumpeter, their Horses, and Arms; but they could not be got on a sudden, which made them very uneasy and much out of Humor, until they perceiv'd that they were Friends who approach'd them.

On Saturday the 15th they marched to Langholme: And their Number being then increas'd to about 180, they proceeded on the 16th to Hawick, where they proclaim'd the Pretender and quarter'd that Night, resolving to penetrate farther into Tiviotdale (or Roxburgh-shire), being advis'd by some of their Friends, That the People of that Country were not at all in a Posture of Defence or Condition to resist them.

My Lord Duke of Roxburgh...having early Intelligence that the Jacobites in the South had formed a Design to take Arms and traverse that Country, his Grace,...as the best Expedient could be thought on to prevent them, ordered Sir William Bennet of Grubbet, Mr Cranstoun, Brother to my Lord Cranstoun, Mr Ker of Cavers, with several other Gentlemen then at Stirling, to return home with all Expedition and put that Shire in some posture of Defence. These Gentlemen accordingly left Stirling on the eleventh of October, and having an Order to get Arms out of the Castle of Edinburgh, came to Kelso on the thirteenth, and made it as tenable as the Shortness of the Time and Situation of the Place would allow.

[Kenmure's[1] force, meanwhile, was at Hawick. At this Place they were alarm'd, which raised some Disputes whether they should proceed. They agreed to return, but had an Express from Mr Forster, about two Miles from Hawick towards Langholm. This Messenger, Mr Duglass, had an Invitation from the Northumberland General to my Lord Kenmure and his Followers to meet him at Rothbury: So they faced about, and marched that Night [October 17] to Jedburgh. Here they received Intelligence of the Macintosh's crossing the Forth[2], and the Duke of Argyle's Resolution to attack them, which put them into mighty Pain how the Consequence would prove. It is to be observed that they were alarmed in marching to Jedburgh: Being late, their Advance Guard was surpriz'd by the Shouts of

[1] P. H. 35.   [2] Supra, p. 98.

one who called out, That the Grey Horse [Portmore's] were
ready to fall on them and had cut the Quarter-Master and those
with him into pieces. Those acquainted with the Quarter-Master
assured Lord Kenmure that he would by no means be so easily
ensnar'd, being better used to Military Affairs; so they continued their March and entred the Town without Opposition.
Here, as in most other Towns, they proclaimed the Pretender;
next Morning [October 18] proceeded to Rothbury, perhaps
such a March as few People are acquainted with, being very
mountainous, long, tedious, and marshy. From Rothbury they
dispatched Mr Burnett of Carlips to Hexam to Mr Forster, to
know his Mind, Whether he would come towards them, or
they should advance? He returned an Express, that he would
join them....Upon this News, but more especially on the aforesaid News of General Carpenter preparing to attack them, they
[Forster's force] march'd out of Hexam, Wednesday the 19th
of October, and making a long March, they joined them and
their Men that Night, and both of them next Day march'd to
Wooler, in the County of Northumberland. Here they rested
all Friday [October 21], where I[1], with some Men which I
had inlisted, being Keel-men, overtook them upon Rothbury
Forest....Here [at Wooler] Mr Errington brought them an
Account of the Highlanders being also coming to join them,
and that they were advanced to Dunse [on October 20], of
which a full Account has been given already. On this News
they march'd[2] for Kelso in Scotland....A little before they came
to Kelso they made a Halt upon a Moor; and there the Gentlemen, formed into Troops, were drawn out by themselves and
called over, not only by their Names but by their design'd Offices
for the several Troops: And it is to be observed, that to each
Troop they assigned Two Captains, being the only Way they
had to oblige so many Gentlemen. Whilst they were thus employed, there came some Townsmen from Kelso, and acquainted
the Rebels that Sir William Bennett of Grubbet, who had been
in Kelso and had barricado'd the Town, pretending to keep
Post there, had gone off in the Night with his Men, who were

[1] Patten acted as Forster's Chaplain.
[2] On October 22, early in the morning.—R. 267.

only Militia and Servants, and that they might enter the Town
without Opposition; so they continued their March, and crossing
the River Twede, tho' very deep at that time and rapid, they
entred the Town. The Highlanders came into the Town
presently after from the Scots Side, with their Bag-pipes playing,
led by old Macintosh, but they made a very indifferent Figure;
for the Rain and their long Marches had extremely fatigued them,
tho' their old Brigadier, who march'd at the Head of them,
appeared very well.

Next Day being Sunday the 23d of October, my Lord
Kenmure, having the chief Command in Scotland, ordered me
to preach at the Great Kirk of Kelso, and not at the Episcopal
Meeting-House, and gave further Orders that all the Men
should attend Divine Service. Mr Buxton read Prayers, and I
preached on these Words, Deut. xxi. 17, the latter part of the
Verse, The Right of the First-born is his....

Next Morning the Highlanders were drawn up in the Church-
yard, and so march'd in Order to the Market-place, with Colours
flying, Drums beating, and Bag-pipes playing, and there form'd
a Circle, the Lords and other Gentlemen standing in the Centre:
There was an inner Circle formed also by the Gentlemen
Voluntiers: Then Silence being enjoined, the Trumpet sounded;
after which the Pretender was proclaimed by one Seaton Barnes,
who assum'd the Title of Earl of Dumferling[1]....

Then the Highlanders returned to their Quarters, where they
continued till Thursday [October 27]; during which time
nothing material happened, but that they failed not here, as well
as in all Places, to demand all the Publick Revenues, viz. of
Excise, Customs, or Taxes, and to search for Arms, of which
they found very few, unless some small Pieces of Cannon of
different Size and Shape, which formerly belonged to Hume-
Castle, and had been employ'd in former Ages in that strong-
Hold against the English, but were at this time brought thence
by Sir William Bennet aforesaid, to be placed at the Barricadoes
which he had made in the Streets leading to the Market-Place:

---

[1] The Earldom of Dunfermline had lapsed in 1690, upon the
attainder of James Seton, the fourth Earl.

They likewise found some broad Swords hid in the Church, and a small Quantity of Gunpowder....

Before I leave this Town, I shall give some Account of what Force the Rebel-Troops now consisted, as well because they were more in Number at that time, and better armed Men, than at any time after; as also because so many different Accounts of their Numbers have been made publick, that it is not easy to know what may be depended upon. The Lord Viscount Kenmure...had a Troop of Gentlemen with him, which, as he was General, was call'd the First Troop, the Command of which he gave to the Honourable Bazil Hamilton of Beldoun [Baldoon], Son to the Lord Bazil Hamilton, Brother to the late Duke Hamilton....

The Second Troop was called the Merse-Troop, commanded by the Honourable James Hume, Esq., Brother to the Earl of Hume, who at that time was Prisoner in Edinburgh Castle....

The Third Troop [was] call'd the Earl of Wintoun's Troop, and commanded by himself....The Command of this Troop he assigned, under himself, to Captain James Dalziel, Brother to the Earl of Carnwath, who had been in King GEORGE's Service formerly....

The Fourth Troop belonged to Robert Dalziel, Earl of Carnwath....The Command of this Troop he gave over to his Uncle, James Dalziel Esq....

The Fifth Troop was under the Command of Captain Lockart, Brother to Mr Lockart of Carnwath....This Troop was composed of several Servants belonging to the Laird of Carnwath, besides several of his own Horses: The Men were payd by Mr Auxton, a Merchant of Edinburgh, who was intrusted in all Mr Lockart's Concerns....

These Troops were well Mann'd and indifferently Arm'd, but many of the Horses small and in mean Condition: Besides these Troops, there were a great many Gentlemen Voluntiers who were not formed into any regular Troop.

The Foot designed to cross the Forth[1] were Regimented under these Colonels, being Six Regiments in all.

The First, the Earl of Strathmore's; but he and his Lieutenant-

<hr />

[1] i.e. Mackintosh's command.

Colonel Walkinshaw of Barrowfield were forced back in their Passage by the King's Men of War, with several others, and obliged to go on Shore in the Isle of May[1]. This Regiment was not in Highland-Dress as the others were....

The Second Regiment was the Earl of Mar's...His Regiment came not entire over the Forth; for...the rest were driven back by the King's Men of War upon the Coast of Fife.

The Third [was] Logie Drummond's. This Regiment came not entire over the Forth, being driven back on the Fife-side with many more; for of the 2500 designed to cross the Forth, the better Half were prevented....

The Fourth [was] the Lord Nairn's, Brother to the Duke of Athol....

The Fifth Regiment was commanded by Lord Charles Murray, a younger Son of the Duke of Athol's....

The Sixth Regiment was called Macintosh's Battalion, a Relation of the Brigadier's....

Besides these Six Regiments...there were a considerable Number called The Gentlemen Voluntiers, commanded by Captain Skeen and Captain Mac-Lean, Lieutenant David Stewart, and Ensign John Dunbar, formerly an Exciseman.

The English were not altogether so well regulated nor so well armed as the Scots. The Troops were these:

First, the Earl of Derwentwater's, commanded by his Brother Charles Radcliffe Esq., and Captain John Shaftoe....

The Second Troop was the Lord Widdrington's, commanded by Mr Thomas Errington of Beaufront....

The Third Troop was commanded by Captain John Hunter, born upon the River North-Tyne in the County of Northumberland....

The Fourth Troop was commanded by Robert Douglass, Brother to the Laird of Fin[g]land in Scotland....

The Fifth Troop was commanded by Captain Nicholas Wogan, an Irish Gentleman, but descended from an ancient Family of that Name in Wales; he joined the Rebels at their first Meeting....

Having thus given an Account of their Troops and Foot

[1] *Supra*, p. 90.

Regiments, which might then amount to 1400[1], I shall give a farther Account of their Marches, and what happened in the Way, till I bring them to the Place of Action.

Having continued in Kelso so long as they did, which was from Saturday the 22d to Thursday the 27th of October, it gave General Carpenter, who, as is said, was sent down to pursue them, the Advantage of Time to advance by the easier Marches, and to observe their Motions: That General...had march'd from Newcastle, and lay now at Wooler the 27th, intending to face Kelso the next Day; of which Lord Kenmure...having notice, called a Council of War, wherein it was seriously considered what Course they should take. And here again my Lord Wintoun...press'd them earnestly to march away into the West of Scotland; but the English opposed and prevailed against that wiser Opinion[2]: Then it was proposed to pass the Twede and attack the King's Troops [under Carpenter]....This also was Soldier-like Advice, and which if they had agreed to, in all Probability they might have worsted them, considering how they were fatigued, and not half the number the Rebels were[3]. But there was a Fate attended all their Councils, for they could never agree to any one thing that tended to their Advantage. This Design failing, they decamped from Kelso, and taking a little to the Right[4], marched to Jedburgh....They stay'd in this Town till Saturday the 29th: And here it being apparent that

[1] Rae computes the united force at fourteen hundred foot and six hundred horse, 'whereof about 200 were menial Servants.'—*R.* 268.

[2] Mackintosh supported Wintoun in his proposal to join hands with the Clans in Argyllshire, and to attack Dumfries and Glasgow in their way thither.—*R.* 269.

[3] According to Rae, Carpenter had not above nine hundred men; while two regiments of dragoons under his command were newly raised and had never seen active service.—*Ibid.*

[4] Rae adds [p. 270] that the foot 'kept the ordinary Road' between Kelso and Jedburgh, and that they observed on 'Forniton' [? Fairning-ton] Moor a party of their own men whom they mistook for Carpenter's force. Presumably, therefore, they followed the main road from Kelso to Maxton, which runs along the south bank of the Tweed, and then, bearing south-east, crosses the Teviot at Ancrum towards Jedburgh.

an Opportunity offering to get the Start of General Carpenter, who would be three Days March behind, and the English Gentlemen earnestly pressing, it was resolv'd, in an ill Hour for them, to cross the Mountains and march for England....

But here began a Mutiny; the Highlanders could not be perswaded to cross the Borders, and tho' many Perswasions were used with them, would not stir a foot. Hereupon the first Resolution was altered....From hence they marched to Hawick. ...Upon this March to Hawick, the Highlanders, supposing still that the March for England was resolv'd on, were disgusted, separated themselves, and went to the Top of a rising Ground, there rested their Arms, and declared that they would fight if they would lead them on to the Enemy, but they would not go to England, adhering to the Lord Wintoun's Advice, that they would go through the West of Scotland, join the Clans there, and either cross the Forth some Miles above Sterling, or send word to the Earl of Mar that they would fall upon the Duke of Argyle's Rear whilst he fell on his Front, his Number being then very small....This Breach held a great while[1]; however, at last they were brought to this, tho' not 'till after two Hours Debate, that they would keep together as long as they stay'd in Scotland, but upon any Motion of going for England they would return back: So they continued their March to Hawick, where they were sore straitned for Quarters....Next morning, being Sunday [October 30], they made their March to Langholme.... From hence there was a strong Detachment of Horse[2] sent in the Night for Achilfichan [Ecclefechan], with Orders to go and block up Dumfreis till they could come up and attack it....But ...the English Gentlemen were positive for an Attempt upon their own Country...and urged the Advantages of a speedy

[1] 'Upon this Dispute, the Horse surrounded the Foot, in order to force them to march South; whereupon the Highlanders cocked their Firelocks and said, if they were to be made a Sacrifice, they would choose to have it done in their own Country...[and] would allow none to come speak with them but the Earl of Wintoun, who had tutor'd them in this Project.'—R. 271.

[2] About four hundred, under the Earl of Carnwath's command.— R. 275.

March into England with such Vehemence that they turn'd the
Scale, and sent an Express after the Party of Horse they had
order'd to Achilfichan for them to return and meet them at
Langtoun in Cumberland.

So the Design of continuing in Scotland was quitted. But the
Highlanders, whether dealt with underhand by the Earl of
Wintoun, or whether being convinced of the Advantages they
were going to throw away and the Uncertainties they were
bringing upon themselves, halted a second time, and would
march no farther. It is true they did again prevail with their
Leaders to march, making great Promises and giving Money to
the Men: But many of the Men were still positive, and that to
such an Extremity that they separated, and about 500 of them
went off in Bodies[1], chusing rather, as they said, to surrender
themselves Prisoners than to go forward to certain Destruction.
...The Earl of Wintoun went off likewise with good part of his
Troop, being very much dissatisfy'd at the Measures, and
declaring that they were taking the way to ruin themselves:
However, in a little time he return'd and join'd the Body, tho'
not at all satisfied with their Proceedings, and afterwards was
never called to any Council of War, which incensed him mightily
against the rest of the Lords and Commanding Officers....

They left the small Pieces of Cannon which they had brought
from Kelso at Langholm, having nailed them up and made them
unfit for Service; then they marched for that Night [October 31]
to Longtoun, which is within seven Miles of Carlisle, and was
a very long and fatiguing March. Here they had Intelligence
that Brigadier Stanwix, with a Party of Horse from Carlisle,
had been there that Day to get Intelligence of their Numbers
and Motions; but that upon notice of their coming towards him,
he had retired to his Garrison, which then consisted of but a very
few Men....This Night the Party ordered to Achilfichan returned and join'd us, sore fatigued with their long and dismal

[1] This large body made off through the moors by Lockerbie and
Moffat. Then, dividing into parties near Crawford, some of them made
towards Douglas, and others towards Lamington. In the neighbourhood
of those places, and at Sanquhar, about three hundred of them were
made prisoners and sent to Glasgow.—*R.* 278.

March. Next Day [November 1] they entered England and marched to Brampton, a small Market-Town, and the second they came to on the English side, belonging to the Earl of Carlisle. Here nothing happened but proclaiming the Pretender, and taking up the Publick Money, viz. the Excise upon Malt and Ale. Here Mr Forster opened his Commission to act as General in England, which had been brought him from the Earl of Mar by Mr Douglass aforenam'd: And from this Day the Highlanders had Sixpence a Head per Day payed them to keep them in good Order and under Command....

They halted one Night at Brampton to refresh the Men after their hard Marches, having march'd above 100 Miles in five Days. The next Day [November 2] they advanced towards Penrith....As they drew near Penrith, they had notice that the Sheriff with the *Posse Comitatus* were got together, with the Lord Lonsdale and the Bishop of Carlisle, to the Number of 14,000 Men[1], who resolv'd to stand and oppose their penetrating farther into England....But they gave the Rebel Army no occasion to try whether they would stand or no; for as soon as a Party, who they sent [out] for Discovery, had seen some of our Men coming out of a Lane by the side of a Wood, and draw up upon a Common or Moor in Order and then advance, and that they had carried an Account of this to their Main Body, they broke up their Camp in the utmost Confusion, shifting every one for themselves as well as they could, as is generally the Case of an arm'd but undisciplin'd Multitude....

Having stay'd at Penrith that Night[2], as is said, refresh'd themselves very well, the next Day they march'd for Appleby. It is to be observ'd that there were none of any Account had yet join'd them on this March[3]; for all the Papists on that

[1] Clearly an exaggeration; though Clarke places their number so high as twenty-five thousand men.

[2] They entered Penrith about three o'clock on the afternoon of the 2nd, proclaimed the Chevalier, and collected the excise.—*P. C.*

[3] 'Only one man joyned them in their march from Penrith to Apleby. This man stole a horse about one houre before he joyned them, and diserted from them the next day, and at August Asizes 1716 was found guilty and executed at Apleby for stealing the said horse.'—*P. C.*

Side the Country were secured before-hand in the Castle of Carlisle....

Being come to Appleby the 3d of November, they halted again, and stay'd there till the 5th....Here, during their Stay, nothing material happen'd but as usual, Proclaiming the Pretender and taking up the Publick Money....

On the 5th they set out for Kendal, a Town of very good Trade.

About[1] 12 a'clock of the same day [Saturday, November 5], 6 quartermasters came into the towne of Kendall, and about 2 aclock in the afternoone, Brigadeer Mackintoss and his man came both a horseback, having both plads on, their targets hanging on their backs, either of them a sord by his side, as also either a gun and a case of pistols. The said Brigadeere looked with a grim countenance. He and his man lodged at Alderman Lowrys, a private house in Highgate street in this towne.

About one houre after came in the horsemen and the footmen at the latter end. It rained very hard here this day, and had for several days before, so that the horse and the footmen did not draw their swords nor shew their collours, neither did any drums beat. Onely six highland bagpipes played. They marched to the coldstone, or the cross, and read the same proclamation twice over in English, and the reader of it spoke very good English, without any mixture of Scotish tongue.

I had for about one month lived [in this towne], and was clerke to Mr Craikenthorpe, attorney at Law, and as a spectator I went to heare the proclamation read, which I believe was in print and began after this manner, viz[t]: Whereas George Elector of Brunswick has usurped and taken upon him the stile of the king of these realms, etc. Another clause in it I tooke particular notice of, which was this, viz[t]: Did imedietly after his said fathers decease become our only and lawful leige. At the end of the proclamation they gave a great shout. A Quaker who stood next to me not puting of his hat at the end of the said ceremony, a highlander thurst a halbert at him, but it fortunatly went between me and him, so that it did neither of us any damage. So they dispersed.

[1] *P. C.*

In this towne the Earl Derwentwater and his servant lodged at Mr Fletcher's, the signe of the White Lyon in Strickland Gate, the other lords at Mr Thomas Rawlandsons, who was at that time the mayor of that towne, and kept the signe of Kings Armes in the street above named. Thomas Foster Esquire, then stiled Generall Foster, lodged at Alderman Simpsons, a private house in the said street.

They compeled the belman here to go and give notice to the tanners and inkeepers to come and pay what excise was due to the crown, or else they that denyed should be plundred by Jack the highlander. They received of the innkeepers and tanners here the summe of eighty pounds and some od shillings, and gave receipts to each person.

About six o'clock this night, the mayor was taken into custody for not telling where the malitia armes were hid (the said mayor was a leivetenant in the malitia). But next morning Mr Crosby, the minister of this towne, went to Earl Derwentwater and Thomas Foster, and got the mayor discharged out of custody.

Madam Belingham (who was godmother to Thomas Foster) and tabled in Mr Simpsons house, wood not admitt her said godson to see her, and he going upstairs for that intent, she met him on the stairs, gave him two or three boxes on the eare, called him a rebel and a popish toole, which he tooke patiently.

They made the gunsmiths here work very hard all night, and a Sunday morning likewise, for little or no pay.

In the house where I lived, two Northumberland gentlemen stiled captains lodged, who behaved themselves very civily.

Some malitious persons had falsely reported that the malitia armes were in the church, and on Sunday morning some of the highlanders broke into the church in expectation of finding armes there. They also went into the vestry in the church. The plate and ornaments belonging to the said church were in the vestry, but finding no armes there, returned without taking any of the plate.

In this towne the horse gentlemen paid their quarters, but the foot highlanders paid little or nothing; and about 8 a clock this morning, the foot marched out, no drums beating nor collours flying, only the bagpipers playing. Most of the horsemen waited at Foster's quarters. I stood close to Mr Simpson's doore, and the six lords, Brigadeere Mackintosse, and Thomas Foster had their hats in their hands. The Brigadeere looked still with a grim countenance, but the lords, Foster, and most of the other horsemen were dishartned and full of sorrow.

About 9 aclock the same morning they marched out of the towne, but not in ranks.

A jorniman weaver joyned them here.

[Leaving[1] Kendal on] Sunday the 6th, they set forward for Kirbylonsdale, a small Market-town in Westmorland. This Day's March was short, so they came early to their Quarters, and had time to proclaim the Pretender, and in the Afternoon to go to Church, where Mr Patten read Prayers, the Parson of the Place absconding. There was one Mr Guin who went into the Churches in their Way, and scratched out His Majesty King GEORGE's Name, and placed the Pretender's so nicely, that it resembled Print very much, and the Alteration could scarce be perceived. In all the March to this Town, which is the last in Westmorland, there were none joined them but one Mr John Dalton and another Gentleman from Richmond, tho' we had now march'd through two very populous Counties; but here Friends began to appear, for some Lancashire Papists with their Servants came and join'd them[2]. Next Day, being the 7th of November, they marched to Lancaster, a Town of very good Trade, very pleasantly seated, and which, had they thought fit to have held it, might easily have been made strong enough to have made a Stand for them; and having an old Castle for their Arms, Stores, and Provisions, and a Sea-Port to have received Succours, it might have been very useful to them; but our Infatuations were not yet over.

In the March from Kendal to Lancaster the whole Army drew up upon a Hill, and lay some time upon their Arms to

[1] *P. H.* 90.

[2] 'Esquire Carus and his two sons, Thomas and Christopher, all papists, who lived at Hatton Hall, joyned them at this towne. It was this Carus that first brought them word that the towne of Lancaster had left of making any preparations for a defence, so they marched for Lancaster.' —*P. C.*

rest the Men. During which time, Mr Charles Widdrington, second Brother to the Lord Widdrington, came from Lancashire, whither he was sent some Days before the Rebels advanc'd, to acquaint the Gentlemen of that County with their marching that Way; he returned with the News of their Cheerfulness and Intention to join them with all their Interest, and that the Pretender was that Day proclaimed at Manchester, where the Town's-People had got Arms to furnish a Troop of Fifty Men at their sole Charge, besides other Voluntiers. This rouzed the Spirits of the Highlanders and animated them exceedingly; nor was it more than needed, for they had often complained before, that all the Pretences of Numbers to join were come to little, and that they should soon be surrounded by numerous Forces. But on this News they pluck'd up their Hearts, gave three Huzza's, and then continued their March into Lancaster. Colonel Chartres, and another Officer who was then in the Town, would have blown up the Bridge which leads into the Place, to hinder us from entring[1]; but the People of the Town shewing their Unwillingness, and especially because, as they said, it would no wise hinder our Entrance into the Place, seeing the River at Low-Water was passable by Foot or Horse, and that we could easily find Boats to pass into the Town, and that as it would be a vast Charge to rebuild the Bridge so strong and fine as before, so it would be a Loss to no manner of End. Then these two Gentlemen, finding a Quantity of Powder in some Merchants[2] Hands, order'd it to be thrown into a Draw-well in the Market-place, lest it should fall into our Hands....

At this time there were some Dragoons in Preston, who were advis'd to advance to Lancaster; but having no Orders for that

[1] 'The inhabitants of that towne had taken up the pavement of the bridge and the side of the north arch of Lancaster bridge. This towne wood have oposed the Earl Derwentwater and his men, and, for that purpose, the inhabitants intended to fetch the 6 guns belonging to the Merchants there, which were at Sunderland, in a ship called the *Robert*, if Sir Henry Houghton, colonel of the malitia, and who was at Preston with his men, had come to Lancaster.'—*P. C.* Some of the approaches to the town were also flooded, to hinder the insurgents' approach.— *R.* 317.   [2] Samuel Saterthwaite.—*P. C.*

March, continued there 'till they were order'd to Wigan. Upon this, Sir Henry Haughton[1] having Intelligence that the Rebels were within 16 Miles of him, he went from Lancaster with 600 Militia, and with them retired to Preston. Before he left Lancaster, finding that the Cannon...could be of no Use to him, having not a sufficient Number of Men to cover that Town, he order'd Mr Lawson[2] to fall down the River with his Vessel out of the reach of the Rebels, so that his Cannon might not fall into their hands. Which Mr Lawson did not obey; for the Rebels having entred Preston, they had Intelligence, by a Gentleman of no mean figure, of the Cannon and of all that passed in the Town.

After all this, as said, we entred[3] the Town [Lancaster] without Opposition in very good Order, and march'd to the Market-place, where the whole Body was drawn up round the Cross, and there with sound of Trumpet Proclaimed the Pretender: Then the Men were Billeted and Quartered in every part of the town, which was very well able to entertain them all....

They continued at Lancaster from Monday the 7th to Wednesday the 9th, during which time they seized some new Arms which were in the Custom-House, and some Claret and a good Quantity of Brandy, which was all given to the Highlanders to oblige them: They likewise took up all the Money belonging to the Revenue which was either in the Excise-Office or Custom-House, six Pieces of Cannon[4], which they seized and mounted upon new Carriages (the Wheels that mounted these Cannon belonged to Sir Henry Haughton's Coaches) and carried them to Preston; of which hereafter. During their Stay at Lancaster they had Prayers read in this Church by Mr Patten, the Parson of the Place[5] excusing himself....

It was time now to advance and open the Way for their other

[1] M.P. for Preston.

[2] He was part-owner of the *Robert*, a ship in the river, whose guns Sir Henry Houghton had tried unsuccessfully to obtain.

[3] About one o'clock in the afternoon of November 7.—*P. C.*

[4] They were the guns from the *Robert*.

[5] James Fenton.—*P. C.*

Friends to come in; for as they had News daily of Troops
gathering to oppose them, it was time to extend themselves that
they might join all those who had promised their Assistance. To
this end they moved from Lancaster, taking the Road to Preston,
and designing to possess themselves of Warrington-Bridge and
of the Town of Manchester, where they had Assurances of
great Numbers to join them, and by this means they made no
doubt of securing the great and rich Town of Leverpool, which
would be cut off from any Relief if they were once possess'd of
Warrington-Bridge. According to these Measures the Horse
reach'd Preston that Night; The Day proving Rainy and the
Ways Deep, they left the Foot at a small Market-Town called
Garstang, half-way between Lancaster and Preston....The
Horse, as is said, entred Preston that Night, and found that two
Troops of [Colonel William] Stanhope's Dragoons[1], formerly
quartered there, had removed upon their Approach. This
encouraged them exceedingly, and made them imagine that the
King's Forces would not look them in the Face. The Foot
coming up next Day, being Thursday the 10th of November,
they marched straight to the Cross, and were there drawn up as
usual whilst the Pretender was proclaimed. Here they were also
joined by a great many Gentlemen[2], with their Tenants,
Servants and Attendants, and some of very good Figure in the
Country, but still all Papists....

Mr Forster spared neither Pains nor Cost to be acquainted
with all General Carpenter's Motions, of which he had constant
and particular Accounts every Day, and sometimes twice a Day;
but the Lancashire Gentlemen gave him such Assurances that
no Force could come near them by Forty Miles but they could
inform him thereof, this made him perfectly easy on that side,
relying entirely on the Intelligence he expected from them:
And therefore, when on the Saturday Morning [November 12]

[1] The regiment was reduced in 1718.

[2] 'Esquire Townley, a papist, joyned them here, and Mr Shuttleworth,
who lived in Preston, as also did aboundance of Roman Catholicks.

The laydys in this towne, Preston, are so very beautyfull and so richly
atired, that the gentlemen soldiers from Wednesday to Saturday minded
nothing but courting and feasting.'—*P. C.*

he had given Orders for his whole Army to march from Preston towards Manchester, it was extremely surprising, and he could scarce credit the Reports, that General Wills was advancing from Wigan to attack them[1]....

The Alarm being now given, a Body of the Rebels marched out of the Town as far as Ribble-Bridge, posting themselves there[2], and Mr Forster with a Party of Horse went beyond it to get a certain Account of Things; when, discovering the Vanguard of the Dragoons, he returned another Way, not coming back by the Bridge. He ordered Mr Patten with all haste to ride back and give an Account of the Approach of the King's Army, and to give Orders to prepare to receive them, whilst he went to view a Ford in the River, in order for a Passage to come behind them. The Foot that were advanced to the Bridge were about an 100; but they were choice, stout, and well-armed Men, and commanded by Lieutenant-Colonel John Farquharson of Innercall, belonging to Macintosh's Battalion: He was a good Officer and a very bold Man, and would have defended that important Pass of the Bridge to the last Drop, and till the rest had advanced and drawn themselves out of the Town; but he was order'd to retreat to Preston. This Retreat was another wrong step....As for the Bridge, they might have barricado'd it so well, that it would have been impracticable to have pass'd there, or to have

---

[1] General Wills, who commanded the troops in Cheshire, marched from Manchester to Wigan on the 11th with the cavalry regiments of Wynne [9th Dragoons], Honywood [11th Dragoons], Munden [13th Dragoons], Dormer [14th Dragoons], and Preston's regiment of foot [The Cameronians]. Pitt's [H.R.H. The Princess of Wales' Own] and Stanhope's [reduced 1718] cavalry regiments awaited him at Wigan. Newton's dragoons [disbanded in 1718], who were marching from Worcester to join him, were ordered to remain at Manchester. Wills arrived at Ribble Bridge about one p.m. on Saturday, November 12. —*R. 318.*

[2] The detachment consisted of about three hundred horse and foot, and took up its position at Ribble Bridge about eleven o'clock; 'but about one hour after, Generall Wills and his men came into Walton in Le dale, neare unto the said Rible Bridge, [and] the said Earl Derwentwaters men retired into Preston.'—*P. C.*

dislodged them from it; also they had Cannon, which General Wills wanted....

General Wills did indeed expect some Difficulty and Opposition at this Place...but understanding by his Advance-Guard that the Rebels had abandon'd that Post, he was surprized, and suspected that then they had some Stratagem in hand, and perhaps had lined the Hedges and so made the Lane unpassable for his Men. The Lane is indeed very Deep, and so narrow that in several Places two Men cannot ride a-breast. This is that famous Lane at the end of which Oliver Cromwell met with a stout Resistance from the King's Forces, who from the Height rolled down upon him and his Men (when they had entred the Lane) huge large Mill-stones; and if Oliver himself had not forced his Horse to jump into a Quick-Sand, he had luckily ended his Days there[1]. General Wills, on these Suppositions, proceeded with Caution, and caused the Hedges and Fields to be view'd, and the Ways laid open for his Cavalry to enter; but finding the Hedges also clear, he concluded then the Enemy was fled, and expected that they had abandon'd the Town and all, and would endeavour by their long Marches to return to Scotland, tho' he thought it impossible for them to do it. But he was soon inform'd that they were retreated to the Town only, and that they resolv'd to receive him there with a resolute Countenance; so he had nothing to do but to prepare for the Attack, which he went about immediately. Having advanced nearer the Town, he ordered his Troops to pass at a Gate which leads into the Fields which lie on the back of the Town, and immediately spreading the Enclosures with the utmost Expedition and Diligence, so disposed of his Forces as best to be able both to attack them in the Town, and to prevent them from Sallying or making a Retreat[2].

[1] There is no hint of this incident in the authorities for the battle.

[2] Wills arranged for two attacks from opposite ends of the town. Upon the Wigan side, Brigadier Honywood was stationed in command of his own dragoons, Preston's foot, commanded by Lord Forrester, and two hundred and fifty dismounted cavalry, besides officers. Upon the Lancaster side, Wynne's and Dormer's regiments and a squadron of Stanhope's were ordered to dismount. The regiments of Pitt, Munden,

During this time the Rebels were not idle in the Town, nor did they appear in the least discouraged, but applied themselves resolutely to their Business, barricadoing the Streets, and posting their Men in the Streets, bye-Lanes, and Houses, to the greatest Advantage for all Events. The Gentlemen-Voluntiers were drawn up in the Church-yard, under the Command of the Earl of Derwentwater, Viscount Kenmure, Earls of Wintoun and Nithsdale. The Earl of Derwentwater signally behav'd, having stript into his Waistcoat, and encouraged the Men by giving them Money to cast up Trenches, and animating them to a vigorous Defence of them: When he had so done, he order'd Mr Patten to bring him constantly an Account from all the Attacks, how things went, and where Succours were wanted; which Mr Patten did 'till his Horse was shot under him. The Rebels formed four main Barriers; one, a little below the Church, commanded by Brigadier Macintosh; the Gentlemen in the Church-yard were to support that Barrier in particular, and Lord Charles Murray that which was at the end of a Lane leading to the Fields: The third Barrier was called the Windmill; this was commanded by Colonel Macintosh: And the fourth was in the Street which leads towards Leverpool, commanded by Major Miller and Mr Douglass. The three former were all attack'd with great Fury by His Majesty's Forces: The first Attack was made upon that Barrier below the Church[1], commanded by Brigadier Mackintosh; but they met with such a Reception, and so terrible a Fire was made upon them, as well from the Barricado as from the Houses on both sides, that they were obliged to retreat back to the Entrance of the Town. During the Heat of this Action, some of Preston's Officers being inform'd that the Street leading to Wigan was not barricado'd, and that the Houses were not possess'd on that side, they presently

and a squadron of Stanhope's remained on horseback. Brigadiers James Dormer and Richard Munden were in command.—*R.* 319.

[1] 'About 2 a clock this afternoone, 200 of Generall Wills men entred the Churchgate street, and the Highlanders, firing out of the cellers and windows, in 10 minuits time kiled 120 of them. The Highlanders also fired the said 2 ship guns, but the bulletts flew upon the houses, so that no execution was done thereby.'—*P. C.*

entred that Street with great Bravery, pushing all before them. Preston's Regiment of Foot were commanded upon this Service, supported by Honnywood's Dragoons. It is true the Rebels had at first taken Possession of that Street and posted Men in the Houses on both sides, but were, against their Inclination, called off to other Service; nor were they left, as some desir'd, to post themselves at the extreamest Ends of the Town, even at that End which leads to the Bridge, where the first and hottest Attack was made. Several Houses were left, particularly one which belonged to Sir Henry Haughton: Captain Innis with Fifty Highlanders had taken Possession of this House, and had he been allowed to have continued there, he would have given a good Account of it; but he being obliged to leave that Post, some of Preston's Men got Possession of that too, tho' it cost them dear, for many of their Men were kill'd there from other Houses. It is a high House over-looking the whole Town: There was also another House opposite to it, which they entred, and posted several of their Men in it. And from these two Houses came almost all the Loss the Rebels sustained during the Action. Mr Forster cannot be blamed for this Oversight, but it must be charged upon the Brigadier, who, when the Regiment of Preston's Foot made this brave and bold Attack and Attempt, withdrew his Men from those Houses. The Attack was thus— Preston's Men, led by their Lieutenant-Colonel the Lord Forrester, did not come up the Head of the Street, but marched into a straight Passage behind the Houses, and then made a Halt 'till their Lieutenant-Colonel the Lord Forrester came into the open Street with his drawn Sword in his Hand, and faced Macintosh's Barrier, looking up the Street and down the Street, and viewing how they were posted. There were many Shots fired at him, but he returned to his Men and came up again at the Head of them into the middle of the Street, where he caused some to face the Barricade where the Brigadier was posted and ply them with their Shot, at the same time commanding another Party to march cross the Streets to take Possession of those Houses. It was a very desperate Attempt, and shews him an Officer of an undaunted Courage. Whilst this was doing, the Rebels, from the Barrier and from the Houses on both sides, made a terrible Fire upon them, and a great many of that old and gallant Regiment were killed and wounded: The Lord Forrester received several Wounds himself. Besides the Damage they received on that side, they were sore galled from some Windows below them, by Captain Douglass and Captain Hunter's Men. Preston's Foot fired smartly upon the Rebels, but did little Execution, the Men being generally cover'd from the Shot, and delivering their own Shot securely and with good Aim; yet some were kill'd and some also wounded....

The next Barrier which was attack'd was commanded by Lord Charles Murray: He behav'd very gallantly, but being very vigorously attack'd, wanted Men, and order'd Mr Patten to acquaint the Earl of Derwentwater therewith; who immediately sent back Mr Patten with Fifty Gentlemen Voluntiers from the Church-yard to reinforce him, who came in very good season. Immediately Mr Patten was order'd over the Barrier to view the King's Forces, who, appearing in a Clergyman's Habit, was not suspected nor fired on. He soon returned back and gave Lord Charles an Account, that by what he saw, they were resolved to attack him again; whereupon Lord Charles gave Orders to his Men to be ready to receive them, and accordingly they came on very furiously: And tho' the King's Forces that made this Attack were for the most part raw, new-listed Men, and seem'd unwilling to fight, yet the Bravery and good Conduct of experienc'd Officers supply'd very much that Defect. However, Lord Charles Murray maintain'd the Post, and oblig'd them to retreat with Loss; nor had they been all old Soldiers could they have beaten Lord Charles from that Barrier, which was very strong; the Number they had slain from the Barn-holes and Barrier it self added very much, so that at last the Officers themselves thought fit to give it over....

Hitherto the Rebels seem'd to have had some Advantage, having repulsed the King's Forces in all their Attacks, and maintained all their Posts; and Night drawing on, no new Action happen'd; but during all this time, and all Saturday-Night and Sunday, and a good part of that Night, the King's Forces kept incessantly Plattoons firing upon the Rebels from Sir Henry Haughton's and Mr Ayre's Houses....There were several Houses

and Barns set on fire by both Parties, both for covering them-
selves among the Smoak and dislodging Men; so that if the
Wind had blown almost from any Quarter[1] that Town had
been burnt to the Ground, and the Rebels had been burnt to
Ashes in it. I shall, as I design'd, impartially hint at all the
Mistakes on both Sides, and this was one—the King's General
had order'd Illuminations to be set in all the Windows of the
Houses where they had possession, which, as long as they continued burning, exposed the Rebels that were crossing the
Streets upon all Occasions to the plain view of those possessed
of the Houses aforesaid, and gave them a good Aim at their
Mark. This was the Occasion of the Death of some and Wounds
of others, even on both Sides; so that after a short time, Orders
were given for some to go to all the Houses and call aloud to the
People to put out their Candles. Which being shouted aloud (as
is said) in the Streets, for the People had shut all their Doors,
they mistook the Command, and instead of putting out or ex-
tinguishing their Lights, set up more, which amused both Sides,
but did no harm to either.

The third Attack was at the Windmill in the Street which
leads to Lancaster, where the Barrier was defended by near 300
Men under the Command of Mr Macintosh, who, with his
Men, behaved very boldly, and made a dreadful Fire upon the
King's Forces, killing many on the spot, and obliging them to
make a Retreat, which, however, they did very handsomely.
This was owing to the Common Men, who were but new-
listed; tho' the Officers and old Soldiers behav'd themselves with
great Bravery. After this the Rebels began to see their Error, by
being impos'd on to give Credit to the many Falshoods told them,
of which this was one, That they might be assured that the
King's Forces would all come over to them: Yet not one Man
offer'd to do so....Nay, Major Preston[2] and Captain [Robert]
Ogleby[2], as well as several common Soldiers that were made
Prisoners, being wounded, assured us that not one Man belonging
to the King's Forces but would die in their Country's Cause,
and told us we could not be able to hold out, for that more

[1] The wind was from the north.—*P. C.*
[2] Both Preston and Ogilvy belonged to the Cameronian regiment.

Forces were also coming from all Quarters; they inform'd us of the Arrival of General [George] Carpenter with three Regiments of Dragoons to surround us.

This Brave General, after his long, troublesome, and dismal Marches after the Rebels, had very much weary'd his Men, but more the Horses for want of good Forage, returned to Newcastle, having Intelligence that the Rebels were gone over the Mountains to join Mar, which was impracticable for his heavy Horse. Having scarce refreshed himself, he had an Express from Sir Henry Haughton, that the Rebels were marching towards Lancaster. Upon which, with all imaginary speed[1], over high Mountains and deep Ways, he at last came to Clithero, a Town 12 Miles from Preston, on Saturday Night that the Action was begun. Whilst he was here, he receiv'd another Express from Sir Henry Haughton of all the Affair, which made him use his wonted Vigilance to have the Horses taken care of, so that they might be able early in the Morning to hasten towards Preston; which they performed with the greatest Expedition, for they came before Preston betwixt nine and ten on Sunday Morning....

The General, having an Account from General Wills of what had pass'd, approved very well of what had been done, but found it necessary to make some small Alterations in the Dispositions of the Troops: He found three Attacks had been made, though not with the desir'd Success, and yet that the Rebels would be forced to surrender at last, or be taken Sword in Hand[2]....

Lieutenant-General Carpenter...finding most part of the Horse and Dragoons of the King's Troops posted on one side of the Town very incommodiously on many Accounts, being crouded in a deep, narrow Lane near the end of the Town, and besides that, so inconvenient for the Service, that it was impossible to draw up above three or four in the Front, he brought them off in Parties to several other Places. Also, going to view Ground

[1] He left Durham on November 7, with Cobham's [1st Dragoons], Molesworth's [disbanded 1718], and Churchill's [disbanded 1718] dragoons.—*R.* 318.

[2] Though Forster possessed six cannon he made no effective use of them, being without experienced gunners.—*P. H.* 116.

towards the River, he found to his great Surprize, that no
Troops were posted at the End of Fishergate-street to block up
that part of the Town, and that for want of it, several of the
Rebels had escaped there, and more rid off that Way even before
his Face. This Street leads to a Marsh or Meadow which runs
down to that part of the River Ribble where there are two good
Fords, being the High-way towards Leverpool. At the upper
end of this Street there was another Barricade, with two Pieces
of Cannon (as is already said): But no Attack had been made on
this side, nor indeed could it be so, the few Troops consider'd.
Here the Lieutenant-General order'd Colonel [Thomas] Pitt
to post his two Squadrons of Horse and extend themselves into
that Marsh, in order to prevent any more escaping that Way,
as it effectually did; for some bold Fellows, attempting to escape
after this, were all cut to Pieces by the Horse: Also the General
caused a Communication to be open'd through the Inclosures
on that side, that his Post might be relieved in case the whole
Body should attempt to force their Retreat that Way, as it was
given out they would, and as indeed they might have done; but
they had no such good Measures in their Heads.

The Rebels being thus invested on all sides, so that they
found themselves entirely block'd up, and being now sensible,
tho' too late, of their Condition, and also that they were short of
Powder for an obstinate Resistance, began to consider what to
do. The Highlanders were for sallying out upon the King's
Forces, and dying, as they call'd it, like Men of Honour with
their Swords in their Hands; but they were over-ruled, and were
not allowed to stir: Nor was the Motion communicated to the
whole Body; but General Forster, prevail'd upon by my Lord
Widdrington, Colonel Oxburgh, and some few Others, resolv'd
upon a Capitulation, flattering themselves with obtaining good
Terms from the King's Officers. Colonel Oxburgh, pretending
Acquaintance with some of the Officers, made an Offer to go
out and treat of a Surrender.

As this was done without the Knowledge of the Rebel Army,
the Common Soldiers were told that General Wills had sent to
offer honourable Terms to them if they would lay down their
Arms; so blinded were we with their Tory Lyes to the last:

But certain it is, that Gentleman, had his Design been known, had never seen Tybourn, for he had been shot dead by the Consent of all the Common Men before he had gone out of the Barrier. However, go he did[1]...to the General, who allow'd him to come and go freely, but told him, They might expect no other Terms than to lay down their Arms and surrender at Discretion. The Colonel, to give him his due, urg'd all the Arguments he could for better Terms, but was told, That they must submit to the King's Mercy, there was no other Terms could be made with them....The Colonel coming back with this Answer, a second Message was sent out by Captain Dalzeil to desire Time to consider of it[2]. About Three in the Afternoon, Colonel Cotton[3], with a Dragoon and a Drum beating a Chamade before them, came up the Street from the King's General: The Colonel alighted at the Sign of the Mitre, where the chief of the Rebel Officers were got together, and told them he came to receive their positive Answer. 'Twas told him, There were Disputes betwixt the English and Scots, that would obstruct the Yielding, which Others were willing to submit to; but if the General would grant them a Cessation of Arms 'till the next Morning at Seven, they should be able to settle the Matter, and that the Gentlemen promised they would then submit. Colonel Cotton sent the Drum to beat a Chamade before the Doors of some Houses where the King's Men continued firing, to cause them to cease, on account of the Cessation which was agreed to[4], and to order them to with-hold 'till they had Notice from the General; but the poor Fellow was shot dead upon his Horse as he was beating his Drum. It is said this was...done by some of the Rebels who were averse to all thoughts of Surrender....

The Common Men were One and all against Capitulating, and were terribly enraged when they were told of it, declaring that they would Die fighting, and that when they could defend

[1] About two o'clock on Sunday afternoon, November 13.—*R*. 321.

[2] Wills had demanded an answer within one hour.—*R*. 322.

[3] Probably Colonel Stanhope Cotton, commanding 13th Foot. He was Wills' Staff Officer at Preston. He died 1725.

[4] Brigadier Mackintosh and the Earl of Derwentwater returned with Cotton as hostages for the fulfilment of these conditions.—*R*. 322.

their Posts no longer, they would force their way out and make a Retreat....In this Dilemma many exclaimed against Mr Forster, and had he appear'd in the Street he would certainly have been cut to pieces; but as he did not appear publickly, yet he had been actually kill'd in his Chamber by Mr [Alexander] Murray, had not I with my Hand struck up the Pistol with which he fired at him, so that the Bullet went through the Wainscot into the Wall of the Room. And since I mention Mr Forster, I cannot but justifie him against the many Aspersions he lies under in this part of the Action, I mean as a Coward. It must be own'd he was no Soldier, nor was the Command given to him as such, but as he was the only Protestant who could give Repute to their Undertaking, being of Note in Northumberland, of an Ancient Family, and having for several Years been Member of Parliament for that County, and therefore very Popular: For if the Command had been given to either of the two Lords, their Characters as Papists would have discouraged many of the People and been improved against the Design in general....

But I return to the Account of the Surrender at Preston. Before the appointed Hour came, several of the King's Forces entred that part of the Town which the Rebels held, and began to plunder, looking upon what they got [as] their own by Rule of War. But Complaint being made, they were stopped for some time. At last[1] the two Generals entred the Town in Form at

---

[1] Rae adds the following episode here:—'The next Day, about Seven o' Clock, Mr Forster sent out to acquaint General Wills, that they were willing to give themselves up Prisoners at Discretion, as he had demanded. But [Brigadier] M'Intosh, being by when the Message was brought, said, He could not answer that the Scots would surrender in that Manner, for that the Scots were People of desperate Fortunes, and that he had been a Soldier himself, and knew what it was to be a Prisoner at Discretion. Upon this the General said, Go back to your People again, and I will attack the Town, and the Consequence will be, I will not spare one Man of you. After this, M'Intosh went back, but came running out immediately again, and said, that the Lord Kenmure and the rest of the Noblemen, with his Brother, would surrender in like Manner with the English.'—R. 323.

the Head of the Troops; one Party under General Wills entred at that End which leads to Lancaster; Brigadier Honnywood, at the Head of the remaining Part of the Troops, entred at that End which leads to Manchester. They came in with sound of Trumpets and beat of Drums, both Parties meeting at the Market-Place. Here the Highlanders stood drawn up with their Arms; the Lords, Gentlemen, and Officers were first secured and placed under a Guard in several Rooms in the Inns, where they remain'd some time. The Highlanders laid down their Arms in the Place where they stood drawn up, and then were put into the Church under a sufficient Guard. When all was safe, by the Rebels being thus disarmed and secured, General Carpenter...went off the 15th with the Earl of Carlisle, Lord Lumley[1], Colonel Darcy, and the rest of the Gentlemen, who, having been now with him ten Days, had been very serviceable in procuring constant Intelligence of the Rebels, by the great Interest they have in that Country. The Slain on both Sides were buried, and then General Wills prepared to march.... There were a great many private Men[2] of his Majesty's Forces kill'd; how many it is hard to determine, but the Number has been esteem'd above 200[3], tho' the publick Lists say not so many.

Of the Rebels there were 174 kill'd and 25 wounded, and no more, for they were every-where under Covert....

There were taken at Preston seven Lords, besides 1490 others, including the several Gentlemen, Officers, and private Men, and two Clergymen[5]....

The Rebels being thus made Prisoners, I shall add an Account how they were dispos'd of afterwards, which take as follows.

[1] Richard Viscount Lumley was Colonel of the 1st Troop of the Horse Grenadier Guards.

[2] Of the officers, three Captains and one Ensign were killed.—*P. H.* 131.

[3] Two hundred and seventy according to Clarke. Rae gives the number as one hundred and forty-six killed and wounded, of whom ninety-two were in Preston's regiment.—*R.* 323.

[4] Eighteen or nineteen, according to Clarke.

[5] An account of the surrender at Preston is in *The Life of the Right Honourable George Lord Carpenter* [Lond. 1736], pp. 22–32.

For the better preventing Escapes, they were order'd to several Places of Confinement: The Lords were secured in the most commodious Houses or Inns. The Scotch Officers and Gentry, divided into three Parties, were set under a Guard at the Sign of the Mitre, the White-Bull, and the Wind-Mill. The Highlanders and common Men were put into the Church, where they continued about a Month, the Town's People being obliged to find them Water and Bread; whilst they took what care of themselves they could, unripping all the Linings from the Seats or Pews, and making thereof Breeches and Hose to defend themselves from the Extremity of the Weather. Several of them were sent under Guard to Wigan the 23d of November, and afterwards sent to Chester, whilst others were sent to Lancaster-Castle till their Trials came on; when some were found guilty and executed, others transported by their own Choice, others acquitted, others repriev'd, and those untry'd or reprieved continued as Objects of His Majesty's most Gracious Clemency. A great many of the Northumberland and Lancashire Gentlemen were confin'd in Mr Wingleby's House till Sunday the 21st, when a great part of the Chief Officers and all the Lords were sent to Wigan. The Lancashire Gentlemen followed them on Tuesday the 23d, and continued there till Thursday, when all of them, being divided into four Parties, were sent under the Guard of several Detachments to Warrington.... Having continued at Warrington all Night, they march'd forwards for London by easy Marches....At Barnet we were all Pinion'd, more for Distinction than any Pain that attended: And at Highgate we were met with a strong Detachment of Horse Granadiers and Foot-Guards, each Man having his Horse led by one of the Foot. Setting forward from Highgate, we were met by such Numbers of People that it is scarce conceivable to express, who with Long live King GEORGE! and Down with the Pretender! ushered us throughout to our several Apartments....

The Names of the Lords, Prisoners, are well known, viz.

James Radcliffe, Earl of Derwentwater, Beheaded on Tower-Hill, February 24, 1715–16.

William Widdrington, Lord Widdrington.

William Maxwell, Earl of Nithsdale, made his Escape out of
the Tower, Febr. 23, 1715–16, dress'd in a Woman's
Cloak and Hood, which since are called Nithsdales[1].
(These Three were Papists.)

George Seaton, Earl of Wintoun, made his Escape also out
of the Tower, Aug. 4, 1716.

William Gordon, Viscount Kenmure, Beheaded with Lord
Derwentwater.

William Nairn, Lord Nairn[2].

[1] The Countess of Nithsdale's story of the Earl's escape is in the
Transactions of the Society of Antiquaries of Scotland, vol. i, 523–38,
and in Sir William Fraser's *Book of Carlaverock* [Edin. 1873], vol. ii,
221 *et seq.*

[2] Of the inferior officers less than thirty were hanged. Thomas
Forster and Brigadier Mackintosh escaped from prison.

Under the provisions of the Act of Grace of 1717, Lords Carnwath,
Widdrington, and Nairn, and the Jacobite insurgents imprisoned in
England and Scotland were released. The Macgregors and a com-
paratively few individuals were excluded from the benefit of the Act.—
Mahon, *History of England*, vol. i, 419.

CHAPTER IV

GLENSHIEL, 1719

The[1] King's affairs for a long time made little or no noise, but on breaking out of the war with Spain[2], people began to hope that something in his favours would cast up, and whilst wee were fed with these hopes in very general terms by letters from abroad, all of a sudden wee received the joyfull news of the King of Spain's having declared for our King[3]. What correspondence King Philip had in England I cannot particularly tell, but sure I am there was not the least intimation of such a design to any in Scotland untill a very little befor it was publick over all Europe. About which time the Earl of Wigton writt a letter to me from his country house, desireing me to meet him without fail next day exactly at four in the afternoon at a certain private place in Edinburgh, and I having accordingly keept the tryst, His Lordship introduced me to Mr Francis Kennedy; this gentleman was sent express to acquaint the King's friends of the attempt that was to be made by Spain on Britain, and he was directed to goe first to my Lord Wigton, who thought fitt to call me to be present at the conference. Mr Kennedy produced a small peice of parchment writt and sign'd by the Duke of Ormond, desireing entire credit might be given to the bearer therof; and then he told us that the Duke was actually embarked with a considerable body of Spanish troops, designing to land them in England, and that the Earl Marishall was sail'd with a battalion, accompanyd by the Marquis's of Tullibardin and Seaforth and some of the heads of the Highland clans, and was to land in the Highlands; that the troops design'd for England and Scotland were sufficient to make a stand till the Kings friends

[1] *L. P.* ii, 17.
[2] Great Britain declared war upon Spain on December 17, 1708.
[3] February 20, 1719.—*H. R.* 188.

could gett togither; that he durst say Marishall was landed befor that day, and that wee would soon hear of the like of Ormond; and he desired wee would consider what was to be done for the King's service at this criticall juncture. After having fully talked over the affair, wee judged it highly necessary to conceal this intelligence as long as it was possible, because wee perceived the Spainards design'd to catch the British Government naping. Besides, as there were many accidents to which the Spanish fleet might be exposed in so long a voyage, wee did by no means think it adviseable to move in Scotland till wee were sure the Duke of Ormond was landed; for if any appearance should be made for the King in Scotland, and the grand design fail in the execution, wee could meet with no quarters from the Government, and the King at the same time reap no benefit.

A few days after this, the Spanish design[1] against Britain was known every where, and that the Earl Marishal was actually landed in the Highlands.

Its[2] necessary to go back to the month of August of this year [1718], when the English, without any previous declaration of

---

[1] The Spanish design was the creation of Cardinal Alberoni. Since the Treaty of Utrecht, Spain had become very restless. By that Treaty the Emperor gained at her expense in Italy, while he refused his recognition of Philip Bourbon as King of Spain. In spite of the kinship of their reigning Houses, Alberoni's policy was hostile also to France, in that he dreamed of a possible union of the two kingdoms in contravention of the Treaty of Utrecht. He was obliged to reckon upon the opposition of England, who in 1716 guaranteed the integrity of the Emperor's dominions in the Treaty of Westminster, and in January 1717 concluded a Triple Alliance with France and Holland for the preservation of the peace of Europe upon the lines of the Treaty of Utrecht. Alberoni, however, resolved to make war upon Austria. Early in 1718 the Spanish fleet seized Sicily. The British Ministry consequently despatched a fleet under Sir George Byng, who destroyed the Spanish fleet off Cape Passaro in August 1718. On December 17, 1718 Great Britain declared war on Spain. To cripple England, or at least to disable her from thwarting his designs upon Italy, became now Alberoni's chief purpose. In order to achieve it, he resolved to rouse the Jacobites in England and Scotland, and to support them with Spanish forces.

[2] K. M. 35.

war, or even any good ground for it[1], had attacked the King of
Spain's fleet [off Cape Passaro] on the coast of Sicily, and entirely
ruined it, which so exasperated the Cardinal Alberoni, who then
governed Spain with the title of first Minister, that he resolv'd
to assist King James, and so revenge himself on the Whigs, who
had been the occasion of the breach of faith he complained of.
To concert the proper methods for this, he wrote to the Duke of
Ormonde, who was then in Paris, inviting him to come to
Madrid.

[On[2] my arrival] Alberoni came to me privately and informed
me that he had sent Sir Patrick Lawless to the King of Sweden
to engage him to enter into an alliance with the King of Spain;
that the Chief Article was to endeavour to dethrone the Elector
of Hanover their common enemy; that he carryed Bills with
him to enable the King of Sweden to make the attempt, with
promises of an Annual Subsidy, provided he enter'd into the
Allyance.

The next time I saw Alberoni, he asked me what I demanded
as necessary to make an attempt to restore the Chevalier de St
George. I told him seven or eight thousand men, with 15,000
arms and Ammunition proportionable. He answered that the
King of Spain wou'd be willing to grant that number if he were
in a condition, but considering that the greatest part of their
Troops are in Sicily, and that they are threatned with an Invasion
from France[3] in two Places, that is, by the way of Roussillon
and Navarre, they cou'd not spare a man, but that they wou'd
give 15,000 arms and Ammunition proportionable, and that
money shou'd not be wanting to enable the King of Sweden to
invade England[4]....

I made Alberoni another visit at his desire, and after some
discourse he told me that the King of Spain wou'd give five
thousand men, of which four thousand are to be foot, a thousand

---

[1] See note, *supra*, p. 224.

[2] *J. A.* 15. From a letter of Ormonde's, dated December 17 [N.S.],
1718, to the Chevalier at Rome.

[3] France declared war on Spain on January 9 [N.S.], 1719.

[4] Charles the Twelfth's death on December 11 [N.S.], 1718, put
an end to hopes of Sweden's co-operation.

Troopers, of which three hundred with their horses, the rest with their Arms and Accoutrements, and two months pay for them, ten field Pieces, and a thousand Barrels of Powder, and fifteen Thousand Arms for foot, with every thing necessary to convoy them.

I told Alberoni that it wou'd be necessary to have a Diversion made in Scotland, and since he cou'd not spare any more men, I desired him to let us have two or three thousand arms to send thither. He asked me if there was any man of consideration to go with them. I told him of the Earl Marischal, who was in Paris, and he desired me to write to him to come with all despatch and as privately as possible. I will write to Brigadier Campbell[1] to come hither as soon as I know where he is. As to the Gentlemen at Bordeaux, they shall have timely notice.

I am now in Valladolid, where the King of Spain thought fitt I shou'd reside. Alberoni desired me to let him have one in whom I cou'd confide to send to the King of Sweden to press him to invade England before the Spring, especially since the King of Spain had come to a resolution of sending Troops, which he had not done when Sir Patrick Lawless was despatched. George Bagenal[2] is the person I left with Alberoni. I expect him here every hour in his way to Sweden, and his Instructions are to tell the King that no money will be given by the King of Spain unless he consents to make an Attempt upon England in the time proposed.

Bagenal will have Instructions to propose to Sweden to send two Thousand men to Scotland with five Thousand Arms.

Alberoni seem'd very uneasy at your Situation in Italy. He fears that your person is not in Safety, considering the late inhuman Proceedings against the Princess[3]. He thinks Rome the worst place for you to be in, because of the Emperor's Spys

[1] Of Ormidale. He had been imprisoned at Carlisle for taking part in the '15, but escaped. He was at this time with other Jacobite exiles at Bordeaux.

[2] Ormonde's A.D.C.

[3] The Princess Clementina Maria Sobieska, on her way to join the Chevalier, to whom she had been recently betrothed, was arrested by the Emperor's orders at Innspruck.

and the Difficulty you will have of getting privately from thence, and he does not think your person safer there than elsewhere. Upon what he says, and the letter I received from James Murray[1] of the ninth November, it is my humble opinion that you ought to come to Spain with all expedition, that you may be out of the Emperor's power; and your presence is necessary here, either to Embark with the Troops, if you can arrive in Time, or to follow as soon as possible, for Alberoni is of opinion that the Opportunity must not be lost tho' you shou'd not arrive in due time, and if it be possible, you ought to be here to go to England with the Troops.

Alberoni desires that this design may be the Strictest Secret, and I beg of you not to acquaint Cardinal Aquaviva[2] with it, and when you come away [from Rome to Spain], to give it out that it is for your own Safety.

The[3] Duke of Ormonde...having discover'd the design to the Earl Marischall of Scotland, had promised him that if there was any thing to be done in Brittain, or if the Cardinal [Alberoni] wou'd take him into the Spanish service, he wou'd immediatly write to him; and accordingly, in the beginning of December [1718] following, he received a letter desiring him to come to that country and to bring me along with him[4].

I was not at that time in a very fit condition to begin so long a journey, being not quite recover'd of a fit of sickness; however, I set out as I was, and before I had got to Marseilles, the travelling and change of air had entirly recover'd me.

We embarcked at that place in the beginning of the year 1719, and after some bad weather, arrived at Palamos on the coast of Catalonia.

Howsoon we landed, we were carried before the Commandant, who asked us what we were and whence we came from. We told him we came from France, but as to the other question, answer'd only that we were English officers who were going to

---

[1] The Hon. James Murray, second son of the fifth Viscount Stormont; created Earl of Dunbar by the Chevalier in 1721.

[2] In charge of Spanish interests at Rome.

[3] *K. M.* 36.

[4] The letter, dated Madrid, December 8 [N.S.], 1718, is in *J. A.* 9.

Madrid to seek employment in the army, for the Duke of Ormonde had desir'd us to keep our journey private. He then asked us if we had any recommendation to any at the Court of Madrid, and finding we had, or at least wou'd own, none, he told us he cou'd let us go no farther, for that coming from an enemies country, and giving so lame an account of ourselves, he must send us to the next governor, who was D^n Tiberio Caraffa, Governor of Giron, who might dispose of us as he thought fit, and that there being then an Irish regiment in that place, commanded by the Duke of Liria[1], perhaps we might find some of our countrymen there who might answer for us. The news of the Duke of Liria's being so near was no little agreeable to us, and we told him we ask'd no better, for that the Duke wou'd answer for us.

Accordingly, next morning we were sent to Gironne with a letter to the governor and a soldier, whom he told us he sent along because the roads were infested by robbers, but in reality to take care we did not make our escape. We arrived there in the evening, and having delivered the letter to the governor, he order'd us to be carried to the Duke's quarters to be examined, who was no little surprized at our appearance, and immediatly sent to acquaint the governor that he answer'd for the two gentlemen, but concealed our names at the desire of the Earl Marischal. We loged that night with him, and finding him alltogether ignorant of any intended enterprize on England, we concluded that we were sent for only to enter into the King of Spain's service, and therefore resolved to continue our route slowly to Madrid, without fatiguing ourselves by going post. We accordingly hired chairs there, and two days after arrived at S^n Andreu, hard by Barcelona, and from thence sent a letter from the Duke of Liria to Prince Pio of Savoy, who was then Captain General of that province, begging him to allow us to come in to the toun without being examined at the Ports; and about an hour after, we saw a coach and six mules (the first equipage of the kind I had ever seen) with the Prince's livery at the door of our inn. This surprized us, and still more the

[1] As Marquess of Teignmouth he accompanied James to Scotland in 1716.

respect his Doctor, whom he had sent in his coach to receive us, paid to two strangers he had never seen. The reason, which we did not know till long after, was, that some days before, he had received letters from the Cardinal that King James wou'd arrive very soon in some of the Ports of Catalonia incognito; that he shou'd receive him in the same manner, and take care to provide every thing for the despatch of his journey to Madrid. This, with the Duke of Liria's letter, occasioned our entry into Barcelona in this manner; and I believe he was sorry to have given himself so much trouble about us when he knew who we were; yet he received us very civilly, tho' with some embarras.

As we did not open ourselves farther to him than telling our true names, so he told us no more than that he believed it wou'd be fit we set out immediatly for Madrid, which we did next morning, after vieuing the new citadelle he was building, and which he allowed us to visit; and after fifteen days journey we arriv'd at that place, and the same evening sent to acquaint the Cardinal we were come. He order'd us to attend him early next morning; and we had no sooner made him our reverence than he asked us why we had been so long on the way, it being eight days since he had accounts from Barcelona of our being there. We answered, that tho' we had been desired to come to Spain, yet not knowing that his Eminence had any pressing commands for us, we had come by the ordinary way of travelling of the country. He told us the business pressed; that it was to execute an enterprize on England in favour of its lawfull master; that the Duke of Ormonde was already set out to embarck at the Groine for England; and it was resolved he, the Earl Marischall, shou'd go to Scotland; but that he must know what he wanted for the expedition, and in what manner he designed to act when there; to which the other answer'd, that as he did not know the plan the Duke of Ormonde had layed doun, and as both parts must go in concert, he beged leave to go to Valladolid, where the Duke then was[1], and that in three or four days he shou'd be back, fully instructed in every thing which might conduce to the good of the affair; to which the Cardinal consented....

[1] Ormonde left Valladolid for Corunna on February 10 [N.S.].— *J. A.* xxxiv.

Five days after, the Earl Marischall return'd, having been obliged to follow the Duke of Ormonde to Benevente[1], and immediatly went to the Cardinal and setled the plan of the undertaking. He asked four thousand arms and ten thousand pistolls; but the furnishing the Duke of Ormonde had so drained their magazins as well as their treasury, that all he cou'd get was 2000 arms and 5000 pistolls, with six companies of foot[2] to cover his landing.

[Meanwhile[3], ten days earlier, the Chevalier] finding that it was no longer fitt for him to be in Italie, resolved to leave it, but some adress was necessary to make his passage out of it practicable and safe[4]. He determined to go by sea and with only a very few of his servants who attend his person. He was pleased to order that the Duke of Perth and I should go togither by another rout and endeavour to join him at a place appointed. His Majesty toke the advice of those who he thought fittest to advise with as to the way he was to go, and also as to the rout for the Duke of Perth and I, both which were followed accordingly. The rout we went was once thought of for his Majesty, but happie it was that he chose the other, as you 'll see by what happend to us. After the Kings choseing to go the other way, it was thought that our going off about the same time he did, in chairs by the way of fflorance and so to Bologna, as if intending to meet the Princess [Clementina] (the reason which was given out for the kings leaveing of Rome), was the way to blind the publick and prevent for some time the discovery of his real designe; so that his Majesty sett out from Rome towards the

[1] Ormonde writes to Alberoni on February 13 [N.S.] from Astorga, announcing that Marischal had met him there the previous evening.— *J. A.* 60.

[2] They were a composite force, consisting of twelve men drawn from each of the 24 companies of Don Pedro de Castro's regiment of foot, and numbered three hundred and seven, including officers.—*H. R.* 281.

[3] *J. A.* 207. From a letter of Mar's to Lord Panmure, dated from Rome, March 21 [N.S.], 1719.

[4] After his return from Scotland in 1716 James had resided in Lorraine. Thence he proceeded to Avignon and eventually to Rome, where he spent the rest of his life.

cost the 8th of ffeb. [N.S.] very airly, and imbarkt and sailed that evening in a shipe that was reddy prepared for him[1]. The Duke of Perth and I, about two hours after his Majesty, sett out in three chairs with our servants on purpose to make it appear as if the King had been in the company, and the bite toke as you'll see. We continued our journie to Bologna without endeavouring to make great heast, as was concerted, in case his Majesty had not got saild so soon as he intended....

ffrom Bologna we went the rout that had been given us, towards Genoa by Modena, Parma, and Piacensa; and when we came two posts further to Vogera, on fryday morning, 17th of ffeb., a post short of Tortona, where there is a German garison, and where we apprehended difficulty if we met with any, we were told at the posthouse that we could have no horses without an order from the Majestrats of the toun. As we were thinking upon this, what was next to be done, The Podesta of the Toun, as they call the chife Majestrat for the Emperour, an Italian, and a German Livetenant Colonel came into the room where we were and askt if we had a passport, and whither we were a going, and who we were; we told that we were going for ffrance by Turin; that one of us was a ffrench man, Mr Le Brun (the name the Duke of Perth went by), and the other two English, Mr Johnston, and Robertson (the names for me and Paterson); that we had mett at Rome, where we had been for severall months for our diversion and curiosity, and were now a returning to our own countrys; that we did not know a passport to be necessary, haveing had none when we came into the country, and knew of severall of our acquentances who had o' late gone back for ffrance without any. Then said they, we cannot help stoping you here til we give an account of you at Millan...[and] so on we were caried to the Podesta's house, which is in the toun house, and there we were keept til Sunday morning the 19th under a gard of ten or twelve souldiers....An express was immediatly sent upon our comeing into the Podesta's house to Millan with an account of us....They lookt much at us the time they were writeing their letters, and particularly at

[1] He embarked at Nettuno on a ship prepared for him by Admiral George Camocke, an Englishman in Spanish service.—*J. A.* xxxiii.

the D. of Perth, by wch we imagind they belived the King to be in the company....When we shall find a way of going to our Master is more than we yet know[1].

King[2] James landed at Rosas [on March 9, N.S.], and to day I expect he will set out from Barcelona on his way to Madrid, where he will hardly arrive before the 25th or 26th of this month....He has risked destruction a hundred times from the Storms he experienced. For three days he remained at Marseilles, concealed in the house of the Master of the Ship on which he had embarked. He was bled for a Fever, and was obliged to lie close hidden at Villafranca for 24 hours. At the islands off Hyères, near Toulon, he was compelled to share the accommodation of a Miserable Inn with a crowd of dirty Wretches, and though he was suffering from sea-sickness, to dance with the Landlady, it being Carnival time. He was pursued, also, by two English Vessels.

Advice[3] [of the Chevalier's arrival] being brought to the Spanish Court, the King immediately sent his own Officers to attend him in his Journey to Madrid, and Orders were given to prepare an Apartment for him in the Palace of Buen-Retiro: He was receiv'd at Madrid with all imaginable Honours: The King of Spain sent his own Coaches to take him at four Leagues Distance from that City, went out of Town himself to meet him, and treated him as a crown'd Head, with the Style of King of England, and his Majesty....He continu'd some Days with the King of Spain at Buen-Retiro, and on the 3d of April set out for Valadolid, which Palace had been fitted up for his Reception.

[But[4] already, two days before the Chevalier's arrival in Spain], the Spanish Fleet [destined to escort Ormonde to England] had sailed from Cadiz on the 7th of March and proceeded on its course without Mishap until the 27th, when it was dispersed by Northeasterly gales. As the ships were victualled only for 30

---

[1] Mar's letter relates the remainder of the journey. After a short imprisonment he and Perth were released and returned to Rome.

[2] *J. A.* 219. From a letter of Alberoni's to Ormonde dated from Madrid, March 18 [N.S.].

[3] *H. R.* 189.   [4] *J. A.* 245. From various reports.

days, their Captains made the best of there way back to port, serving out half rations of food and water for fear they should perish of Hunger and Thirst, and seeing themselves almost at the end of their Provisions. The Horses suffered a good deal, though of 57 on board [four vessels returned to port] only three died. Two of these ships encountered no other units of the Fleet in their course. The other two—the *Comte de Toulouse* and the small frigate *Rebecca*, passed the Flag ship. The Captain of the former says that he had lost all his spars except the Mainmast. The other, however, declares that not even the Mainmast was standing, and that the Admiral had been obliged to throw overboard the greater part of his artillery. However, he had found means to hoist a small sail, and attended by an escort carrying provisions, was making progress to the North. The Soldiers have Suffered severely and are in a pitiful Condition. Of the fifteen Companies aboard the *Comte de Toulouse* 40 are sick and eight are dead.

On [April] 9 the *Mercure* reached Vigo with 200 Troops on board whose sufferings have been terrible—for the last 4 days of the voyage they were without food and water and several Soldiers are ill in consequence. On the 10th the *Guadaloupe* and the frigate *El Rosino* entered that port having on board Seven companies of Infantry and three of Grenadiers, many of them Sick. The *Guadaloupe* is the Vice-Admiral's and has on Board the Intendant, Treasurer, and 14,000 pistoles, all of which has been landed. On the 11th two Ships named the *Susanne Marie* and *Vedon* arrived at Muros, having on board some Infantry detachments and 13 Horses in bad condition. They had been obliged to throw nine overboard which had collapsed for want of water. There is no news of the rest of the Fleet. But it is reported from Portugal that an English Squadron has left Lisbon to search for it.

[The[1] preparations for the Scottish expedition meanwhile proceeded] One difficulty still remain'd, which was, to get the chiefs of the King's friends who were in France advertised of this, which the Cardinal desired me to undertake. The Earl Marischal had brought with him from the Duke of Ormonde

[1] *K. M.* 41.

a little billet containing these words—'Pray have entire confidence in the bearer,' and signed Ormond[1], to be given to him who shou'd be sent; and with this and about 18,000 crowns, I set out from Madrid the 19 of February [N.S.], and three days after arrived at St Sebastian, where I deliver'd 12,000 crowns to the Prince [of] Campo Florido for the equipement of the frigats destin'd for Scotland, and with the little money which remained, enter'd France privatly. I...pass'd without any difficulty, and got to Bourdeaux in the end of February, where I mett General [Alexander] Gordon, Brigadeer Campbell [of Ormidale], and some others, to whom I deliver'd my message, and left them some money to hire ships to transport themselves to Scotland; only Brigadeer Campbell went to Spain to embark at S^n Sebastian with the Earl Marischall. The greatest difficulty I had in my journey was how to get post horses from this place....To obviate this difficulty I made use of another person, who, not being suspected, asked horses for himself and one servant to go to Paris, and as such I set out with him, and the 3d of March arrived at Orleans, where I found the Marquess of Tullibardine, who, according to my orders, I carried along with me to Paris next day.

Howsoon I got there, I advertised the Marquess of Seafort, who immediatly came to the house where I was, and brought along with him a brother of Lord Duffus's, and some whille after came in Campbell of Glenderuel. I told them the reason of my coming, and showed them the short credentials I had brought from the Duke of Ormonde. Glenderuel smiled at reading them, and told me that that billet wou'd have been of little weight with them, had they not been already advertised by the Duke of Marr to obey what orders the Duke of Ormonde shou'd send. This plainly let me see that we had two factions amongst us, and which proved the occasion of our speedy ruin when we landed in Scotland. However, they agreed to obey the orders, and I went away next day to Rowen [Rouen] to provide a ship for them, which in ten days I got fitted out by the help of a merchant there, and ready to put to sea. Howsoon this was done, I wrote to them to come down with all hast, the ship

[1] Dated February 15 [N.S.], 1719.—*M. D. A.* 451.

being already at Havre de Grace. When they arrived, Glenderuel asked me if I had seen General Dillon[1] whille I was at Paris. I told him I had not; that General Dillon being at St Germains, I durst not venture to go there, being too well known not to be discover'd; and that tho' the interest of those there was the same as ours, yet their imprudence was so great that they were not to be trusted with a secret, which, shou'd it take vent, must occasion our being stopt at the instance of the Earl of Stair, then Embassador from the Court of England; that besides, having no instructions to communicate any thing to him, I made no doubt but he had been advertised by some other canal[2].

Glenderuel declared he did not think those reasons valid, and that Dillon shou'd be advertised of this, and desired to let us know if the King (whose affairs he was then intrusted with at Paris) had given him no particular instructions on this head. This was the pretence; the true reason was, to get a commission which they knew he had in his hands, and was design'd for the King of Sweden's expedition in the year 1717, by which the King constituted the Marquess of Tullibardine Commander in chieff of his forces in Scotland. This Glenderuel thought absolutly necessary for his own private ends, being surer to govern the easy temper of the Marquess than of those who otherwise wou'd naturally have the command of the army, and particularly to prevent its falling into the hands of General Gordon, with whom he was not in very good intelligence.

The day before we embarked, the express they had sent to Paris returned with a pacquet from General Dillon, of which they showed a letter full of common place advices relating to the conduct we shou'd hold in Scotland, but not a word of the commissions, which they keept to be drawn out on proper occasions.

All things being now ready, we embark'd[3] the 19th of March [N.S.], in a small barck[4] of about 25 tunns, in the mouth of the Seine, and shaped our course to pass betwixt Dover and Calais,

[1] The Chevalier's agent at Paris.
[2] Dillon had been informed of the project in a letter from Mar, dated January 30 [N.S.], 1719. It is printed in *J. A.* xxxii.
[3] At Honfleur.—*M.D.A.* 453. Mar gives the date as March 20.
[4] Named the *Fidele*.—Oliphant, *Jacobite Lairds of Gask*, 465.

and so round the Orkneys to the Isle of Lewis, which was our place of rendezvous; but the wind continuing at east forced us the Friday after, March 24, to alter our course and stand away for St George's Channel, or the back of Ireland, as we shou'd think best. Two days after, we came up with the land's end in the evening, and about two hours after found our selves in the middle of a fleet, seven of which had out lights and the others none; these we conjectured to be men of war, and the rest transports; and finding the number of the former to agree with what the Duke of Ormonde had, I made no doubt but it was his fleet; however, the wind being favourable, we passed thro' them without speaking to them, in which we were very lucky, for it proved a squadron of English men of war transporting a body of troops from Ireland to England, where they had at last got the news of the invasion intended against them[1].

From thence we stood for Cape Clear and the west coast of Ireland, and after favourable but blowing weather, arrived the 4 of April, N.S. [March 24, O.S.][2] in the isle of Lewis, where we enquired if no ship had touched there lately from Spain, or if there was no particular news in the country; but finding them ignorant of any thing that cou'd give us light into what we wanted to be informed of, we remain'd there some days, and at last had accounts that two frigats were come to an anchor on the other side of the island, on which I went with all hast there, not doubting but it was those we were longing for[3]. I found them allready sailed, but a gentleman of the country informed me that they were the same, and were gone some miles farther

[1] Since January the English Government had a general knowledge that some hostile enterprise was contemplated by Alberoni. On March 4 [N.S.] Stair was able to give precise information of the destination of Ormonde's fleet. Prompt measures were taken. Fleets were sent to cruise off the Lizard and in the Bay of Biscay, and troops were summoned from Ireland and Holland.—*J. A.* xxxviii *et seq.*

[2] The date was April 5 [N.S.], or March 25 [O.S.], according to Tullibardine (Oliphant, *op. cit.* 465), April 2 [N.S.] or March 22 [O.S.] according to Mar.

[3] *i.e.* Marischal and his party from Spain. They sailed from Passage on March 8 [N.S.] with a force of 307 Spaniards.—*H. R.* 281.

to Stornoway, the only toun, or rather village, on all the island. I went the same night there, and found them in the harbour at an anchor, and the men still aboard.

Next[1] day [March 30] Ld Marishall produced his instructions from the Duke of Ormond, which gave power to him or any supperiour officer to make war upon the usurper when and where they thought most convenient; accordingly his L^{op} proposed immediately goeing to arms without any regaird to a landing [by Ormonde] in England, which for many reasons was against the oppinion of the others present, except Brig: Campbell of Ormadale—Considering what a blow the Highlands had received very few years before, which was so fresh in the people's memory, that they would not be easily brought to the field againe without greater encouragement than what his L^{op} brought; for to press things rashly on so slender a foundation might disconcert the King's affairs when a reall opportunity offer'd, besides ruine any that would be so foreward as to stirr if the designes on England should happen to miscarry, which would prove a mighty disadvantage to his Majesty's interest, as well as bring destruction on the countrey. My Ld Marishall alleadged the Duke of Ormond might be landed, and time would be lost if the Highlanders were not immediately call'd to arms[2]. The others sustain'd that a general riseing might be as quick and easier upon the certainty of a landing in England, a partiall riseing being precarious; besides that, it could not answer the end of people's appearing for the service as things were stated. The day after, my Ld Tullibardine by advyce produced his Commission of Lieutennent Generall, on which Ld Marishall quite his pretensions to a sole command, but still insisted in haveing the charge of the ships[3], which created a good dale of

[1] *M. D. A.*

[2] Marischal's party supported 'the project which the Earl Marischall had proposed to the Cardinal, to land as soon as possible in Scotland, and with the Spaniards and Highlanders who shou'd first join us, march straight to Inverness.'—*K. M.* 47.

[3] Marischal contended that he had received positive orders from Alberoni as to the ships. Tullibardine's superior commission as Lieutenant-General had come to him from Dillon. The Earl Marischal

trouble, tho he was likeways oblidged to renounce any particullar authority over them, & allso to give up most things else; only his L^{op} retain'd a fifth part of the money which was sent for the publict use. He told, the Duke of Ormond had desired him not to ask much of the Cardinall, lest he should grant nothing, and that he only required the 300 men for a guaird to the arms and ammunition.

Ld Seafort, seeing what slender encouragement there was for riseing disarm'd people, was not only against goeing to arms before a landing in England, but allso would by no means hear of stirring out of the Louis till the account came; all were against that, because it might prove of ill consequence by contrare winds hindering the news to come, and opposite gales would allso stop goeing to the mainland; besides, if friggats came on the cost, it would then be impossible to waft over at any rate. However, it was with the greatest difficulty his L^{op} was perswaded to move; at length, April the 4th, O.S., the wind permitting, they sail'd to the main land, but could only fetch Garloch, where there was only a rumour of the landing in England. However, supposeing it certaine, Ld Tullibardine wrote to the Clans and Gentlemen in the Highlands, requireing them to goe to arms, and Glenderuell went by land to gett the letters deliver'd. On the 6th, the wind favouring[1], they lous'd from Garloch, but a storm riseing in the night, they were drove back on the 7th to Stornoway, and could not saile till the 11th, and then only made the poynt of Garloch; the next day the wind drove them againe within 4 leagues of Stornoway, but on the 13th, the wind changeing, they came safe to ane anchor that night at Ileandonnan[2], which was thought the fittest place for debarquation, tho it was the 28th before the arms and everything

held a Major-General's commission in Jacobite and Spanish service.— *Ibid*. 46, 48.

[1] According to Keith, the pilots 'declared that the wind was still contrary for the port we intended,' but Tullibardine's impatience compelled them to sail.—*K.M.* 48.

[2] Castle Eilean Donan, a stronghold of the Mackenzies, stands on an island at the head of Loch Alsh, and overlooks Loch Long and Loch Duich.

else could be gott ashoar, for want of boats and other conveniences[1].

The 14th, Glenderuell return'd with a Gentleman of no small consideration, who was hearty and very ready for the service the minute there came any certainty of the Landing, and told that was the advyce came from the King's freinds both in Scotland and England. On the 17th, the Lords Seafort and Marishall with severall Gentlemen of the Mackenzies came to see Ld Tullibardine, and amongst other discourse, Ld Marishall began to talk of goeing to arms without expecting the Duke of Ormond's landing, and without more adoe alleadged the meeting was a Councill of war, haveing no ways apprys'd those who were then chiefly concern'd in calling it or officers on such occasions, which appear'd to Ld Tullibardine the more extraordinary that there came at the same time a letter from Brig: Campbell of Ormadale, who it seems was not weell, however, thought fitt to send his oppinion to a Councill of war that had never been thought of, wherin he declares it was his oppinion that it appear'd most advantageous to the King's interest not to waite for any further news of the D. of Ormond's landing or a General assembly of the Clans, but that the Marquis of Seafort and ane other Gentleman should rise some of their men, not doubting but Clanranald and Lochiell (who were then landed and comeing) would joyne their men for secureing some post with the Spainards to favour the diversion intended; on which Ld Marishall would likeways let the Company know his mind in wryteing, as it seems was before concerted, that as he had declar'd at Stornoway, his oppinion was, that according to the D. of Ormond's instructions, his Majesty's forces ought to be assembled, it being for the King's service that they should be immediately employed in secureing some post where not only the Highlands, but the Gentlemen of the Low countrey might more securely joyn, or whatever other expedition is judged most for the service, and that they were not to waite any news of the

[1] 'A Person who came this day [May 8] from the Rebels Quarters, which he left the first Instant, reports, That they are lodg'd in Houses and Huts built by themselves, within two Miles of the Place where they landed.'—*H. R.* 279.

D. of Ormond's landing, considering the distance; however, the Generallity did not think his Grace's instructions meant that people should endeavour to force a riseing at all hazards on so small a foundation, especially since there was no directions how to behave on all events in case of any accident or disappointment as to the main designe.

My Ld Seafort was not against giveing oppinions in wryteing, but declar'd his mind was still the same as he had told in the Leuis, thinking it folly and destraction to stirr without a landing in England, and the Gentlemen of his name agreed that all their endeavours would be to no purpose for men could not be brought in earnest to the field before that time; & since Clanranald with Lochiell were expected in a day or two, they could certainly give the best account of their oun people. On the 20th Clanranald and Lochiell being arrived, as allso Mackinnon and the Chisme [Chisholm], everybody mett. Brig: Campbell then proposed that the Spainards and Chieffs of Clans should continue where they were till the account of a landing in England, and that about 1000 men should be rised out of the estates of the attainted and sent to attaque Innerness under the command of the Earle Marishall, whose reputation and character might make ane attempt of that kind succeed. Clanranald answered, they were first to consider what way such a number of men was to be rised, since those that were not attainted would not readiely follow their Chiefs without a generall riseing, The people over all the Kingdome being equally safe, tho the persons of some Gentlemen were attainted; besides, the Highlanders could not fight against walls; that all Clyton's regiment[1] would be there long before them, and the toun [Inverness] could rise six or seven hundred militia, whose fire from the houses would quickly disperse their men, the consequence of which may be easiely imagined; but supposeing they succeeded, how could they keep it if there was not a speedy landing in England. The Brigadeer answered, in that case (it being a seaport) they could easiely save themselves and the men by transporting all to Spain. The gener-

---

[1] Colonel Jasper Clayton's 14th Foot was stationed in the West Highlands 1716–19. For a return of the troops in Scotland at this time cf. *J. A.* 284. The effective strength was 482 horse and 2015 foot.

allity thought makeing a bustle with such views as these would doe more disservice to the King than any of them could weell answer for. The discourse continued thus till it was late; next day every one mett againe except Ld Marishall. All who had followings saw projects of that kind were distructive to the service, and were entyrely against a riseing before it could be generall; but in case of being attaqu'd where they were, they would endeavour to defend themselves, that all might be preserved against the landing which they dayly expected; and least that miscarryed, it was thought necessary the ships should be sent to a place of safety to carry back the Spainards. In the mean time, Clanranald with Lochiell went away to secure their proportion of arms and ammunition.

Nevertheless on [April] the 28th (before all the stores were weell gott on shoar) Lord Tullibardine was inform'd that the captains of the friggats, having Ld Marishall's dispatches, were resolved to waite no longer on any account whatsoever[1], and accordingly next morning fell doun to the Calliach's Stone in their way out to sea. Lord Tullibardine, finding nothing could make them stay hardly one day for his letters, however necessary, was therefore oblidged to give them his consent on [April] the 30th.

The 29th, my Ld Seafort wrote a note to Ld Tullibardine, that a party was come from Innerness and were to be joyned by some disafected Highlanders to surprize them in Lochalsh, desireing proper measures might be taken to prevent any such attempt; on which Ld Tullibardine acquainted his L^{op}, that if he would rise some of his men, he would wryte desireing Clanranald and Lochiell, with any others that would joyn, to doe the

[1] Keith asserts, and the caution which characterised Tullibardine's conduct supports the suspicion, that Tullibardine contemplated embarking his force and returning to Spain forthwith, and that Marischal despatched the frigates to prevent him from putting his design into execution.—*K. M*, 49. A Spanish lieutenant, captured at Eilean Donan, informed Lord Carpenter at Edinburgh that his Colonel was resolved to return to Spain when he saw how few Highlanders were ready to join, but that 'at last he was prevail'd with to stay, and to let them [the frigates] sail.'—*H. R.* 282.

same. My Ld Seafort agreed; upon which orders were wrote accordingly, and the more pressing, that on the first of May there came confident reports that the D. of Ormond was landed; but on the 4th, Mr Wallace[1] arriv'd from the King's freinds at Edin^r, assureing that the Spanish fleet was dispersed and drove back by storme, advyseing by all means they should imediately reembarque the 300 men, and everybody gett off as quickly as possible. But the ships being gone, there was no retreating; at the same time there was a letter from a person of consequence, telling it would ruine the King's freinds and affairs if they pretended to make a stirre as things stood; on which Ld Tullibardine sent to Clanranald and Lochiell, desireing they would come to Isleandonan, that joynt measures might be taken how to behave most for the service under such a precarious situation; at the same time advysed them to leave such directions that their men might on all events be in the same readyness to follow them as if they had been present. On the 9th they returned, and the same evening three English men of war came to anchor at Caliach's stone[2]. While there was hopes of a landing, the great quantity of ammunition was lodged in a countrey house near the Crow of Kintaile, but when the accounts came of the fleets being dispers'd, there was no way of preserveing it in ane open place; upon which the Castle of Isleandonan being visited, it was found, by putting it there with a small guiard, the old walls and vaults would be sufficient to keep it from any flying party by land or attaque by sea. Accordingly it was put there in the best manner with all the dilligence the difficultys they had to struggle with could permitt, and Capt. Stapletone with a Spainish Lieutennent and above 40 souldiers were sent to garrison the place.

On the 10th in the morning, the three ships came up and anchor'd within musquet shot of the Castle[3]. They were no

---

[1] ? Hew Wallace of Inglestoun. Cf. *Stuart Papers*, vol. iii.

[2] The ships were the *Worcester*, Captain Boyle; the *Enterprize*, Captain Herdman; the *Flamborough*, Captain Heldesley.—Captain Boyle's despatch of May 12, in *H. R.* 281.

[3] Captain Boyle's despatch gives the following account: 'At nine in the morning [of May 10], I sent my Lieutenant towards the Fort with a Flag of Truce to demand them to surrender; but they firing at the

sooner moor'd than they begun to fire on the place, which continued the whole day, but the walls being very thick they could not make a breach; however, one of the Spainards desearted to the Ennimy, informing them that their lieutennent would deliver the place at discretion. Captain Stapleton imediately sent a Highlander ashoar with the account of what had pass'd among the Spainards, on which their Cap: Commandant was ordered to goe and comand them with more men, and directions to blow up the place if he found it could not be kep'd, which migh have very much shatter'd the ships, if not sunk them; but the tyde would not allow him to enter before ten of the Clock at night, and they surrender'd to the ship's boats at 8, without any resistance nor so much as one man kill'd or wounded. In the afternoon the smallest ship[1] sail'd up to the Crow, and fir'd so hard on a detachment of 30 Spainards who guarded some of the Ammunition there, that they were obliged to blow it up.

In short, when Clanranald, Lochiell, and all had mett, my Lord Seafort declar'd he could bring out no men while the men of war were about his cost, on which Clanranald and Lochiell went home to be ready against the first favourable accounts from abroad to make ane effectuall riseing; for as things stood, there was no possibility of bringing people togeather, especially since there was none but Clanranald and Lochiell would so much as receive any proportion of arms, except my Lord Seaforth, who did not send for his till after the men of war came upon them.

Boat, he return'd. About Four in the Afternoon, a Deserter wav'd to us from the Side of the Camp, who, being brought off, inform'd us that the Camp was of about 4700 Men and daily increasing. At eight in the Evening we brought our Ships to play upon the Castle with a great Fire, under the Cover of which I detach'd two Boats mann'd and arm'd, under the Command of two Lieutenants, who, landing at the Foot of the Castle, attack'd and took it after a small Resistance. Thinking it proper (as the Camp lay within two Miles) to blow the Place up, I sent Captain Herdman of the *Enterprize* on that Service, who perform'd it effectually, after having first sent off the Prisoners, with 343 Barrels of Powder, 52 Barrels of Musket-Shot, 200 Weight each, and some Bags of Meal.'—*H. R.* 280.

   [1] The *Flamborough.*—*H. R.* 281.

The way by sea being cutt off to the Crow, they were oblidged to march on [May] the 13th by the head of Loch Long[1], and transported all the arms with 3 or 4 boatfulls of ammunition thither, thinking to have carryed the whole from thence by land to the Crow, but could at no rate gett any baggage horse, therefore were oblidged to return it with great difficulty by sea under night, least they should be stopt by the ships, and so got the stores past Isleandonan to the Crow. A day or two after they came to Gleneligag [Glen Elchaig] at the head of Loch Long, my Ld Marishall, the Brigadeers Campbell of Ormadale & Mackintosh[2], who were still endeavouring a riseing at any rate, acquainted Ld Tullibardine that Ld Seafort was then satisfyed to march to a Randezvouse out of his own countrey, upon which Ld Tullibardine went[3] to know of his L^{op} how the matter stood, and what new resolutions he would have taken. The answer was, that Ld Tullibardine might march with the Spainards to Killiwhiman [Fort Augustus], and that Clanranald and Lochiell should joyn at that place with their men, and his L^{op} would meet them with 100 men, and that he would order as many to follow as could be spar'd from guairding the coast. Ld Tullibardine said that to stirr out of the countrey so near the Ennimy without a body of men would expose their weakness, and show the world that none would join them, but if his L^{op} would allow him to acquaint Clanrald and Lochiell, that he would meet them on a day of Randezvouse to be named with 3 or 400 men, or else a battalion, without mentioning the number of which it should consist; in that case there was a probability these Gentlemen would undertake something effectually, and then they might stand their ground till others joyn'd, if there was still

[1] A portion, at least, of the force made its way to the head of Loch Carron, near Loch Kishorn, where two British men-of-war, the *Assistance* and *Dartmouth*, were at anchor. Several encounters took place between the ships' boats and the insurgents.—*H. R.* 282.

[2] Mackintosh of Borlum.

[3] The disagreement between Marischal and Tullibardine appears to have resulted in their occupying different camps at three miles' distance from each other. The Spaniards encamped with Tullibardine. —*H. R.* 283.

hopes of a quick descent, otherways they would have a very difficult task. Ld Seafort said there was no promiseing on any number of men; however, he would try what could be done, and took a warrand to that effect. However, the execution of what regairded that designe was lay'd aside for a few days by a rumour which was spread abroad and confidently reported, that the Regullar troops, with the Frazers and other Highlanders who were thought to be disafected, were marching against them, and would be at Gleneligag in two days at farthest; on which Ld Seafort sent desireing to meet with Ld Tullibardine, and proposed, that since there was no possibility to oppose them, they too should leave everything and immediately goe off togeather. Both agreed there was no opposeing such a force, but Tullibardine said, that tho it were certaine, they ought once to see them and at least endeavour some way to secure the arms, ammunition, &c.: and if better could not be, even tho they were forced to give all up, yet it was necessary they should endeavour to abscond amongst the hills till the King's orders came how to dispose of themselves, which his L^{op} agreed to, and charged himself with acquainting my Ld Marishall of what had pass'd; on which, next day, that Lord and Brig: Campbell of Ormadale came to Ld Tullibardine, desireing under his hand that they might goe and doe for themselves. He answer'd he had seen nothing certaine of the Ennimy's motion, but if they were so near as was given out, there would be no occasion for liberty to dispose of themselves, since it would soon but too plainly appear impracticable that any of them could keep togeather under such difficultys as they were unavoydably oblidged to wrestle with. The story proveing false, and the arms being transported, as is said, before they marched to the Crow of Kintaile [on] May the [13th], the same day Ld Tullibardine received a letter from the King's freinds att Edin^r dated the 11th, telling private letters seem'd positive that the Spainsh fleet was repair'd and might be allready sail'd, or at least quickly would; allso there was ane article from London of the 7th which said, at last a lyne is come from the D. of Ormond, and his freinds here recomend and wish that those in the north of Scotland may keep possession and support themselves the best way they can, for that the Duke will certainly send them supplys; besides, about the same time, there were other encourageing letters from different hands, which gave Ld Tullibardine a handle of wryteing on the 21st to severall as weell as to Clanranald and Lochiell, earnestly desireing they would come, if it were but with few of their people, and more might follow by degrees, which would give little umbrage, and could hardly be observed; but on the letter from Edinburgh, he could not help sending fresh orders to them and others, requireing without loss of a minute they would march immediately with what people could be gott togeather, and leave directions for the rest to follow by degrees as they should be ready[1]. Lord Seafort then went to Loch Carron, and by his presence endeavour'd to bring up his people, which he found would be no easie task.

At length on the 4th of June, Lochiell came up first with above 100 men to Glensheall, where Ld Tullibardine with the Spainards mett him on the 5th, takeing up their quarters there, it being the strongest ground in those parts. On the 7th they had severall accounts, particullarly from the Chisme of Strathglass, that the Ennimy were marching from Innerness, calling for arms and ammunition to the Laird of Glenmoristone and himself, who were comeing with about 100 men and designed to observe the Ennimy's motion, and would joyne before they could be near them. The arms and ammunition were sent according to his desire, but there came no further accounts from either of them after. The passes in little Glensheall being view'd [on] the 6th, it was belived that rough ground might be mentain'd till the people who were expected could come, which Ld Seafort did next day to the Crow with about 400 men, who it was thought would briskly defend their own countrey.

Late on the 8th there were accounts that the Ennimy had moved from Killiwhiman[2] to the Braes of Glenmoriston. Lord Tullibardine haveing acquainted Ld Seafort, next day he came from the Crow, 3 miles distant, with his men to Glensheall,

[1] 'Not above a thousand men appeared,' says Keith, 'and even those seemed not very fond of the enterprize.'—*K. M.*, 51.

[2] Fort Augustus. Wightman marched from Inverness on June 5, halted a day at the head of Loch Ness, and on the 10th proceeded from Strath Clunie to the Pass of Glenshiel.—*H. R.* 283, 284.

REFERENCES TO THE PLAN.

1. A Sergt. and 12 Grenadiers.
2. An Officer and 24 do.
3. Main Body of Grenadiers, 120 in Num.
4. Col. Montagu's Regmt.
5. Col. Harrison's Detacht Battalion.
6. Huffel's Regmt. and 4 Companies of Amerongen's.
7. Dragoons.
8. Col. Clayton's Regiment.
9. The Monro's Highlanders.
10. The Sutherlands Right.
11. The first march by ye Right.
12. Clayton's march by the Left.
13. The Dragoons march to the Plain.
14. The Dragoons Halt.
15. The Dragoons advance to the middle of the Plain.
16. Clayton's four Plottoons and the Monro's making ye First Attack on ye Rebels' Right.
17. Cohorn Mortars throwing Granades at the Rebels where ye First Attack was Ordered.
18. Cohorn Mortars throwing Granades at ye Spaniards in their Entrenchments.
19. Part of Clayton's attacks the Barricade of the Pass.
20. 35 Dragoons on Foot attack the Spaniards Breast Works.
21. The Dragoons mount the Hill.
22. Our March in line of Battle to the Rock where the Attack began under ye command of Col. Clayton.
23. Our Right pursue the Rebells.
24. The Plottoons and the Monro's halt upon the Hill, having putt the Ennemy to the Flight.
25. Our Right halts upon ye Mountain.
26. Part of Clayton's takes possession of ye Hill that commanded the Pass.
27. Guard for the Baggage and place for the Hospitall.
28. The Bagage advanced with the wounded men for their security.
29. Majr.-Genl. Whightman giving his directions during the Action.

REFERENCES TO THE ENNEMY.

A. A Spanish Regiment posted on the Hill that commanded the Plain and the Pass.
B. Spaniards march to ye Mount and Halt.
C. The Spaniards retire to the Top of the mountain.
D. The Barricade that defended the Pass on the River Side.
E. The Breastworks on the Side of the Hill.
F. The Highlanders drawn up before the attack.
G. A straggling number of Highlanders fire upon the Plottoons of Clayton's and the Monro's behind them in the time of the attack.
H. A Body of Highlanders going to sustain their Right.
M. The Flight of the Rebels. The Mount called Skururan the highest in Scotland except Benevis.

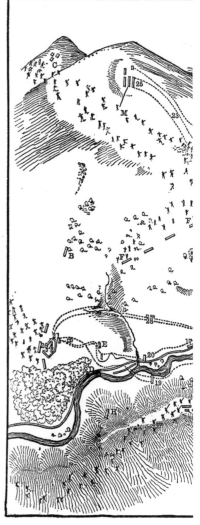

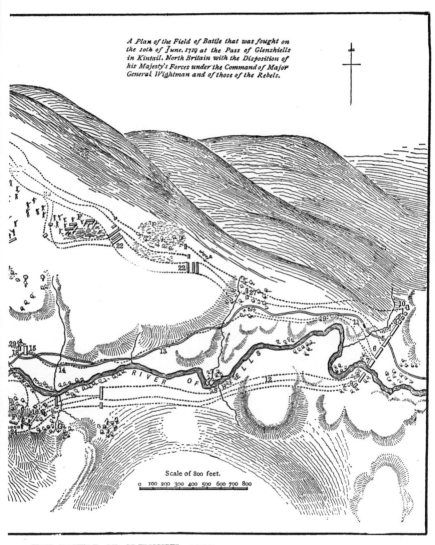

A Plan of the Field of Battle that was fought on
the 10th of June, 1719 at the Pass of Glenshiells
in Kintail, North Britain with the Disposition of
his Majesty's Forces under the Command of Major
General Wightman and of those of the Rebels.

THE BATTLE OF GLENSHIEL, 1719

from whence they all marched with the Spainards (except about 50 who were sick and left at the magazine) to the Little Glen, where all posted themselves in the pass which was thought properest for defence. That evening ane hundred men of a friend's[1] joyn'd them, and Lord George Murray, who was on the out guaird, sent word he saw the Ennimy encamp on the head of Lochelumie [Loch Clunie], which was about 4 miles from them. Next morning he sent againe to tell they were decamped and moveing slowly foreward. Soon after, 50 men of the nighbourhood joyn'd them, and likeways some of Lochiell's, besides Mackinnon with 50 more, which were the last, for the severall men that ought to have been with them were on both sides of the Glen on the tops of the mountains, many by 12 of the Clock, and the rest before four; yet they did not descend to incorporate as was expected; perhaps they thought the Ennimy too near[2], who as they advanced, Ld George retyr'd, keeping about half a mile from them, till they came in sight of the pass, which was near two in the afternoon, when they halted at above a quarter of a mile's distance to refresh their men and make a disposition for the attaque, which began at full six at night.

The King's people[3] had drawn up to the right of their main body, on the other side of the little water which runs through the Glen; upon a little hill to the southward about 150 men,

---

[1] In Tullibardine's letter to Mar describing the battle, this 'friend' is called 'Mr Lidcoat.' Mr Dickson suggests 'Lidcoat' as a possible pseudonym for Glengarry (*J. A.* l, 271); but cf. *Portland MSS*, vol. v, 587.

[2] In the official account published in the *London Gazette* this force is described as being 'posted on a Hill in order to make themselves Masters of our Baggage, it being always one of their chief Aims.'— *H. R.* 284.

[3] Keith thus describes the strength of the position: 'Our right was cover'd by a rivulet which was difficult to pass, and our left by a ravine, and in the front the ground was so rugged and steep that it was almost impossible to come at us.'—*K. M.* 51. Wightman states in his despatch:— 'Their Dispositions for Defence were extraordinary, with the Advantages of Rocks, Mountains, and Intrenchments.'—*H. R.* 283. The position entirely commanded Wade's military road, along which Wightman was marching from the east.

includeing 2 companys of Ld Seafort's, besides 80 more, were allotted for that place, who were to have come from the top of the mountaine above them, but tho they sent twice that they were comeing, yet they only beheld the scuffle at a distance. This party to the right on the little hill was commanded by Ld George Murray, the Laird of Macdougall, Major Mackintosh, and John Mackenzie of Augh [Avoch], ane officer of my Ld Seafort's people. At the pass on the other side of the water was, first, the Spainards, who were hardly 200 men; next in the lyne was Lochiell with about 150 men, and then, from the neighbouring bounds, 150 with 20 volunteers; next, 40 of Rob Roy's men, 50 of Mackinnon's; then about 150 of Ld Seafort's commanded by Sir John Mackenzie of Coull; to the left of all, at a considerable distance, Ld Seafort posted himself with above 200 of his best men, where Ld Marishall and Brig: Campbell of Ormadale commanded with him. Brig: Mackintosh was with the Spainish Collonell, and Ld Tullibardine & Brig: Campbell of Glenderuell were in the centre, where all imagined the main attaque would happen, it being by far the easiest ground, besides the only way through the Glen. However, it fell out otherways.

The Rebellious forces[1], who were about 1300 strong, besides

[1] The official account gives the following disposition of Wightman's force: 'On the Right were posted all the Grenadiers under the Command of Major [Richard] Milburn, being above 150 in Number, who were sustained by Montague's Regiment [11th Foot], commanded by Lieutenant-Colonel [Herbert] Lawrence, and a Detachment of 50 Men commanded by Colonel [Henry] Harrison, the rest of his Regiment [15th Foot] being in Garrison at Inverlochy; these were supported by Huffel's Dutch Regiment, and four Companies out of Amerongen's; this [right] Wing had 56 of [William Sutherland] Lord Strathnaver's [d. 1720] Men in the Flank, under the Command of Ensign Mac Cey, and the whole Wing was commanded by Colonel Clayton, who acted as Brigadier upon this Occasion.

'The left Wing consisted of Clayton's Regiment, commanded by Lieutenant-Colonel [John] Reading, and had on the Flank above fourscore Men of the Monroes, under the command of Mr Monroe of Culcairn. The Dragoons [Scots Greys], which were 120 in Number, commanded by Major [Patrick] Robertson, and had made their March from Inverness without the Loss of so much as one Horse or the least

near 200 Highlanders[1], placed their Horse on the low ground, and a Battalion cross the water near them, with most of their Highlanders on their left; all the rest of their foot were at a distance on a riseing ground to the right of the horse. The first attaque[2] they made was on the men with Ld George, by a small detatchment of regular troops with their Highlanders, who fir'd severall times on other without doeing much dammage, upon which they sent a second & third detatchment, which made most of those on the little hill run to the other side of the steep banks of a rivolet, where Ld George and the few rest were afterwards oblidged to follow, continueing there till all was over, it being uneasie for the Ennimy to come at them. When they found that party give way, their right begun to move in three bodys up the hill, from thence to fall doun on the left of the Highlanders; but when they discover'd Ld Seafort's people, who were behind the steep rock, they began to attaque them least they should be flanqued, upon which the Laird of Coull (many of whose men begun to goe off on seeing the Ennimy) marched with his battallion to sustaine the rest of the Mackenzies, which oblidged the Ennimy to push harder that way, on which Lord Seafort sent down for a further reinforcement; at the same time, Brig: Campbell of Ormadale came, saying it was uncertaine if that main body would not just then fall upon their centre, which made Mackinnon, Rob Roy, and the volunteers, with above 50 more, the longer of drawing of after orders to the Mackenzies' assistance, but seeing them begin to give way, they made all the dispatch they could to sustaine them. However, before they could gett up so as to be fairly in hands with the Ennimy, the

Inconvenience to them, were order'd to keep the Road, having four Cohorns plac'd in their Front. The Major-General [Wightman] himself was posted in the Centre.'—H. R. 284.

   [1] The official account gives Wightman eight hundred and fifty foot, one hundred and twenty dragoons, and one hundred and thirty-six Highlanders, a total force of eleven hundred and six men, with four cohorns; and the Jacobites 1640 Highlanders, 300 Spaniards, and the detached corps on the hill.—H. R. 284.

   [2] This and other movements in the battle are shown very clearly on Bastide's plan at p. 246.

most of all Ld Seafort's people were gone off, and himself left wounded in the arme, so that with difficulty he gott out of the place. That detatchment, finding the place abandon'd, begun to retyre likeways, which made them still send fresh supplys from the left, so that Brig: Campbell of Glenderuell with the men out of the neighbouring bounds march'd up from the centre, but seeing everybody retyre before them occasion'd their doeing allso the same, tho severall of them, with Ld Marishall and Brig: Campbell of Ormadale, turn'd twice back on Glenderuell's perswasion; the Ennimy, finding all give way on that hand, turn'd their whole force there, which oblidged them to march up [on] Lochiell and his men, who likeways drew off as others had done. At last Lord Tullibardine with the Spainards were oblidged to follow, and none standing to sustaine them, the Ennimy being possessed of the high ground, they could doe nothing, but moved up the same hill as others did towards the left, where at last all begun to run, tho the half had never ane opportunity to fire on the Ennimy, who were soon heartned at seeing some of them once give way and the rest of their people as much discouraged, so that they could never after be brought to anything, but all went entyrely off till they gott to the top of the mountaine, where it was impossible to bring them into any order, and night soon seperated them all, so that next morning there were hardly anybody seen except some of the Spainards.

I[1] [had] proposed to my Lord Marshall, Locheill, Brigadier Campbell, and all present, that we should keep in a body with the Spaniards and march thro' the Highlands for some time till we could gather again in case of a Landing; or else should the King send instructions, the Highlanders would then rise and soon make up all that was past. But every body declar'd against doing any thing further, for as things stood they thought it impracticable, and my Lord Mairshall with Brigadier Campble of Ormondell went off without any more adoe or so much as taking leave. The Spaniards themselves declared they could

---

[1] *J. A.* 272. From a letter of Tullibardine's to the Earl of Mar. It is dated from Glen Garry, June 16, 1719. Mar's *Distinct Abridgement* follows it almost literally.

neither live without bread nor make any hard marches thro'
the Country, therefore I was oblig'd to give them leave to
Capitulate the best way they could.

Don[1] Nicolas Bolano, who commanded the detachement of
the regiment of Gallicia, offer'd to attack the enemy once more;
but the general officers judging the attempt in vain, the first
resolution was followed, and accordingly next morning [June
11] the Spaniards surrender'd, on condition their baggage shou'd
not be plunder'd[2], and every body else took the road he liked
best[3].

After[4] signing of the præliminarys [of peace with Spain in
1720] and King Georges death [in 1727], all the Kings then
schemes and projects were at ane end, as the affairs and views of
almost all the princes of Europe took a quite different turn, and

---

[1] *K. M.* 52.

[2] Wightman's despatch, dated June 11, states:—'I marched this
Morning to Glenshill, where I now am, and where a Spanish Officer
is come to me with a Proposition from the Spaniards to surrender as
Prisoners at Discretion, which I have granted them, and they are to
come into our Camp at Two a-Clock this Afternoon.'—*H. R.* 283. For
details as to the treatment of the Spanish prisoners at Edinburgh, where
they were confined until their release in October 1719, cf. *L. P.* ii,
23 *et seq.*; *J. A.* liv, 274 *et seq.* They numbered two hundred and
seventy-four men, including their officers.—*H. R.* 285.

[3] In the engagement Wightman lost one hundred and twenty-one
wounded, and twenty-one killed, including Captain [Henry] Downes
of Montague's regiment.—*H. R.* 284, 285. Cf. *J. A.* lii. From a letter
of June 15, 1719 (*Proceedings Soc. Antiq. of Scotland*, vol. vi, N.S.,
p. 66), it appears that the Jacobites lost less than ten killed and wounded.
Cf. *K. M.* 52; *Portland MSS*, vol. v, 586. Seaforth and Lord George
Murray are the only prominent persons mentioned as wounded.

Wightman's letters and other documents relating to his treatment of
the Highlands in 1719 are in *J. A.* 274 *et seq.* On June 17 Wightman
writes from 'Aderhanon,' 'I...am taking a Tour thro' all the difficult
parts of Seaforth's Country to terrify the Rebels, by burning the Houses
of the Guilty, and preserving those of the Honest....There are no
Bodies of the Rebels together, unless stealing Parties in Scores up and
down the Mountains.'—*H. R.* 285.

[4] *L. P.* ii, 403.

their designs in favor of the King were superceded, and must so remain whilst the ruling powrs continue in this pacific disposition.

And here if weẹ look into the state of the Kings affairs, they appear with a more dismall aspect than I ever knew them, as he has no prospect of (at least sudden) assistance from abroad. King George the 2d mounted the British throne [in 1727] with the favor of the populace, whither more from that nationall genius which is constantly pleased with noveltys, or out of odium to his father, with whom he was in bad terms, and whom they heartily hated, I shant say; but so it is, that at first all parties made court to him, and before they began to cool (by discovering the few popular acts he performed were all grimace, as he followd his predecessors measures), he established himself by procuring such a Parliament to be elected as consisted of as well disciplined members as those of his powerfull army, both which being made up of men pickt out and of known zeall to the revolution interest, and truely mercenary, as they were well paid, went thorow stitches to serve him and establish his dominion on the united basis of a military power and legall authority; whilst at the same time the King, Ime afraid, daylie loses ground.

He began the world with the generall esteem of mankind; evry person, freind and foe, allowd him to be a wise, sober, just, good natured prince, of great knowledge and application in business; and such as knew him, both forreigners and subjects, concurrd in portending the happiness of that people over whom he shoud rule, and this charactar he mantaind whilst the Duke of Mar was at the head of his affairs after his return from Scotland [in 1716]. Tis true he was thought to put too much trust and shew too much favor towards His Grace, so as all matters were directed solely by him, wherby the Duke of Ormond and sevrall other persons of quality thought themselves slighted and retired from the Court; yet still affairs were managed with a good decorum and dexterity, and severall well laid projects carryd on and prudent negotiations set a foot, and people excused the Kings having a byass towards a person that had made so great ane effort for him, and who was certainly a very able minister, tho not free of that ambition which overules the minds of most statesmen, by endeavouring to monopolize all power into their own hands. But soon after Mars removall[1], His Majesties charactar and affairs appeard in a quite different light: great blunders were committed in the execution of affairs in Scotland (and the same was alledged and may be reasonably supposed elsewhere), so that people soon saw that they were not carryd on with the dexterity and secresie as formerlie. But that which struck the nail to the head was his allowing these his favorites (which seems to be a curse in a peculiar manner entaild on the royal race of Stewart) to rule under him in so absolute arbitrary a manner, that for their sake and on their account, the prerogatives of a soveraign and a husband are skrewed up to a pitch not tenable by the laws of God or man, or consistent with prudence; in so far as the royall consort, the mother of the royall issue[2], and subjects of the best quality and merit who had served the King with their blood and fortunes, are trampled upon and abused by a parcell of people who never were nor will be capable to do the King any materiall service, and are contemptible in the sight of all that know them, and at last forced to seek a sanctuary in some other place, and on that account deprived of the small pensions they received for supporting themselves, after having lost all for the King. And as all these continued steps of unaccountable proceedings were contrary to the repeated prayers and remonstrances of his Majesties best freinds, princes and subjects, they gave the world a very unfavorable opinion of his prudence, justice, honour, and gratitude, and highlie discouraged such as were inclined and capable to advise and serve him, and created ane universall despair of ever seeing a probality of better dayes.

And thus, whilst no party is acting for his interest, no projects formed, nothing done to keep up the spirits of the people, the old race drops off by degrees and a new one sprouts up, who having

---

[1] Mar was superseded as the Chevalier's Minister in 1724.

[2] Princess Clementina, whom James married in 1719, left him and retired to a convent in 1725. For her treatment at the hands of Lord Dunbar and Lord and Lady Inverness, and correspondence relating thereto, cf. *L. P.* ii, 220 *et seq.* Prince Charles had been born in 1720, and Prince Henry in 1725.

no particular byass to the King, as knowing litle more of him than what the public news papers bear, enter on the stage with a perfect indifference, at least coolness towards him and his cause, which consequently must daylie languish and in process of time be tottally forgot. In which melancholy situation of the Kings affairs I leave them in the year 1728.

TABLE OF PERSONS

* An asterisk denotes an article in the *Dictionary of National Biography*

*ABERDEEN, GEORGE GORDON, 1st Earl of (1637–1720), Chancellor of Scotland 1682–4, Jacobite sympathies alleged 1707.

ABOYNE, JOHN GORDON, 3rd Earl of, married Grace, daughter of George Lockhart of Carnwath, d. 1732.

*ANNANDALE, WILLIAM JOHNSTONE, 2nd Earl and 1st Marquess of, Lord Privy Seal (Scotland) 1702, opposed the Union, supported the Government 1715, d. 1721.

*ARGYLL, JOHN CAMPBELL, 2nd Duke of, see *supra*, p. ix.

*ATHOLL, JOHN MURRAY, 2nd Marquess and 1st Duke of (1660–1724), opposed Union, suspected of Jacobite sympathies 1707, sided with the government 1715, while his sons and brother joined Mar.

*BALFOUR, ROBERT, 5th Baron Balfour of Burleigh (1687–1757), 'out' in 1715, attainted.

BELHAVEN AND STENTON, JOHN HAMILTON, 3rd Baron, commanded East Lothian troops at Sheriffmuir 1715, d. 1721.

*BERWICK, JAMES FITZJAMES, Duke of (1670–1734), natural son of James II by Arabella Churchill, defeated the English at Almanza 1707 and defended France against Prince Eugene 1709–10, supported the English alliance after Treaty of Utrecht 1713.

*BLACKADDER, JOHN (1664–1729), Colonel of Cameronian regiment 1709, commanded Glasgow volunteers 1715, deputy governor of Stirling Castle 1717.

*BORGARD, ALBERT (1659–1751), served in Danish, Polish, and Prussian armies, chief Fire Master in England 1712, served under Argyll 1715, Lieutenant-General 1739.

*BREADALBANE, JOHN CAMPBELL, 1st Earl of (1635?–1716), imprisoned as a Jacobite suspect 1695, encouraged a French invasion 1707, joined Mar without enthusiasm 1715.

BUCHAN, DAVID ERSKINE, Earl of, joined Argyll in suppressing the '15, d. 1745.

*BUCHAN, THOMAS, Jacobite General, Major-General in Ireland 1689, defeated at Cromdale 1689, retired to France 1692, Jacobite agent in Scotland 1707, d. 1720.

*BYNG, Sir GEORGE, Viscount Torrington (1663–1733), Vice-Admiral 1705, repulsed the French invasion 1708, active during the '15, destroyed Spanish fleet off Cape Passaro 1718.

*CADOGAN, CHARLES CADOGAN, 2nd Baron (1691–1776), served under Marlborough in Flanders, and under Argyll in Scotland 1715.

*CADOGAN, WILLIAM CADOGAN, 1st Earl (1675–1726), Colonel of 'Cadogan's Horse' 1703–12, Major-General 1706, Lieutenant-General 1709–12, succeeded Argyll in command in Scotland 1716.

CAITHNESS, ALEXANDER SINCLAIR, 9th Earl of, d. 1765.

*CAMERON, DONALD, of Lochiel (1695–1748), son of John Cameron of Lochiel, took over the estates 1706, and the chieftaincy 1719, 'out' in 1745 and attainted.

CAMERON, JOHN, of Lochiel (d. 1747), son of Sir Ewen Cameron of Lochiel, 'out' in 1715, 1719, and 1745, after 1715 resided principally in France.

*CAMOCKE, GEORGE (1666?–1722?), Rear-Admiral in Spanish service, Jacobite partisan 1718, defeated at Cape Passaro 1719, banished to Ceuta 1719.

CARNWATH, ROBERT DALZELL, 6th Earl of, captured at Preston 1715, forfeited and pardoned, d. 1758.

*CARPENTER, GEORGE CARPENTER, Baron (1657–1732), suppressed the insurrection in England 1715, Commander-in-Chief in Scotland 1719.

CATHCART, CHARLES, 8th Baron (1686?–1740), served under Argyll 1715.

CLAYTON, JASPER, Colonel of 14th Foot, June 1713, engaged at Sheriffmuir, employed in West Highlands 1716–19, killed at Dettingen 1743.

*COCKBURN, ADAM, Lord Ormiston (1656–1735), Lord Justice Clerk 1705–10, 1714–35.

CRANSTOUN, WILLIAM CRANSTOUN, 5th Baron, d. 1727.

*DERWENTWATER, JAMES RADCLIFFE, 3rd Earl of (1689–1716), brought up at St Germain as companion to the Chevalier de St George, returned to England 1710, made prisoner at Preston 1715, beheaded 1716.

*DILLON, ARTHUR (1670–1733), General in French service, the Chevalier's agent in Paris, died at St Germain.

DORMER, JAMES, raised the 14th Dragoons 1715, wounded at Preston 1715, d. 1741.

*Drummond, James Drummond, Marquess of, 5th Earl and 2nd titular Duke of Perth (1673?–1720), imprisoned as a Jacobite 1708, planned capture of Edinburgh Castle 1715, commanded Jacobite horse at Sheriffmuir 1715, attainted, died at Paris.

Duffus, Kenneth Sutherland, 3rd Baron, voted for the Union 1707, joined Mar 1715, imprisoned and liberated 1717, d. 1734.

Dunbar, James Murray, titular (1721) Earl of Dunbar, served in 1715–16, Governor to Prince Charles 1727, d. 1770.

Dundonald, John Cochrane, 4th Earl of, d. 1720.

Echlyn, Thomas, son of Robert E. of Ardquin, Co. Down, Colonel of Inniskilling Dragoons 1691, sold commission on account of Jacobite proclivities, joined Mar 1715, employed with Seaforth and Huntly to reduce Inverness 1715.

*Eglinton, Alexander Montgomerie, 9th Earl of (1660?–1729), Jacobite sympathies alleged 1707, Scottish representative peer 1710 and 1713, raised the Ayrshire Fencibles for the Government 1715.

Errol, Charles Hay, 13th Earl of, strongly opposed Union 1707, imprisoned under suspicion as a Jacobite 1708, d. 1717.

*Forbes, Duncan (1685–1747), Advocate Depute 1715, Lord Advocate 1725, President of Court of Session 1737, actively supported the government 1715 and 1745.

Forbin, Comte de, see *supra*, p. xi.

*Forfar, Archibald Douglas, 2nd Earl of (1692–1715), Colonel of the 10th regiment of infantry 1713, mortally wounded at Sheriffmuir 1715.

Forrester, George Baillie, 5th Baron (1688–1727), served at Oudenarde and Malplaquet, commanded Cameronians at the capture of Preston 1715, succeeded to command of 30th Foot 1716.

*Forster, Thomas (1675?–1738), M.P. Northumberland 1708–16, surrendered at Preston 1715, escaped from Newgate 1716, died in France.

*Galway, Henri de Massue de Ruvigny, 2nd Marquis de Ruvigny, 1st Earl of (1648–1720), in French military service, accompanied the Chevalier to Scotland 1708.

Gordon, Alexander, of Auchintoul, joined Mar 1715, received command-in-chief on the Chevalier's flight from Scotland 1716.

*Gordon, George Gordon, 1st Duke of (1643–1716), held Edinburgh Castle for James II 1689, refused to sign Jacobite Memorial to Louis XIV 1707, but favoured the Chevalier.

*Grant, Alexander, Laird of Grant (1679–1720), Brigadier-General and Constable of Edinburgh Castle 1715.

*Guest, Joshua (1660–1747), Brevet-Colonel 1713, served under Argyll 1715, held Edinburgh Castle against Prince Charles 1745.

*Haddington, Thomas Hamilton, 6th Earl of (1680–1735), member of the Squadrone Volante, wounded at Sheriffmuir, 1715.

*Hamilton, James Douglas, 4th Duke of (1658–1712), leader of Scottish national party during Union debates 1702–7, imprisoned for complicity in the Jacobite plot 1708, killed in duel with Lord Mohun 1712.

*Hay, John, of Cromlix, titular Earl of Inverness (1691–1740), son of the 7th Earl of Kinnoull, brother-in-law of Earl of Mar, engaged in the '15, succeeded Mar as Secretary to the Chevalier de St George 1724, created Earl of Inverness 1725.

Home, Alexander Home, 7th Earl of, imprisoned under suspicion as a Jacobite 1715, d. 1720.

Honywood, Philip, Colonel of 11th Hussars July 1715, commanded brigade at Preston 1715, commanded a division at Dettingen 1743, d. 1752.

*Hooke, Nathaniel, see *supra*, p. ix.

*Huntly, Alexander Gordon, 5th Marquess of (1678?–1728), 'out' in 1715, submitted to and pardoned by government, succeeded as 2nd Duke of Gordon 1716.

*Innes, Lewis (1651–1738), Principal of the Scots College at Paris 1682–1713, Lord Almoner at the Court of St Germain.

*Islay, Archibald Campbell, Earl of (1682–1761), brother of John Campbell 2nd Duke of Argyll, raised Argyllshire for the government 1715, at Sheriffmuir 1715, succeeded as 3rd Duke of Argyll 1743.

*James Francis Edward Stewart, Chevalier de St George (1688–1766), only son of James II and Mary of Modena, recognized by France as king 1701, attempted invasion of Scotland 1708, retired to Lorraine after Peace of Utrecht 1713, arrived in Scotland after Sheriffmuir 1716, returned to Lorraine 1716 and thence to Avignon and finally Rome, visited Spain to further Alberoni's plot 1719, married Maria Clementina Sobieska 1719, received Papal pension 1727, buried in St Peter's at Rome.

*Keith, James, Field-Marshal, see *supra*, p. x.

*Kenmure, William Gordon, 6th Viscount, appointed to Jacobite command in south of Scotland 1715, captured at Preston 1715, beheaded 1716.

*Ker, John, of Kersland, government spy 1707, died in King's Bench prison 1726, memoirs published 1726.

KILMARNOCK, WILLIAM BOYD, 3rd Earl of, supported the Union 1707 and government 1715, d. 1717.

KILSYTH, WILLIAM LIVINGSTON, 3rd Viscount, opposed Union 1707, arrested under suspicion as a Jacobite 1708, at Sheriffmuir 1715, forfeited, died at Rome 1733.

KINGSTON, JAMES SETON, 3rd Viscount, joined Mar 1715, forfeited, d. c. 1726.

KINNAIRD, PATRICK KINNAIRD, 3rd Baron, opposed Union 1707, d. 1715.

KINNOULL, THOMAS HAY, 7th Earl of, imprisoned under suspicion as a Jacobite 1715, d. 1719.

LAWLESS, Sir PATRICK, an Irishman in Spanish service employed by Alberoni 1719.

LINLITHGOW, JAMES LIVINGSTON, 5th Earl of, joined Mar 1715, died at Rome 1723.

*LOCKHART, GEORGE, of Carnwath, see *supra*, p. x.

*LONSDALE, HENRY LOWTHER, 3rd Viscount (d. 1751), son of Sir John Lowther, 1st Viscount (d. 1700).

*LOUDOUN, HUGH CAMPBELL, 3rd Earl of (d. 1731), Lord Lieutenant of Ayrshire 1708, fought at Sheriffmuir 1715.

*LOVAT, SIMON FRASER, 11th Baron (1667?–1747), assumed title 1699, outlawed for outrage on Dowager Lady Lovat 1701, implicated in Scots Plot 1703, raised his clan for government 1715 and recovered estates and recognition of his title, in hope of a dukedom joined in invitation to Prince Charles Edward 1737, arrested as hostage for fidelity of his clan 1746, beheaded 1747.

LUMLEY, RICHARD, Viscount (1688?–1740), and (1721) second Earl of Scarborough.

MACDONALD, ALEXANDER, of Glencoe, signed address to George I 1714, joined Mar 1715.

MACDONALD, ALLAN, of Clanranald, succeeded his father 1686, exiled in France after Killiecrankie 1689, returned to Scotland 1696, joined Mar 1715, killed at Sheriffmuir.

MACDONALD (MACDONELL), ALEXANDER, of Glengarry, succeeded 1694, joined Mar 1715, submitted after Sheriffmuir 1716, not directly involved in the '19, d. 1724.

MACDONALD, Sir DONALD, of Sleat, joined Mar 1715, d. 1718.

MACDONALD (MACDONELL), COLL, of Keppoch, succeeded 1682, fought at Killiecrankie 1689, joined Mar 1715, escaped to France, returned to Scotland 1719, d. c. 1729. His son and successor Alexander also joined Mar 1715, and Prince Charles 1745.

MACDONALD, RANALD, of Clanranald, brother of Allan Macdonald (*supra*), fought at Sheriffmuir 1715, held aloof 1719, died at St Germain *c.* 1727.

*MACGREGOR (or CAMPBELL), ROBERT (Rob Roy) (1671–1734), followed but did not join Mar 1715, surrendered to Argyll 1717, pardoned 1727.

*MACKINTOSH, WILLIAM, of Borlum (1662–1743), Brigadier in Jacobite service 1715, surrendered at Preston 1715, escaped from Newgate 1716, returned to Scotland and was 'out' in 1719.

MACLEAN, Sir JOHN, 4th Baronet (1674), fought at Killiecrankie, brought out his clan 1715.

*MAR, JOHN ERSKINE, Earl of, see *supra*, p. xi.

*MARISCHAL, GEORGE KEITH, 10th Earl (1694–1778), as 'Chevalier Keith' in communication with Hooke 1707, succeeded to title 1712, joined Mar 1715, led Spanish expedition to Scotland 1719, took no part in the '45, named Prussian ambassador at Paris 1751, pardoned by George II 1759, recalled to Prussia by Frederick the Great 1764.

MARISCHAL, WILLIAM KEITH, 9th Earl, opposed the Union 1707, imprisoned as a Jacobite 1708, d. 1712.

*MARY OF MODENA, queen of James II (1658–1718), after Revolution resided at St Germain.

*MELFORT, JOHN DRUMMOND, 1st Earl and titular Duke of (*c.* 1649–1714), brother of James 1st titular Duke of Perth, attainted 1695, suspected of treachery to Jacobite interests 1707, died at Paris.

*MIDDLETON, CHARLES MIDDLETON, 2nd Earl of (1640?–1719), chief adviser to the Court of St Germain, active in the plot of 1707–8.

*MONRO, Sir ROBERT, 6th Baronet of Foulis, stood for the government in the '15 and '45, killed at Falkirk 1746.

MORAY, CHARLES STEWART, 6th Earl of, d. 1735.

MUNDEN, RICHARD, raised 13th Dragoons in July 1715, present with his regiment at Preston 1715.

*MURRAY, Lord CHARLES, fourth son of John Murray, 1st Duke of Atholl, Cornet of Royal Irish Dragoons, joined Mar 1715, made prisoner at Preston 1715, tried as a deserter and pardoned, d. 1720.

*MURRAY, Lord GEORGE, sixth son of John Murray, 1st Duke of Atholl (1694–1760), 'out' in '15 and '19, Lieutenant-General under Prince Charles 1745–6, retired to France and died in Holland.

MURRAY, Lord JAMES, son of John Murray, 1st Marquess of Atholl, d. 1719.

*Nairn, William Murray (Nairn), 2nd Baron, son of John Murray, 1st Marquess of Atholl, succeeded his father-in-law as 2nd Baron, opposed the Union, made prisoner at Preston, death sentence remitted, d. 1726.

*Nicholson, Thomas Joseph, first Vicar-General of Scotland 1695, d. 1718.

*Nithsdale, William Maxwell, 5th Earl of (1676–1744), made prisoner at Preston 1715, escaped from the Tower by his wife's aid, joined the Chevalier at Rome, where he died.

Ogilvy, James, Lord, 'out' in 1715, attainted 1717, d. 1731.

*Ogilvy, Sir Patrick, of Boyne, signed the Jacobite memorial to Louis XIV 1707. His son 'Brigadier Ogilvy' joined Mar 1715.

*Ormonde, James Butler, Duke of, see supra, p. x.

*Oxburgh, Henry, received Colonel's commission under Thomas Forster 1715, surrendered at Preston, executed 1716.

*Oxford, Robert Harley, 1st Earl of (1661–1724), Secretary of State, dismissed 1714, corresponded with Chevalier de St George, but refused to head English Jacobites.

*Panmure, Harry Maule, titular 5th Earl of, joined Mar 1715, fled to Holland 1716, d. 1734.

*Panmure, James Maule, 4th Earl of (1659?–1723), made prisoner at Sheriffmuir and rescued by his brother (supra), escaped to Holland 1716, declined restoration of his estates at the price of swearing allegiance to George II, died at Paris.

*Patten, Robert, see supra, p. xi.

*Perth, James Drummond, 4th Earl and 1st titular Duke of (1648–1716), attended the Chevalier at St Germain, accompanied him to Scotland 1708.

*Perth, James Drummond, 5th Earl and 2nd titular Duke of (1673?–1720). See Drummond, James (supra).

*Petit (des Etans), Lewis (1665?–1720), military engineer, settled in England after revocation of Edict of Nantes, distinguished in War of Spanish Succession, served under Argyll 1715.

*Portmore, Sir David Colyear, 1st Earl of (d. 1730), Colonel of Scots Greys 1714.

*Preston, George (1659?–1745), Commander-in-Chief in Scotland 1715.

*Queensberry, James Douglas, 2nd Duke of (1662–1711), Secretary of State for Scotland 1702, involved in Simon Fraser's 'Scots Plot' (1703), carried the treaty of Union in Parliament 1707.

*Radcliffe, Charles (1693–1746), took part in the '15 with his brother James 3rd Earl of Derwentwater, surrendered at Preston 1715, escaped from Newgate, assumed title 1731, secretary to Prince Charles Edward 1745, captured and beheaded 1746.

REAY, GEORGE MACKAY, 3rd Baron, supported government 1715 and 1745, d. 1748.

ROLLO, ROBERT, 4th Baron, voted for Union 1707 but joined Mar 1715, surrendered and pardoned, d. 1758.

*ROTHES, JOHN LESLIE, 8th Earl of (1679–1722), supported the Union 1707, fought for the government 1715, Governor of Stirling Castle 1716–22.

*ROXBURGHE, JOHN KER, 5th Earl and 1st Duke of (d. 1741), Lord Lieutenant of Roxburgh and Selkirk, fought at Sheriffmuir 1715.

*SABINE, JOSEPH (1662?–1739), served under Argyll 1715, Governor of Gibraltar 1730.

*SALTOUN, WILLIAM FRASER, 11th Baron (1654–1715), opposed Union, in communication with Nathaniel Hooke 1707.

*SEAFORTH, WILLIAM MACKENZIE, 5th Earl of, 'out' in 1715, escaped to France 1716, returned to Scotland with the Earl Marischal 1719, pardoned 1726, d. 1740.

SELKIRK, CHARLES DOUGLAS, 2nd Earl of (1663–1739), opposed Union 1707.

*SINCLAIR, JOHN SINCLAIR, Master of, see *supra*, p. xii.

SOUTHESK, JAMES CARNEGIE, 5th Earl of, joined Mar 1715, d. 1740.

*STAIR, Sir JOHN DALRYMPLE, 1st Earl of (1648–1707), Viscount 1695, Earl 1703, supported Act of Union.

*STAIR, JOHN DALRYMPLE, 2nd Earl of (1673–1747), son of 1st Earl, Ambassador at Paris 1715, revealed Alberoni's plots 1719, Commander-in-Chief in South Britain 1744.

*STANHOPE, JAMES STANHOPE (1673–1721), Brigadier-General 1704, M.P. for Cockermouth 1702–13, took leading part in securing the Hanoverian Succession 1714, created Viscount 1717, Earl 1718.

*STANWIX, JOHN (1690?–1766), entered army 1706, Brigadier in the '15 campaign.

STEWART, ROBERT, of Appin, succeeded to the chiefship *c.* 1685, joined Dundee 1689, arrested and released 1690, joined Mar 1715, died between 1730 and 1739.

STORMONT, DAVID MURRAY, 5th Viscount, opposed Union 1708, cited to Edinburgh as suspect of Jacobitism 1715, d. 1731.

*STRATHALLAN, WILLIAM DRUMMOND, 4th Viscount (1696–1746), made prisoner at Sheriffmuir, released 1717, joined Prince Charles Edward 1745, killed at Culloden 1746.

STRATHMORE, JOHN LYON, 4th Earl of, opposed Union 1707, suspect as a Jacobite 1708, d. 1712.

STRATHMORE, JOHN LYON, 5th Earl of, son of 4th Earl, killed at Sheriffmuir 1715.

SUTHERLAND, JOHN SUTHERLAND, 15th Earl of (1660–1733), a Commissioner for the Union, held the North for the government 1715.

*TORPHICHEN, JAMES SANDILANDS, 7th Baron, served under Argyll 1715, d. 1753.

TRAQUAIR, CHARLES STEWART, 4th Earl of, d. 1741.

*TULLIBARDINE, WILLIAM MURRAY, Marquess of, second son of John Murray 1st Duke of Atholl, joined Mar 1715, attainted, commanded the Jacobites at Glenshiel 1719, accompanied (as titular Duke of Atholl) Prince Charles to Scotland 1745, surrendered after Culloden and died in Tower of London 1746.

TWEEDDALE, CHARLES HAY, 3rd Marquess of, supported Hanoverian succession, d. 1715.

*WADE, GEORGE (1673–1748), stationed in Bath 1715, made military roads in Highlands 1726–33, Field-Marshal 1743, opposed Prince Charles in England 1745.

WHETHAM, THOMAS, Commander-in-Chief in Scotland 1712, commanded Argyll's routed left wing at Sheriffmuir 1715, Colonel of 27th Foot 1715, General 1739, d. 1741.

*WIDDRINGTON, WILLIAM WIDDRINGTON, 4th Baron (1678–1743), joined Thomas Forster 1715, attainted 1716, pardoned.

*WIGHTMAN, JOSEPH, Commander-in-Chief in Scotland 1712, commanded centre at Sheriffmuir 1715.

WIGTOWN, JOHN FLEMING, 6th Earl of, opposed Union 1707, imprisoned as a Jacobite suspect 1715, d. 1744.

*WILLS, Sir CHARLES (1666–1741), Lieutenant-General 1710, participated in defeat of Forster at Preston 1715.

*WINTON, GEORGE SETON, 5th Earl of, made prisoner at Preston 1715, broke prison, died at Rome 1749.

*WOGAN, CHARLES (1698?–1752?), made prisoner at Preston 1715, escaped from Newgate 1716, secured release of Princess Clementina Sobreska from Innspruck 1719, Brigadier in Spanish service.

*WOGAN, NICHOLAS (1700–70), brother of Charles Wogan (*supra*), found guilty of high treason for complicity in the '15, pardoned, naturalised French subject 1724, with Prince Charles in Scotland 1745–6.

INDEX